Florida's Black Public Officials, 1867–1924

Florida's Black Public Officials, 1867–1924

Canter Brown, Jr.

THE UNIVERSITY OF ALABAMA PRESS
Tuscaloosa and London

Text and Cover Design by Lucinda Smith

∞
The paper on which this book is printed meets the minimum requirements of American National Standard for Information Science-Permanence of Paper for Printed Library Materials, ANSI Z39.48-1984.

Library of Congress Cataloging-in-Publication Data

Cloth ISBN 0-8173-0915-2
Paper ISBN 0-8173-0916-0

Brown, Canter.
Florida's Black public officials, 1867–1924/ by Canter Brown, Jr.
p. cm.
Includes bibliographical references and index.
ISBN 0-8173-0915-2 (cloth). —ISBN 0-8173-0916-0 (paper)
1. Afro-Americans—Florida—Politics and government. 2. Afro-American leadership—Florida—History—19th century. 3. Afro-American leadership—Florida—History—20th century. 4. Florida—Race relations. 5. Florida—Politics and government—1865–1950.
I. Title
E185.93.F5B76 1998
305.896'073075—dc21 97-43612

British Cataloguing-in-Publication Data Available

With gratitude to
my friend and mentor,
William Warren Rogers

Contents

Introduction

Black Leadership in the Post–Civil War Era

Beginning in 1867 and continuing into the twentieth century, African American men contributed to the South, the state of Florida, and their local communities through service in public office. Their total numbers in Florida may have reached close to 1,000, yet the state's black political leadership has received relatively little attention from historians. Works such as Joe M. Richardson's *The Negro in the Reconstruction of Florida, 1865–1877*, as well as period histories by William Watson Davis, Jerrell H. Shofner, and Edward C. Williamson, have offered important information and context, but they have not delved deeply into the lives and careers of specific black leaders nor attempted to treat the broader subject over more than a short period of time.[1] The Florida studies that have attempted a broader treatment deal only with the city of Jacksonville and its suburban neighbor, LaVilla.[2]

On the regional and national level, the picture appears no brighter. As Howard Dodson noted in his foreword to Eric Foner's 1993 work, *Freedom's Lawmakers: A Directory of Black Officeholders During Reconstruction*, "Until recently, little was known about black Reconstruction lawmakers."[3] Some readers doubtlessly will be surprised to learn, for example, that Florida's African Americans, in a pattern probably repeated in other southern states, resisted disfranchisement and political exile for a generation or more after the end of Reconstruction. Perhaps a majority of Florida's black officials served after 1876.

Foner's volume represents the most ambitious attempt to date to focus on the individuals who held office. Nonetheless, it adopts a very narrow scope, limiting the meaning of Reconstruction to "a date that varies from state to state and that I define as the election that produced simultaneous Democratic control of both houses of the legislature and the governorship."[4] Thus, the author excludes all individuals—in Florida's case, hundreds of men—who first entered office after Redemption (as Democratic resumption of power was called). Further, Foner insists that his book includes "all major state officials, members of constitutional conventions, and legislators." He adds, "This volume does not encompass *every* black person who held public office during Reconstruction, although it does include a substantial majority."[5] About sixty Florida officials are mentioned, including forty-two state legislators. Yet, hundreds of black men held office in the state during Reconstruction, well over one dozen of whom were legislators not listed in *Freedom's Lawmakers*.

Very little is available in published form concerning the particular individuals who held public office in Florida. The single monograph-length biography is Peter D. Klingman's *Josiah Walls: Florida's Black Congressman of Reconstruction*, although Lee Warner's recent work, *Free Men in an Age of Servitude: Three Generations of a Black Family*, provides a careful look at the politically active Proctor family. Otherwise, essay-length biographical sketches are available for only six leaders: Charles H. Pearce, Jonathan C. Gibbs, Robert Meacham, John Wallace, John Willis Menard, and James Page. The single account of consequence *from* a black leader, John Wallace's *Carpetbag Rule in Florida*, has been shown to be heavily influenced by white Democratic leader William D. Bloxham.[6]

My interest in this subject evolved from research on the life of Republican Governor Ossian Bingley Hart.[7] Although during the past decades historians have portrayed black leaders in a kinder light, few have suggested that African American leadership took on a dynamic quality, much less was bold or successful. Yet, beginning in 1870 a group of politically powerful African Methodist Episcopal ministers and laymen, with the cooperation of key black veterans of the Civil War, essentially revolted against carpetbag "rings" led by United States Senator Thomas W. Osborn and Governor Harrison Reed to force, first, the nomination and election of Josiah Thomas Walls to the United States House of Representatives and, then, to bring about the election of southern Loyalist and former slave owner Hart as governor in 1872.[8]

With this intriguing information in hand, I naturally wondered about the rest of the story, including how long African Americans served in office, the nature of their accomplishments, and the obstacles they faced. I confess that at the outset I thought that I probably was dealing only with a few hundred individuals. Estimates for the number of black legislators, for instance, ran from the upper thirties to fewer than fifty. Research soon disabused me of such ideas, as the number climbed to well over 100 and black officeholders showed up in county and municipal offices in places and at times previously unknown or ignored.

Given the wealth of information that surfaced, the need for a decision confronted me. Limited time and resources compelled restrictions on the study's scope. As a result, I centered upon the most significant elective and appointive offices: United States Congress; the governor's cabinet; constitutional convention delegates; the state legislature; the Reconstruction-era county offices of judge, clerk, sheriff, superintendent of schools, tax assessor, tax collector, treasurer, county commissioner, and justice of the peace; and elected municipal officers in the towns and cities of largest size or having the greatest likelihood for African American office holding. I did not comprehensively survey post-Reconstruction county offices. Under the 1868 Florida constitution they were appointive, and Bourbon Democrats made few designations of blacks to the positions. Where individual appointments came to my attention, I have included them. Omitted also were militia officers, most constables (an elective office, but one for which the state kept no records), boards of education, boards of public health, port wardens, county surveyors, perhaps a majority of postmasters, and a myriad of other minor offices. In the end, the identities of about 600 different individuals who held substantive office came to light, but the omissions and (especially in the case of municipal officials) a paucity of records likely resulted in the exclusion of several hundred others.

The lives and careers of the identified officeholders are presented in three segments. First, a brief narrative in five chapters surveys the beginnings and evolution of black leadership in post–Civil War Florida, providing context and introducing the most prominent officials. Then come brief biographical sketches of the officeholders. I have attempted, where information was available, to give place and date of birth and death, occupation, religious affiliation, offices held, and a notation as to whether the individual was black or mulatto. In the case of state officials, constitutional convention delegates, and legislators, I have checked for military service and, where applicable, have included a notation of unit of service. For the leading officeholders, entries also contain quotations by or about the individual to provide additional depth concerning the individual and the dynamics of black leadership generally. Finally, an appendix lists officials by reference to political subdivision and office held. Municipal officers are enumerated by town name but appear after the county in which the municipality is (or was) located.

Readers should take care in placing too much reliance upon some of the specific information given for officeholders in the biographical directory, especially dates of birth and whether black or mulatto. Many freedmen did not know their birth dates (or, often, birth years) and later adopted dates as a convenience. Military authorities, to cite an example, sometimes considered inductees to have celebrated their twenty-first birthday on the date of enlistment. Occasionally the same individual might list several different dates over a period of time. Also, census takers accepted information given them by family members or neighbors or else made their own estimations. Errors in recording information also occurred. Wide variation in reported information naturally resulted.

Scores of individuals and institutions assisted me with the preparation of this book. William Warren Rogers, professor of history at Florida State University, Larry E. Rivers, professor of history at Florida A&M University, John T. Foster, Jr., professor of anthropology at Florida A&M University, James M. Denham, associate professor of history at Florida Southern College, and Leland M. Hawes, of the *Tampa Tribune*, reviewed the manuscript and improved it with their helpful suggestions. The personal generosity of Leland M. Hawes and Walter M. Manley II permitted me the time to undertake and complete the project. My thanks go to the following individuals for their generous research assistance and encouragement: David J. Coles, Florida State Archives; Joan Morris and Jody Norman, Florida Photographic Collection, Florida State Archives; Mary Ann Cleveland, Cynthia C. Wise, and Randi Bailey, Florida Collection, State Library of Florida; Nathan Woolsey, Milton; Stephen Prine, Library of Congress, Washington, D.C.; Kenneth J. Nemeth, Atlanta, Georgia; Joyce Ann Tracy, American Antiquarian Society, Worcester, Massachusetts; Roy E. Goodman, American Philosophical Society, Philadelphia; Elizabeth Alexander and Bruce Chappell, P. K. Yonge Library of Florida History, University of Florida; Mark I. Greenberg, then at the University of Florida and now at the Museum of the Southern Jewish Experience, Jackson, Mississippi; Tom Hambright, Monroe County May Hill Russell Library, Key West; Vernon Peeples, Punta Gorda; Hal Hubener, Lakeland Public Library; Julius J. Gordon, Hillsborough County Historical Commission; David Nolan, St. Augustine; Taryn Rodriguez-Boette and Charles A. Tingley, St. Augustine Historical Society Research Library; Janice S. Mahaffey and Aisha Canty, Office of the Putnam County Clerk of the Circuit Court, Palatka; Willie Mae Ashley, Fernandina Beach; James M. Perry and Suzanne D. Hardee, Amelia Island Museum of History, Fernandina Beach; David St. John, Baker County Historical Society, Glen St. Mary; Vi Ballentine, city clerk, DeLand; Mary Mizell, Cedar Key; Doris Enloe, city clerk's office, Leesburg; JoAnn B. Crawford, Leesburg Public Library; Fay Farmer and Bonney A.

McClellan, Keystone Genealogical Library, Monticello; Charles Carroll Fishburne, Jr., Quincy; Miles Womack, Quincy; Willie Speed, Apalachicola; George Chapel, Apalachicola; Del E. Jupiter, Atlanta, Georgia; Catherine King, Walton County Clerk of the Circuit Court, DeFuniak Springs; Elba Wilson Carswell, Chipley; Brian R. Rucker, Pensacola Junior College; and Tom Muir and Marshall L. Emerson, Historic Pensacola Preservation Board. A special word of thanks should be added to editor Beverly Denbow and to the director and staff of The University of Alabama Press.

Mention should be made of a number of technical matters. Documentation of material in endnotes is the same as that for the text unless otherwise indicated. Incorrect spellings and usages within direct quotations appear as they do in the original; I have avoided using *[sic]*. Finally, responsibility for the interpretation of events and for errors of fact is mine alone.

Florida's Black Public Officials, 1867–1924

1

"We are all looking for the day when we shall vote"

The Founders

When on May 10, 1865, Union authorities accepted Confederate Florida's surrender at Tallahassee, some segments of the state's African American population already had asserted demands for the right to participate in political decision making. Thereafter, blacks struggled until well into the twentieth century to maintain an influential voice in public affairs. They did so in spite of poverty, violence, betrayal, poor opportunities for education, and—in the end—insurmountable legal obstacles. Still, representatives of their communities held public office along with whites from 1867 to, in at least one instance, 1924. In the process, they left an imprint upon Florida the legacies of which remain visible today.[1]

The story began at least as early as April 1865, when the town of Fernandina prepared to elect new municipal officers in the wake of General Robert E. Lee's surrender at Appomattox, Virginia. Likely in furtherance of United States Supreme Court Chief Justice Salmon P. Chase's presidential ambitions (he advocated granting voting rights to freedmen), the jurist's local friends supported black desires that they be allowed to participate. Chase's allies overcame local white resistance. When the polls opened on May 1, 160 blacks and 9 whites appeared to cast ballots. They elected an all-white ticket, whose members were sworn into office personally by Chase.[2]

The promise of black political participation initiated at Fernandina evaporated within days. On May 29 President Andrew Johnson published two Reconstruction proclamations that effectively excluded blacks from voting and soon placed most southern states back into the hands of secessionists and Confederate sympathizers. In Florida, Johnson's gubernatorial appointee William Marvin called elections for a constitutional convention to meet in October. After hearing Marvin proclaim that "the governing power is in the hands of the white race," that body met the president's minimum requirements for readmission to the Union and set state officer elections for late November. When the legislature met thereafter in mid-December, the solons enacted, with Governor David S. Walker's encouragement, a series of restrictions upon freed slaves that came to be known as the black code. The laws touched virtually every aspect of their lives, and many African Americans viewed them as reinstitution of slavery in all but name.[3]

The political and social climate fostered by the actions of conservative white officials in 1865 and 1866 met heated resistance from blacks and some members of Florida's white Loyalist minority. Meeting at Tallahassee's African Methodist Episcopal (AME) church, for example, local blacks purported to select Governor Walker's former slave Joseph E. Oates as their congressman in an ill-fated attempt to secure national leaders' attention. A Fernandina gathering blasted the legislature's actions. Not long afterward, hundreds of freedmen marched at Quincy to demand their rights.[4]

As resistance built to the repressive policies, some whites reacted with threats and violence against blacks and Loyalists. By June 1866 the situation had grown so severe that military authorities proclaimed martial law in Escambia, Santa Rosa, Levy, Madison, and Alachua Counties. Historian William Watson Davis noted, "Throughout the state during 1866 affairs moved along amid some vague talk of race war and some disorder."[5] In the circumstances many blacks turned their attention toward advocates of radical policies. One man in particular voiced opinions that found growing audiences. Northerner Daniel Richards had served in Florida during the Civil War as a United States tax commissioner and was well known in the state's northeastern towns. By mid-1866 he was speaking out against the prevailing postwar conditions, proclaiming "the war not ended" and that "it must be continued through the ballot box until the Southerners are completely subjugated."[6]

In his attempt to influence Florida's blacks and the direction of their political thinking, Richards did not stand alone. Conservative white leaders such as Marvin and Walker spoke to black audiences, counseling acceptance of the status quo. Some northern whites, soon to be called carpetbaggers, agreed. For instance, Harrison Reed, editor of Jacksonville's *Florida Times*, declared, "We say that sound policy requires that the freedmen of the South should not be admitted immediately to the right of suffrage."[7] Conversely, at least one prominent Loyalist leader advocated black enfranchisement. "When the rebellion closed," recalled Tampa and Jacksonville lawyer Ossian Bingley Hart, a former slave owner, "I asked our people to extend the right of suffrage at once."[8]

While seeking to influence African Americans, Marvin, Walker, Reed, and Hart failed to create an organizational structure within the black community. Others, such as one-time Union army officer Thomas W. Osborn, were more successful. A New Yorker, Osborn had received appointment in 1865 to head the United States government's Bureau of Freedmen, Refugees, and Abandoned Lands in Florida. Associating in his work other former officers such as Marcellus L. Stearns, William J. Purman, and Charles M. Hamilton, Osborn organized within the black community a secret league named the Lincoln Brotherhood. The society coalesced strongly in the plantation-oriented and black-majority Middle Florida counties of Jackson, Gadsden, Leon, Jefferson, and Madison.[9]

Osborn's white-run league necessarily required black leaders' cooperation. He often relied upon Baptist ministers and located the Lincoln Brotherhood's headquarters at Tallahassee's Baptist church. "[Preachers] were looked upon as the leading colored men of each community, and fitted for politics as well as religion," explained black Florida political commentator John T. Shuften in 1877, "and, as they met with no opposition from those whom they lead in spiritual matters, but on the contrary received their support, they soon became the controlling element."[10] Partly because Baptist ministers tended to advocate policies aimed at peaceful accommodation with whites, the brotherhood reflected a more conservative orientation than some other organizing initiatives among the freedmen.[11]

AME church ministers and adherents stood in counterpoint to Baptist influence in the Lincoln Brotherhood. Although AME organizers had entered Florida only in 1865, the black Methodists rapidly expanded their reach in 1866 and 1867. In doing so the churchmen reflected the teachings of Bishops Daniel A. Payne and Henry McNeal Turner. "I shall neither fawn nor cringe before any party nor stoop to beg them for my rights," Turner declared.[12] The church's militancy would help to mold the lives and attitudes of thousands of Floridians; among them, to cite two examples, were Monticello's James William Randolph, who became an AME minister, and his better-known son, A. Philip Randolph.[13] The militancy would provide, as well, the principle around which Florida's most successful black leadership organized.

The African Methodists enjoyed a major advantage over the Baptists when it came to exercising influence among blacks. Their church's hierarchical structure permitted coordinated effort over the state, whereas black Baptists moved slowly to create a formal association. The first steps in that regard came in late 1869 with the creation of the Florida Bethlehem Baptist Association. Even then, politically involved Baptist leaders such as Tallahassee's James Page and John N. Stokes, Jacksonville's Cataline B. Simmons and Thomas Lancaster, Marion County's Samuel Small, and

Charles H. Pearce (1820–1887), presiding elder of Florida's African Methodist Episcopal church. (Courtesy Florida Archives)

Jefferson County's John A. Potter maintained a personal independence that might have invoked church discipline upon their AME counterparts.[14]

Presiding elder Charles H. Pearce, of Maryland, headed the African Methodists' Florida organization during the early post–Civil War years. His views coincided fully with the church's militant stance. "A man in this State," he declared, "cannot do his whole duty as a minister except he looks out for the political interests of his people."[15] The church sent other ministers to assist him, including William G. Stewart and William Bradwell, both of Georgia. Finding some already existing congregations anxious to affiliate with the national organization, Pearce accepted their leaders into the clergy's ranks. Two men proved especially important in that regard. Pearce sent Robert Meacham, who had founded a church at Tallahassee, to lead missionary efforts in nearby Jefferson County. Henry Call similarly brought Florida contacts and experience to AME work in West Florida.[16]

As Osborn's Lincoln Brotherhood and Pearce's AME church extended themselves, men representing another potential source of black leadership began to lay foundations for the future. During the war numerous regiments of African American troops had served in Florida, with perhaps 1,000 of their number originating in the state. Whites had officered the men, but blacks had occupied important noncommissioned officer positions. Having seen Florida, enjoyed its climate, and recognized its potential, many veterans chose to remain or return. Accustomed to leadership from their corporals and sergeants, they continued to look to them for guidance after the conflict. These men located around the state but concentrated in coastal and port towns such as Fernandina, Jacksonville, St. Augustine, Key West, and Pensacola. Additionally, significant numbers could be found at or near Tallahassee and Gainesville.[17]

Even though numerous veterans eventually exercised substantial political power, they tended to do so in a manner less ideological and more pragmatic than did leaders associated with the Lincoln Brotherhood or the AME church. On the other hand, the lines between the groups were not drawn hard and fast. Veterans such as Thomas Warren Long of the Thirty-third United States Colored Infantry and Josiah Haynes Armstrong of the Third USCI emerged, for instance, as prominent AME ministers. Yet the most politically successful veterans maintained careful independence while building organizations loyal to themselves. Often—as in the case of Tallahassee's John Wallace, a North Carolina-born veteran of the Second USCI—they taught school while cultivating relationships within the white community and among students and their parents. Wallace also benefited from the local presence and support of Second USCI Sergeants Owen B. Armstrong of Pennsylvania and William Henry Ford of Maryland.[18]

One former noncommissioned officer deserves particular attention. Born in 1842, Josiah Thomas Walls hailed from Frederick County, Virginia. He soldiered in northeastern Florida in the Third and Thirty-fifth USCI, attaining first sergeant rank. In late 1864 he married an Alachua County woman, settling there after the war. A former white officer of his, William K. Cessna, provided Walls with work as a lumberman. Later Walls taught school at Archer. The veteran's abilities soon attracted the respect of area freedmen, while his connections with Cessna and two other former officers, Sherman Conant and William Birney, offered important support. As was the case with Wallace in Leon County, Walls drew strength from the presence of fellow veterans, such as Sergeants Richard H. Black and Henry S. Harmon, both of Pennsylvania.[19]

While all of these organizations and individuals established their influence during 1865 and 1866, the treatment of blacks and Loyalists worsened in the South. The president's attitudes appeared to harden despite confrontations at New Orleans and Memphis that offered bloody portraits of southern conditions to the northern public. Spurred by Radical Republican calls for decisive measures to overturn Johnson's Reconstruction policies, northern voters in late 1866 elected a new United States Congress with sufficient strength to enact a congressional Reconstruction policy over the president's vetoes. The legislators acted with dispatch. Beginning in March 1867 they passed a series of laws—the Military Reconstruction Acts—to divide the greater part of the Confederacy into five military districts and to direct the officers in charge to oversee a process for rewriting state constitutions to guarantee suffrage rights to adult, male blacks. The statutes provided the first federal mandate for black voting.[20]

The new laws prompted a political revolution in Florida two years after the Civil War's end. "Unexpectedly to them," recorded a resident, "the reconstruction acts of Congress made the great body of the people, black and white, Radical."[21] At Jacksonville on March 14 jubilant freedmen rallied at the Baptist church to nominate a Republican slate in upcoming city elections. Baptist minister Cataline B. Simmons, joined by AME leaders William Bradwell and John Robert Scott, Sr., led eager voters in voicing approval of a white ticket headed by Loyalist Ossian B. Hart. Almost 400 miles to the west, their counterparts voted in Pensacola elections held April 1, despite warnings from former Confederate navy secretary Stephen R. Mallory "against secret political societies, and their organization for party purpose upon the basis of race or color."[22] Elsewhere, mass meetings expressed relief, joy, and widespread enthusiasm for voting rights. The excitement persisted even when military authorities voided Pensacola's election and canceled Jacksonville's, pending further orders.[23]

Meanwhile, white leaders at Jacksonville organized a state Republican Party, hoping to capture Florida's black voters and state government control. Florida had about 154,000 inhabitants, 47 percent of whom were black. When combined with several thousand southern Loyalists and 400 to 500 politically active northern whites, majority control seemed assured for Republicans if blacks joined in the coalition. The events at Jacksonville and Pensacola portended well for this conclusion, as did rallies in Middle Florida counties such as Leon and Jefferson. In June success appeared certain when the Florida AME Conference held its first annual session at Tallahassee. Reported Robert Meacham, "The most exciting question is, what party shall we vote for, but the answer from all quarters of the State is the Republican party."[24] Presiding elder Charles Pearce already had announced his church's goals. "We are hunting for education that will give us a name and position in the nation," he proclaimed. "We have a right to aspire to and claim position with education. We will send to the Legislature men who are qualified."[25]

Amid the euphoria of April, May, and June 1867, Republican Party backers failed to recognize signs of weakness within their organization, problems that boded ill for party rule. Among white Republicans, the largest segment consisted of Loyalists, whose leader Ossian B. Hart became first party chairman. Many northern whites resented Hart's role and desired power for themselves. They saw Hart's political philosophy as too radical. Led by postal chief Harrison Reed of Wisconsin, President Johnson's man in the state, they sought closer relations with the state's conservative white power structure. From Middle Florida, Thomas W. Osborn and his Freedmen's Bureau associates looked askance at party power centering in Jacksonville, away from themselves and their Lincoln Brotherhood power base. At Fernandina, Daniel Richards and his ally, former Union army officer Liberty Billings of New Hampshire, mulled possibilities for an even more radical Reconstruction centered upon their friends. They had begun organizing Union League chapters among blacks, advocating social equality while extracting a commitment not to vote for any southern white. Thanks to Richards's connections, they expected support from national party sources antagonistic to Reed and the president.[26]

The divisions exploded into public view at the state's first Republican convention, held at Tallahassee in early July. Of the eighty-two delegates, fifty were African Americans. As the Osborn and Reed factions maneuvered for position, Billings denounced Hart, insisting that "a southern man cannot be trusted." Two black Baptist leaders from Jacksonville, Cataline B. Simmons and Samuel Spearing, defended the Loyalist, but his opponents combined to deny him the convention presidency in favor of Osborn. The move came despite Charles Pearce's attempt to calm the troubled waters. "We meet here not to abuse each other, or to stir up strife and dissension," he urged, "but to form a platform upon which all the loyal people can stand, and we must begin by making no distinction between the black and white."[27]

Pearce's AME faction warily eyed Osborn's rise. The one-time Union officer's supporters included men such as Reed who maintained close ties with white conservatives. Further, the Lincoln Brotherhood's connections with Baptists concerned the African Methodists. "The [Osborn] Ring controlled the Baptist element," explained one commentator, "and were taught that the members of the Methodist churches were opposed to the Baptists getting any of the offices, which caused much bitterness and much fighting among themselves."[28] The circumstances left Pearce looking for allies with a militant agenda.

Billings and Richards left the convention mulling their own concerns. As did Pearce, they believed Osborn and his associates were too conservative and that the new party power broker intended to deny them influence. Accordingly, they determined to transform party leadership. The arrival in August of Marylander William U. Saunders, a mulatto, aided them greatly. Described as "overcharged with ad captandum eloquence" and able to exert "magnetic influence over a crowd," the orator offered them instant and easy access to black voters for their radical message. By October they had allied with Pearce. Reportedly, they agreed that all the principals would run together for constitutional convention seats. Thereafter they would support an election ticket that named Billings for governor, Richards and Saunders for the United States Senate, and Pearce for lieutenant governor or superintendent of schools. They called their coalition the Mule Team.[29]

November elections for constitutional convention delegates concerned all Republican factions in the months following the party convention. Preparations had been under way since spring. By June they had brought the state its first black public officials. John Pope, the Third Military District commanding officer, had decreed that a board of voter registrars be appointed for each county, to consist of two whites and one black. The first designation was made by John T. Sprague, state military commander, on June 4, 1867, when he placed African American Peter Wright on the Madison County board. The following day Sprague added Willis Johnson and John Kelker, respectively, to the Walton and Santa Rosa County panels.[30]

By mid-June Sprague and Pope had placed Ossian B. Hart in charge of the voter registration process, and the Loyalist named the boards for the remaining thirty-nine counties. Some appointments proved significant for the future. For Charles Pearce's Leon County, the state's most populous, Hart chose Pearce's Baptist rival James Page. Within the AME church a rivalry also had emerged between the presiding elder and Robert Meacham, partly from ill feelings arising out of Pearce's 1866 action in taking over Meacham's Tallahassee church and sending the Florida-born preacher to Monticello in Jefferson County. Hart named Meacham to Jefferson's board. In another black-majority Middle Florida county, Jackson, Hart turned to a locally born mulatto, Emanuel Fortune, neglecting Osborn's Lincoln

Florida Baptist leader James Page (1808–1883). (Courtesy Florida Archives)

Brotherhood in one of its strongest counties.[31]

Florida's summer heat moderated in September and October, but the political climate neared the boiling point. Many conservative whites had opted out of the approaching elections. So, the prizes would be divided between Republican factions. "We are all looking for the day when we shall vote," William Bradwell announced, "to sustain the great Republican party."[32] Mule Team advocates preached social equality to eager audiences. Fearful Lincoln Brotherhood orators countered with demands for confiscation of white lands for distribution to blacks. Southern Loyalists and Jacksonville's carpetbaggers found themselves isolated, a fact borne out by the election results. A Nassau, Duval, and St. Johns County ticket that included Bradwell and Liberty Billings swamped one headed by Hart. Statewide, the Mule Team coalition claimed close to a majority of delegates, among them Pearce, Richards, Meacham, and Saunders.[33]

The convention opened at the state capitol in early 1868 amid high Mule Team expectations. Of the initial forty-six delegates, eighteen were black. Of the eighteen, the religious affiliations of ten can be identified. Four were AME clergymen (Bradwell, Major Johnson, Meacham, and Pearce), and six were AME laymen (Owen B. Armstrong, Auburn H. Erwin, Emanuel Fortune, Frederick Hill, Anthony Mills, and John W. Wyatt). Erwin and Wyatt later became ministers. If these men and other Mule Teamers acted quickly, their leaders reasoned, the faction could seize control of the convention. On January 20 it did just that. With twenty delegates present, the coalition elected Pearce as temporary president and created a permanent organization headed by Richards but with men such as Pearce, Meacham, Saunders, and Armstrong given prominent roles. They adopted rules designed to preserve their power and set about writing a constitution. Of the participating blacks, a New York newspaper correspondent declared: "In spite of all the whips and prisons, there were a few slaves who learned to read and write, as now is evidenced in this Convention. I do not see that one of the 18—and I believe 15 or 16 of them were formerly slaves—is destitute of this desirable accomplishment. Independent of that, their genial demeanor and address shows them possessed of all the attributes of gentlemen—'niggers,' the Rebels call them—but eloquent speakers."[34]

The Mule Team successes spawned harder opposition as ever more heated rhetoric led some white Republicans to conclude that Mule Teamers intended "the positive supremacy of the Colored people throughout the state."[35] The alarming concerns prompted Reed, Osborn, and others to dispatch a private train to Jacksonville in late January to bring Hart to Tallahassee to advise them. Under his guidance, twenty-one delegates (including Columbia County's Auburn Erwin) withdrew to Monticello, denying a convention quorum to the Mule Team. By their return on February 10, three other blacks—Jackson County's Emanuel Fortune and Homer Bryan and Marion County's Alexander [Alonzo] Chandler—had joined the faction. Soon they had captured control of the capitol rooms used by the convention and had revised the rules to permit election of new convention officers. They then secured an agreement with military authorities by which Pearce, Richards, Saunders, and Billings were expelled as failing to meet qualifications for election, to be replaced by Hart, Osborn's ally Marcellus Stearns, Leon County black Richard H. Wells, and one other man.[36]

Flushed with their accomplishment, the Osborn, Reed and Hart group wrote their own constitution. While it established the state's most liberal charter to that date, it incorporated important restrictions on black political power. It permitted most former Rebels to vote, at the same time specifying a legislative apportionment plan that discriminated against black-majority counties in favor of sparsely populated white counties. Effectively the provisions guaranteed a white majority in the state senate and house of representatives. Additionally, the document vested in the governor extensive powers of appointment, permitting him to name all state and county officers except constables, state representatives, and state senators. Many Floridians read the grant of power as implying that the governor would maintain white control of black-majority counties. The drafters retained one item especially important to black leaders. The constitution directed the legislature to create a uniform system of public schools.[37]

The Mule Team's core leadership refused to accept defeat and vowed to fight against public and congressional approval of the constitution. On the chance the document might become effective, the men also named a ticket to participate in state elections and for appointment afterward. Among the individuals named were: Billings for governor; Saunders, lieutenant governor; Meacham, commissioner of immigration; and Pearce, superintendent of schools. Presbyterian minister Jonathan C. Gibbs, an African American, received the honor of nomination to Florida's congressional seat. Born in Philadelphia and educated at Dartmouth College and Princeton Theological Seminary, Gibbs was, in one historian's words, "the most accomplished man of either race in the convention."[38]

The regular Republican organization named its candidates, as well, all of them white carpetbaggers. Reed led the ticket for governor, with fellow Wisconsinite William H. Gleason for lieutenant governor. Osborn associate Charles M. Hamilton received the congressional nomination. Although not on the ticket, Osborn and Hart intended to vie for legislative election to the United States Senate. For weeks Reed declined to promise appointment of a black to his cabinet. In early April, a Jacksonville newspaper excerpted portions of a Reed letter referring to "L. Billings and his niggers."[39] When a furor ensued, Reed announced he would make the appointment.[40]

As Reed's campaign picked up steam, Pearce and the AME church took up the reins of leadership in offering opposition. "Through the stormy existence of our Convention, [he was] as true to the interests of his people as the needle to the pole," recorded Daniel Richards, "and up to the very last battled manfully to save his race and our state from the terrible calamity of the Rebel-Reed constitution."[41] When the Florida AME Conference met at Tallahassee on March 6, Pearce and Bradwell, against Meacham's opposition, committed the church to fighting the constitution. "The action of the

Jonathan C. Gibbs (1827–1874), Florida secretary of state and superintendent of public instruction. (Courtesy Florida Archives)

Conference is of the most vital importance on the colored people," one carpetbagger informed Pennsylvania congressman Thaddeus Stevens. "They regard it as an oracle of their religious persuasion and a guide to their political conduct."[42]

Whatever respect black voters held for Pearce and the AME church in spring 1868, it proved insufficient. As the likelihood of constitutional approval and a Reed victory in the May elections became ever clearer, the Mule Team coalition fractured. Meacham withdrew from its ticket and backed Reed, as later did Saunders. Whether these actions derived from political principle, expediency, or, as Bradwell alleged, bribes is not known. When Osborn announced himself as a candidate for a Leon County state senate seat, even Pearce took his name from the ticket in order to oppose the man whom he had begun to consider an enemy. Meacham and Bradwell likewise entered contests for senate seats in Jefferson and Duval Counties.[43]

The election ended without surprise. The returns indeed handed the governor's chair to Reed and the congressional seat to Hamilton. Republicans captured two-thirds of the twenty-four-member state senate. The three black senators—Pearce, Meacham, and Bradwell—were the state's leading AME ministers. Thirty-seven Republicans claimed seats in the fifty-three-seat lower house. Seventeen of the representatives were black. Ten of the men came from the Middle Florida counties of Jackson, Gadsden, Leon, Jefferson, and Madison. The remainder represented Escambia, Columbia, Duval, Nassau, Alachua, and Marion Counties. Of the nine whose religion is known, one was Roman Catholic and eight were AME ministers or laymen. They included constitutional convention members Auburn Erwin, Emanuel Fortune, Frederick Hill, Anthony Mills, Josiah T. Walls, and Richard H. Wells.[44]

In the new era, black political power soon found its forum. Due to delays in congressional ratification of the new constitution, military officials delayed transfer of authority to Governor Reed until early July 1868. Nonetheless, the legislature convened for its first session on June 8. In the first actions taken by black lawmakers in Florida, the members ratified the Thirteenth and Fourteenth Amendments to the United States Constitution, abolishing slavery and mandating equal protection of the laws and due process of law regardless of race. In mid-June they reconvened to elect United States senators. They first selected Michigan carpetbagger Adonijah H. Welch and then moved on to a contest between Osborn and Hart. Although the Loyalist received support from Pearce and Bradwell, Osborn's carpetbag and Lincoln Brotherhood allies defeated Hart. After watching the African American solons in action, white northern Methodist minister John M. Swaim commented, "There may be very few polished experts in parliamentary procedure, but there is a good deal of that which is an excellent substitute therefore—sound sterling common sense."[45]

Thus, with a measure of sound common sense and a growing knowledge of parliamentary procedure, Florida's black legislators eagerly looked ahead to a new day in politics, law, and society. They foresaw rapid improvement for their race through legislative enactment and the power of the governor's office. From the celebrations of June, it would take them only a few weeks to discover how hard a road remained to be traveled.

2

"African Methodism is about to rule Florida"

The Struggle for Power

Three years after the Civil War's end, Republican government came to Florida in June and July 1868 based upon a foundation of African American suffrage. The process divided white Loyalists, carpetbaggers, the state's principal black churches, and the black electorate generally. Still, hopes ran high that summer. "[The freedmen] are all jubilant over their success," reported one observer, "and expect soon to have things all their own way."[1] Incoming governor Harrison Reed had courted African American support with promises of action, including appointment of at least one black cabinet member. African Americans, in turn, had turned out in substantial numbers to provide the governor with a mandate. The only thing required was the passage of time, or so it seemed.

Reed's ability to accomplish good ends for Florida's African Americans derived in substantial part from two constitutional powers. First, he could veto bills passed by the legislature, giving him a say in its deliberations. More important, he possessed broad powers of appointment. "The Governor of Florida is as much an autocrat as the Czar of Russia," explained one resident. "He has the appointment of every State officer of any importance, and can remove, reappoint, and remove again each and all at his sovereign will and pleasure." The man added, "He can remove and appoint for official or personal reasons or for no reason at all, and there is no one to say him nay."[2]

During his first weeks in office, Reed utilized these powers but with intentions surprising to many black leaders. To the good, he placed some African Americans in county offices, though rarely in any position other than county commissioner or justice of the peace. Even then, he failed to confer control of any commission on African Americans. He also tended to reward men not linked to AME presiding elder Charles H. Pearce. In Leon

County, for example, Reed positioned Baptist minister James Page on the county commission, and in Duval he named Baptist Samuel Spearing as a justice of the peace. Most major appointments went to Reed's fellow carpetbaggers. Alarmingly, though, many brought former secessionists and Rebel officials into the government. Three of the seven circuit judges Reed placed on the bench were white conservatives, as was comptroller Robert H. Gamble. For attorney general, Reed turned to James D. Westcott, Jr., who had been closely linked to Florida's Confederate government. Soon the governor elevated Westcott to the state supreme court. As for Reed's promise to include a black man in his cabinet, he named the well-regarded Jonathan C. Gibbs as secretary of state but withdrew his name before senate confirmation.[3]

The attempt to expand the Reed administration's base of support among conservative whites stoked fears among Loyalists and some black leaders. The concerns deepened when, in early August, the governor vetoed a law guaranteeing blacks equal access to railroad transportation and public accommodations. Reed labeled the measure, a high priority of blacks, as "unnecessary."[4] Further, the governor resisted passage of a law providing for an integrated public school system, another matter of importance to African Americans. "There are certain elements in the Republican party whose interests have not been subserved—who have not been treated with proper consideration," alleged a Hillsborough County legislator. "I refer to the colored people and what is known as the Southern Loyalists."[5] Senator Charles H. Pearce added, "Every appeal for my race has been voted down by the Conservatives, aided by these weak-kneed [carpetbag] Republicans."[6]

The conflicts between Reed, the Loyalists, and Pearce's allies paralleled another and growing split, this one between the governor and his associates on the one hand and United States Senator Thomas W. Osborn and his friends on the other. Reed had aimed some appointments at drawing Osborn supporters into the governor's camp. In the legislature the two forces had come to blows over a number of issues, especially bills to create corporations with state sponsorship for the benefit of private backers including followers of Reed and Osborn. When Reed exercised his veto powers, the differences hardened. The train of events resulted in polarization within the government and the Republican Party. For the next four years, most state government crises would center around or be substantially affected by the clash of the Reed or "state house" faction with the Osborn Ring or "federal officeholders" faction.[7]

As these divisions and complications swirled around them, African American legislators, new to the process, attempted to find their way.

Editor T. Thomas Fortune, a former legislative page and son of representative Emanuel Fortune, remembered most of them as “outstanding characters, intelligent and shrewd.” Noting that “many of them were orators,” he explained that “they could talk at length and with some show of information on any subject proposed in the legislature.”[8] Nonetheless, the lawmakers often found themselves confused, uncertain as to which of the contending camps merited support or which financial schemes deserved public sponsorship.

Other problems confronted the legislators. Most were poor men, living in a state that afforded few economic opportunities for blacks. The constitution provided salaries for General Assembly members, but the state, practically bankrupt, could pay only in scrip that was difficult to negotiate and that rapidly decreased in value. In the circumstances, accusations of improper payments and outright bribery circulated. Similar rumors already had arisen out of the constitutional convention, where Mule Team proponents had maintained a rented home to provide free room and board for their delegates. Harrison Reed and his supreme court chief justice appointee Edwin M. Randall reputedly had dispersed cash received from national Republican sources. Apparently, black and white legislators accepted funds and favors. “[Some black lawmakers had] wide open eyes to the main chance, which was not always reached by the straight and narrow path,” T. Thomas Fortune explained, “and much crooked business went on which helped to bring the Reconstruction government into disrepute and ultimate downfall.”[9]

In late summer and fall 1868, legislative corruption and the ultimate downfall of Republican government remained less of a concern to the governor than did the threat of Senator Osborn. When Reed approved a measure canceling the presidential election in Florida and providing for the legislature to choose presidential electors, he weakened his position by alienating many of the white conservatives he had been courting. Anxious to buttress his administration, he chose that moment to reach out to Senator Pearce and the AME church. In doing so the governor appealed to Pearce’s long-standing dislike for Osborn and insisted that he, Reed, had seen the error of his own ways. “[The governor] had a consultation with him with reference to the conspiracy that Osborn and his officeholders had formed to resist his administration,” recalled black state senator John Wallace. “Pearce was convinced that the Governor was sincere in trying to administer the government with honesty and pledged himself to do whatever he could to enlighten his people as to the true intention of the administration.”[10]

Whatever commitments were made between Reed and Pearce, the

governor in September and October launched a series of initiatives that almost resulted in his removal from office. First, he executed a host of appointments of African Americans to local office, including designation of Pearce as superintendent of schools for Leon County. Then he attempted a preemptive strike against Osborn. On October 28 the governor declared vacant the legislative seats of certain men whom he had appointed to local office. The individuals primarily affected were Osborn men, although it likely caused Pearce little regret that his rival, Robert Meacham, was removed from the senate due to his designation as Jefferson County's circuit court clerk.[11]

To Osborn faction members, Reed's removal action constituted a gauntlet thrown down at their feet. The opportunity for counterattack came within a few days when the legislature met to name three presidential electors (including Meacham). Finding a pretext in the governor's veto of an expenses bill, they pushed a bill of impeachment through the house of representatives on grounds, among others, of embezzlement, corruption, and "declaring many legislative seats vacant."[12] Carpetbagger lieutenant governor William H. Gleason adjourned the legislature before the senate could consider the charges. In the process he assumed power as acting governor with the complicity of Reed's secretary of state George J. Alden.[13]

Reed, with Pearce's assistance, refused to yield. He fired Alden as secretary of state and appointed in his stead Jonathan C. Gibbs, finally making Gibbs the state's first black cabinet official. The governor's support among black voters thus bolstered, Reed pursued redress in the state supreme court, which ruled that he had been removed illegally. The governor also moved against Gleason, winning another victory in December when the supreme court determined that the lieutenant governor did not meet the qualifications for his office. Meanwhile, Pearce irritated the Osborn men by contesting, though unsuccessfully, the Republican congressional nomination with incumbent carpetbagger Charles M. Hamilton.[14]

The impeachers blustered through the setbacks that their quarrel with the governor would be continued when the legislature met in January 1869. New house speaker Marcellus Stearns, still close to Osborn, appointed an impeachment committee that included Emanuel Fortune, Auburn H. Erwin, and Henry S. Harmon, all of whom previously had shown independence from Charles Pearce. The senator and his allies battled on Reed's behalf. Ultimately, Fortune, Erwin, and Harmon opposed removing the governor. After announcement of their stand, impeachment backers called off the attempt. Temporarily, peace reigned between white supporters of Reed and Osborn, but the AME ministers were not so easily assuaged.

"Hon. C. H. Pearce, who had succeeded in rallying the colored members of the Legislature to the Governor," recalled John Wallace, "was very severe on the conspirators, and threatened to alienate the colored voters from the carpetbaggers if this persecution of Reed was continued."[15]

The legislative controversies of 1868 and early 1869 carried important implications and consequences. Divisions between state and federal officeholders had become pronounced, not to mention marked by rumors of corruption. The credibility of Republican government suffered. "This gypsy politics degrades the character of all who are concerned, in taking an interest to sustain it," commented a Madison man, "reducing political life and morals to the sheerest scramble for spoils."[16] On the other hand, African American leaders had emerged as key legislative players. They had to be taken seriously. Symbolic of that fact, newspaper accounts of the governor's capitol reception for legislators in February 1869, where "a very happy interchange of sentiment took place," specified the prominent appearances of "Messrs. Gibbs, Pearce, Bradwell, and others."[17] These men and their colleagues had proved themselves adept at maneuvering and capable of achieving needed results. In the 1869 scramble, for instance, Pearce and his allies had ended up with approval of a public education act that provided for racially integrated schools. The law represented no small accomplishment.[18]

The political truce that ended the 1869 regular session lasted only for a short while. In February the governor telegraphed another overture to white conservatives by appointing Confederate Florida's chief commissary officer, Pleasants W. White, as circuit judge for Leon County, the state's most important circuit judgeship. Also, violence against African Americans had begun to escalate the previous autumn. The problem grew in the new year. In March an attack upon Jackson County court clerk John L. Finlayson and state senator William J. Purman, a close friend of Senator Osborn, initiated what was called the Jackson County War. Into the new decade, the county's black and white Republicans fought with white vigilantes. When Governor Reed declined to send state militia to quell the violence, Purman and Osborn found new grounds for wanting to oust the governor from office.[19]

Reed compounded his problems by calling a special legislative session for the summer of 1869. The Fifteenth Amendment to the United States Constitution—which prohibited a state government from abridging voting rights based upon race, color, or previous condition of servitude—awaited ratification. More important for the governor, he desired to assist his friends Milton S. Littlefield and George W. Swepson in obtaining several million dollars in state bonds for railroad development. Reed succeeded in obtaining legislative approval, but the affair scandalized the public. History has labeled it the Swepson-Littlefield fraud.[20]

The public clamor over the Swepson-Littlefield subsidies offered Osborn and Purman a ready-made excuse for another impeachment attempt. In December 1869 and January 1870 Reed once again successfully appealed to Pearce and the AME church for assistance. During January's legislative session, black representatives John R. Scott, Sr., who was an AME minister, Emanuel Fortune, and Henry S. Harmon led the governor's defense. Because some Democrats had sided with the impeachers, Reed seemingly needed additional support. He negotiated with David L. Yulee, prominent former Democratic United States senator, and with Osborn's men. As a result, impeachment failed. Then the assembly approved numerous laws creating private corporations vested with substantial state subsidies. With minor exceptions they benefited whites and not blacks. Public anger hardly had died down when, in May, Reed cajoled a special session to permit him to transfer $4 million in state bonds to Swepson and Littlefield. Disillusionment with Republican government ballooned. "Taxes are getting to be enormous," recorded one northern-born resident, "and all to enrich a lot of thieves who for the sake of office call themselves Republicans."[21]

At this point, the AME leaders subject to Pearce's influence decided with some other African American leaders that the government's direction needed to be changed by their taking aggressive action to mute the Osborn Ring's power. The final ratification in 1870 of the Fifteenth Amendment, which Florida black leader John Willis Menard called "that righteous measure," offered inspiration. "The South was in a state of great political excitement," Menard explained.[22] At the same time the AME church was experiencing rapid growth due to a wave of religious sentiment called the "Great Revival of 1870," a fact that emboldened its ministers religiously and politically.[23] Finally, some white leaders—namely Osborn—had come to realize that if they were to continue to enjoy black support, offices of importance must be afforded to the race's representatives. The senator decided to back Meacham for United States congressman, seeing the move as an effective way to sap Reed's strength among black voters.[24]

The congressional contest came to its head in August 1870 at a Republican state convention held to nominate candidates for Congress and lieutenant governor. State senator Purman urged renomination of Congressman Hamilton, and Osborn worked for Meacham. Alachua County, where the session convened, presented Henry S. Harmon and Josiah T. Walls. Pearce and Jonathan C. Gibbs also advanced themselves. Because black

State senator and United States congressman Josiah Thomas Walls (1842–1905). (Courtesy Florida Archives)

delegates constituted the assembly's majority and most were unpledged, the nomination remained up for grabs. An African American caucus failed to identify a consensus candidate. A series of nine convention ballots, marked by confusion and wheeler-dealer politics, left Meacham close to nomination but several votes shy. Widely shared sentiment desired to deny Meacham, Osborn, and Hamilton. Accordingly, the remaining black candidates withdrew in favor of Walls who, until then, had received few votes. Walls benefited from several factors: his popularity among veterans, the fact that he was not identified with a church or carpetbagger faction, and his pragmatic political orientation. On the eleventh ballot he obtained his majority. Gibbs saw the event as "not only a vindication of the honor and faith of the Republican party" but also as a triumph for Florida's blacks. "This was the great point sought after and gained," he declared.[25]

The ensuing electoral campaign unfolded tumultuously and sometimes violently. White night-rider groups attempted to intimidate black voters, with mixed results. When they threatened Meacham at Monticello, for instance, blacks armed themselves. "The negroes of the county have shown a desire to fight," the local newspaper declared.[26] Still, terrorism gained the conservatives advantages in key counties, with more than a few black voters opting for their families' safety rather than the ballot. When the votes were tallied, Walls and his running mate—Loyalist lieutenant governor candidate Samuel T. Day—claimed narrow, though contested, victories. Pearce survived a challenge from Baptist minister James Page and returned to the state senate with Meacham and Gadsden County's Frederick Hill, an AME layman. Seventeen blacks claimed house seats. Among them were AME ministers Josiah H. Armstrong, Noah Graham, John R. Scott, Sr., and John W. Wyatt, along with respected AME layman and later minister Alfred Brown Osgood.[27]

Though he had been denied the congressional nomination, Pearce along with his followers and other black leaders interpreted the 1870 election results as a great step forward for Florida's African Americans. When a newspaperman encountered Pearce, Gibbs, Scott, state representative Daniel M. McInnis, and Duval County justice of the peace William W. Sampson the following year at Jacksonville, he reported, "They all believe that there is a bright future to dawn upon this land of flowers, and they are doing all they can do to encourage immigration from other states."[28] That summer AME minister and Gadsden County commissioner William G. Stewart proclaimed to the church's leading journal, "I am glad to inform you that African Methodism is about to rule Florida."[29]

These men believed in a hopeful future, but the present still troubled them. First, Pearce came under attack in December 1870. Senator Frederick Hill and Gadsden representative Harry Cruse, both Osborn Ring men, accused the AME leader of accepting a bribe earlier in the year. The charges likely came as retribution for Pearce's vehement opposition to Ring power. Judge Pleasants W. White, the former Confederate official appointed by Governor Reed, presided over a trial that found the senator guilty and sentenced him to imprisonment and a fine. Pearce appealed. Meanwhile, conservatives and Ring men sought to deny the senator his legislative seat. New lieutenant governor Samuel T. Day blunted the attack.[30]

Other concerns added to the magnitude of problems encountered in 1871. Violence, especially in Jackson County, had continued to plague rural blacks. When Reed appeared before the AME annual conference in June, he insisted that he could do nothing. In frustration, the ministers could only urge African Americans to move out of Jackson County, as state representative Emanuel Fortune already had. The governor persisted, as well, in appointing conservative whites to powerful local offices in black-majority

The Florida senate in 1875. John Wallace appears on the far left leaning on a cane. Thomas W. Long stands in the front row holding his hat, while directly above and to the right of Long likely is Frederick Hill. Robert Meacham gazes from the row next to the top, third man from the right. Standing immediately to the right of Meacham probably is Washington Pope. (Courtesy Florida Archives)

counties. Reed also declined to push for a substantive civil rights act; he and Osborn feuded; and tales of government corruption ran rampant as the governor attempted to deed most state lands to his friend Milton S. Littlefield. "The carpet-bag dynasty of Florida is crumbling," a Democrat gloated in December.[31]

The political crisis intensified during the 1872 legislative session. Osborn Ring men, led by house speaker Marcellus Stearns, proposed impeachment. The governor's allies were diminishing in number, and Jonathan C. Gibbs emerged as a prime defender. "I believe him to be a persecuted man," the secretary of state wrote during the fight, "& I will not desert him in his trouble."[32] Within the Republican caucus, fights erupted. Meacham and Gibbs squared off verbally, although the true pyrotechnics came when Ring member William J. Purman accused Pearce of "a diarrhoea for Congress." Pearce, according to one report, " 'chawed' the senator from Jackson up."[33]

The party breach thereafter widened. Soon the senate's carpetbagger leadership killed another civil rights bill with the governor's apparent blessing. That constituted the last straw for many black legislators. Representative Daniel M. McInnis offered a resolution condemning the carpetbaggers: "We, the colored members, and those who honestly sympathize with us, do unhesitatingly repudiate such friendship, and do now and henceforth withdraw from and decline from ever affiliating with, politically, or to aid in electing any such man or men who have so basely misrepresented our people." McInnis, Scott, and many of their fellows then voted for Reed's impeachment. Lieutenant Governor Day proclaimed himself governor, although the senate adjourned before trying the impeachment.[34]

The legislative excitement paled by comparison with subsequent events. Reed, who had returned to his Jacksonville home, reappeared at the capitol in April, reclaimed his office, and appealed to the state supreme court. Days later, a Republican convention met at Jacksonville to elect national party delegates. Pearce and his men vehemently attacked the Osborn Ring and carpetbaggers in general. They denied Osborn, Stearns, and Purman seats in the national convention while affording them to Walls and Josiah H. Armstrong.[35]

Back at Tallahassee, state tribunals issued several critical rulings. First, the supreme court upheld Pearce's 1871 bribery conviction on technical grounds. The senate, meeting at Day's call, expelled Pearce. Loyalist associate justice Ossian B. Hart thereupon publicly defended Pearce against the arguments of carpetbagger chief justice Edwin M. Randall. Seemingly influenced by Hart, Randall thereafter joined with Hart and other members of the state pardon board to grant Pearce a full pardon. The court subsequently ruled in Reed's favor over Day, placing the governor firmly back in power. In a separate decision, it ousted Day from the lieutenant governor's office by declaring that his 1870 Democratic opponent, William D. Bloxham, actually had won the position by a few votes.[36]

The wild events of spring 1872 served as a backdrop to that year's gubernatorial election. Reed wanted to return to office for another term, several of the carpetbaggers in the Osborn Ring desired the honor, and Lieutenant Governor Bloxham rated his own chances as excellent. The Loyalists spoke of Justice Hart. Pearce and the AME ministers faced a quandary. Reed was better than an Osborn man, but they desired neither. For a while Pearce supported a carpetbagger, state treasurer Simon P. Conover, but Conover withdrew on the nominating convention's eve, convinced that Osborn had rigged the affair. Pearce, himself, would not be a delegate. Leon County's party had split into factions, as a result of which a group led by Baptist minister John N. Stokes eventually represented the county in place of Pearce.[37]

While the AME presiding elder had no official place at the August nominating convention, he and his church intended to influence the proceedings. Stearns emerged as the Ring candidate, and Madison County's African American sheriff and tax collector David Montgomery nominated Reed. Black Hillsborough County delegate Peter W. Bryant named Hart. When Hart showed surprising black strength on the first ballot, Ring allies attempted to steal the nomination for Stearns. "Many of the Hart men, mostly colored, became frantic," one observer recorded. "They rushed about the room, mounted chairs, tables, desks, and everything else that would elevate them, and yelled, and bawled, and shouted, and swore they would not submit to such a nomination; they wanted Hart and intended to have him." Protest leaders included AME ministers John R. Scott, Sr., and Josiah Armstrong. After they threatened to bolt from the convention, Stearns withdrew and Hart received the nod by acclamation. With noise and confusion prevailing in the hall, Ring men urged Stearns for the lieutenant governor nomination. Scott attempted to block the Ring initiative but failed.[38]

Through the insistence of black delegates, particularly AME representatives, the 1872 Republican gubernatorial convention rejected the party's carpetbagger wings in favor of a southerner who had owned slaves and whom Pearce and other church leaders had angrily battled at the 1868 constitutional convention. On the surface the action is difficult to comprehend, but when carefully viewed it reflects shrewd judgment. The AME men desired an honest governor who would consider their interests as having real priority in the state government. Hart had called early for the grant of civil rights to blacks, had opposed President Andrew Johnson's conservative Reconstruction policies, and had defended Charles Pearce at the time of his senate expulsion. One of Hart's most persistent critics, the Democratic editor Charles Dyke, later wrote of him, "His integrity as a man and as an officer of government . . . [was] never questioned."[39] Pearce believed that he could trust the southerner, while experience had proved that he could not trust the carpetbaggers.

Contestants bitterly fought the 1872 gubernatorial campaign, though widespread violence did not mar it as had been the case in 1870. A splinter group of white Republicans—identified as the Liberal Republicans—backed William D. Bloxham, as did the Democrats. Disenchanted with Republican squabbles, corruption, and disappointment or else lured by

Poet, editor, and legislator John Willis Menard (1838–1893). (In possession of the author)

promises of reward, some African Americans opted as well to campaign for the Democrat. On his part, Bloxham argued that he desired only to deliver the state from "the hands of wicked, designing men" and "to assert the equal political rights of all men of every color and condition and [to] see that they are preserved inviolate."[40] Countering the Democrat, Loyalists and black leaders toiled to bring their voters to the polls in record numbers. Their efforts brought success. Hart defeated Bloxham handily in a large turnout. "Elder C. H. Pearce saved this state to the Republican party," boasted J. Willis Menard in the AME newspaper. "He has been triumphantly re-elected to the state senate, and now he stands forth amply vindicated, as the champion of right and duty, the most independent man in the state." Menard concluded, "Florida is destined to become the negro's new Jerusalem."[41]

In January 1873 African American legislators looked forward to the legislature's opening and to Governor Hart's inauguration. They enjoyed enhanced numbers in the General Assembly. Jackson County's Washington Pope and AME minister Thomas W. Long of Marion County joined Pearce,

Meacham, and Hill as senators. The house black delegation increased by two to nineteen, with the notable addition of two strong leaders: AME minister William G. Stewart, now of Leon County, and Madison County's David Montgomery. They believed that they could elect John R. Scott, Sr., as speaker. The Republican caucus approved Scott, but dissident members joined with Democrats to deny him the office.[42]

Disappointment such as Scott's did not typify African American leaders' experiences during the session. Daniel McInnis introduced a strong civil rights act. With the governor's help it became the Hart administration's first new law. Also in January the legislators denied Thomas W. Osborn reelection to the United States Senate and Harrison Reed a first election to the body. Robert Meacham showed strength in the contest, but former state treasurer Simon Conover—who had become speaker in lieu of Scott—took the prize. Before adjournment in February, the assembly had increased support for public education and passed a Hart initiative to revamp state finances. The governor's leadership, combined with black votes and legislative skills, had begun to revolutionize Florida government.[43]

Beyond legislative debates, the governor moved on other fronts to honor his commitments and distinguish himself from his predecessor. In line with their educational concerns, many black leaders wanted Jonathan C. Gibbs designated as superintendent of public instruction. Hart hesitated briefly, unsure of Gibbs's association with Reed and still mindful of the 1868 constitutional convention, before naming the former secretary of state to the post. The governor showed less hesitation in making other appointments of blacks, substantially increasing their involvement in local government. Where Reed in 1872 had handed control in some counties to white conservatives, Hart reversed the trend. In one exceptional example—violent Jackson County from which some African American officials had fled earlier in the decade—he had named by 1874 a black-majority commission and two new black justices of the peace.[44]

In a letter to a friend, Governor Hart explained his beliefs about appointments of blacks to public office. "It is not impossible to find men among those of darker skin than our own who will do well in office," he wrote, "if we accord them such friendly aid in their new and unaccustomed duties, as was always given before the war to ordinary appointees by those of their friends who understood the duties of their offices better than they did." Hart continued: "We are not apt to trouble ourselves much to find men who will do for office with some friendly aid, among any but our own color. But we ought to do it, and the sooner we learn to do it faithfully, the better for our Country." The governor concluded, "Our race will always be the most prominent and aggressive one at any rate, but we ought to act squarely up to our grand political principles, and crush our prejudices under our heels."[45]

Circumstances soon tested Hart's grand political principles. Violence flared in Columbia County, threatening local Republican officials. When similar situations had occurred during Reed's administration, the governor had declined to send military force. Hart's reaction showed a decided difference. He ordered the state adjutant general and six African American troopers to Lake City. They, in turn, armed additional blacks who patrolled the streets, keeping the peace. When the situation did not calm, Hart and his cabinet visited the town. In a public meeting the governor lectured local citizens on their responsibility to help maintain law and order. The black troopers and volunteers remained, and the crisis eased.[46]

The Hart administration brought change to Florida. As early as March 1873 one observer could note, with some exaggeration, "The strife is over; the antagonisms have measurably expended their force; the elements are settling into closer harmony."[47] The governor proudly expressed similar sentiments in his address to the 1874 legislature. "It is . . . very gratifying to know that the spirit of political hatred and bitterness, which was the fruit of the great rebellion, is well nigh extinguished," he declared, "and that the people of all parties are more united and harmonized than they have been for many years."[48] During that session legislators further revamped state finances, approved a series of constitutional amendments to continue reform of state and local government, and supported greater funding for education and social services. "This legislature is the best we have had to be sure," commented a Jacksonville Democrat.[49]

When the legislature departed Tallahassee in February 1874, black leaders looked ahead optimistically. The past fourteen months had brought them enhanced power and solid progress. That fact evidenced itself to all when, in mid-1873, John R. Scott, Sr., had received the lucrative and influential appointment of United States collector of customs for the port of St. Johns (Jacksonville). Their chronically sour relationship with carpetbaggers was one of few immediate political concerns. Then on March 18 Florida's political world turned upside down. Ossian Hart died suddenly at his Jacksonville home, and Osborn Ring carpetbagger Marcellus Stearns became governor. Things would never be the same.[50]

3

"In God's name let the negro have rest and peace"

The Collapse of Dreams

During 1873 and early 1874 Florida's African American leadership came into its own. Josiah T. Walls served his state in the halls of Congress. Jonathan C. Gibbs presided from Tallahassee over Florida's public school system. And enhanced numbers of legislators worked with Governor Ossian B. Hart to protect civil rights, quell racial and political violence, broaden educational initiatives, improve state finances, and reform state and local government. Just when the future began to look brightest, the governor died, leaving his office in the hands of a carpetbagger closely associated with the Osborn Ring. Soon a crisis atmosphere pervaded state politics. "The lines between the Ring and the anti-Ring element in the Republican party," observed John Wallace, "were now drawn more distinctly than were the lines between the Democratic and Republican parties."[1]

A preview of renewed warfare between major black leaders and Florida's northern-born politicians had occurred early in 1874 when the house of representatives elected a white Osborn Ring man, Malachi Martin, as its speaker. "The colored members of the Assembly are justly enraged at the want of faith manifested in the election of Speaker," observed a Savannah newspaper. "Mr. [Alfred Brown] Osgood, a colored man, was nominated by general consent and by a full [Republican] caucus." The account continued, "With no reason assigned of incompetency or anything else, he was denied an election, and enough Republicans withheld their votes to defeat him, and Mr. Martin was elevated, receiving the entire Democratic vote."[2] By midyear leaders, such as one former Jefferson County legislator and constitutional convention delegate, once again openly condemned the northerners. "At a Radical meeting in Monticello the other day," one report noted, "one of the members, a negro named Anthony Mills, made a speech which was loudly applauded. He denounced the carpetbaggers in round terms, and advised his race to support no man for office hereafter who was not born and raised in Florida."[3]

Through the year the situation worsened, as the pressures of adjusting to new political conditions in the wake of Hart's death increased. By summer important splits had developed within the black leadership in key counties, with some African Americans associating themselves with the white northerners. For example, in Duval County John R. Scott, Sr., and J. Willis Menard spatted about broken commitments to support each other for office. Because he occupied the highest level federal patronage position held by a black in the state, collector of customs at Jacksonville, Scott served at the pleasure of carpetbag senator Simon Conover. As such, he came to be identified with the senator's interests and to be seen as his representative in the black community. In that capacity Scott attempted to enforce discipline upon local black leaders such as state representative Daniel McInnis, who had opposed Conover in certain matters. Scott combined with protégé Joseph E. Lee to deny McInnis renomination in 1874 and to assure Lee's election in McInnis's stead. Bitter feelings naturally resulted from such incidents.[4]

As of August the bruised feelings, mistrust, and fears resulted in open political warfare. Florida by then merited two members of the United States House of Representatives. In one district Josiah T. Walls, after resisting a carpetbag attack in his home county of Alachua, easily bested northern-born Dennis Eagan for the congressional nomination. In the other district the situation proved more complicated. White northerner William J. Purman had held the seat for two years, but Robert Meacham, Charles H. Pearce, and Jonathan C. Gibbs all desired to displace him. Gibbs and Meacham both believed that they had Governor Marcellus Stearns's support.[5]

The congressional nominating convention opened on August 11 at Tallahassee. Purman grasped control of its organization, provoking Meacham, Pearce, and Gibbs to revolt. A rump session resulted in Meacham's nomination after several ballots. Purman friends then burst open the doors of the capitol room in which the proceedings had taken place and "commenced an indiscriminate assault upon every person in the lobby who was opposed to Purman."[6] Stearns thereupon ejected Purman and his men from the capitol. On August 13 the congressman convened a meeting of the party's district executive committee and claimed the Republican nomination. Over the next month the two candidates confronted each other as well as the Democratic nominee. Finally Purman and Stearns reached an accord, after which the governor, by withdrawing his support, convinced Meacham to leave the race.[7]

Besides party unity, the Tallahassee nominating convention produced another important casualty. On August 14 Jonathan C. Gibbs died. "Without premonition, and in the enjoyment of vigorous physical and mental powers," explained one newspaper, "he was suddenly stricken down in his office of apoplexy, about the hour of 11 o'clock yesterday morning, and was insensible to the hour of his death." The report further noted: "Mr. Gibbs had slept peacefully and quietly Thursday night, and gave no indication of being unwell on Friday morning. At his accustomed hour he repaired to the Capitol, visited the Executive Office on business connected with his department, and then went to his own office, which is located on the second floor of the building. Here he was found shortly thereafter by Judge [James T.] Magbee, lying insensible on the floor of his office." Physicians labored to revive Gibbs, but their efforts proved unavailing. "No apparent relief was given," the newspaper commented, "and he lay with closed eyes, breathing stentorious and heavily, until late in the afternoon when he was removed to his residence, when, without other change than the steady approach of death, he breathed his last."[8] A Jacksonville editor wrote of Gibbs, "It is doing no injustice to the living to add, that in all the elements that go to make up what is termed a good citizen and a capable and honest public servant, he leaves few superiors."[9]

Gibbs's death fittingly accentuated a mournful period for the Republican Party. Anger at carpetbaggers kept many blacks from voting for the white northerners in November. Yet Purman succeeded in his congressional race, and Walls claimed victory as well. For black legislators, the polling produced pleasing results. In the senate, John Wallace replaced Charles H. Pearce, and Alfred B. Osgood joined Washington Pope, Frederick Hill, Robert Meacham, and Thomas W. Long. For the carpetbaggers the totals appeared not so appealing. Republicans controlled only half the senate's seats, and the body ended up with a Democrat as presiding officer. Eighteen African Americans sat in the house of representatives, but it contained only a narrow Republican majority. Upon organization, the lower chamber again chose a white man, Independent Democrat Thomas Hanna, as speaker over an African American, David Montgomery. It did so, though, with the votes of black members wary of Montgomery's ties with Governor Stearns and the Osborn Ring. "The colored brother was now even with the Ring for the defeat of Osgood for Speaker in 1874," recorded John Wallace.[10]

In this situation African American leaders searched out some way to preserve their power in state government to ensure that Reconstruction gains would not be lost amid party splits and bitter feuds. One strong trend of thinking called for more blacks in political and party office, particularly major state positions. "The next Convention of the Radical party in this State will witness the presentation of a number of colored aspirants for the higher offices in the gift of the people," forecasted a Jacksonville newspaper in July 1875, "and the display of a degree of independence which will entitle them to respect and consideration."[11] Somewhat to the contrary, some formerly Radical leaders decided that, in the interest of party unity or personal preference, they must accommodate themselves to certain carpetbag officials. Charles H. Pearce, to cite one example, associated himself more closely with Governor Stearns. In similar circumstances, John R. Scott, Sr., and Josiah T. Walls cemented their relationships with Senator Conover, although Walls later shifted again toward Stearns.[12]

One prominent voice began to speak out in favor of abandoning attachment to the Republican Party in favor of issue-oriented cooperation with leaders of each of the major parties. J. Willis Menard by early 1875 had been editing the state's principal black newspaper for several years. "The color line which divides political parties is, in the words of Homer, 'the direful spring of woe unnumbered,' " he wrote in that period, "and it is to be hoped that the time is not far distant when it will be abolished." Menard continued: "The quickest way to solve the Southern problem is to make the negro no longer an issue in politics. Let citizenship mean one thing all over the Union, and to all men and races." He added: "In God's name let the negro have rest and peace. Give him 'a fair field,' and free water, and let him sink or swim."[13]

As different men sought different answers to the dilemma, added complications arose. Some of them involved the AME church and carried a long-term impact that diminished its ability to influence politics. The first problem involved personalities. Since the church's advent in Florida, its two most powerful ministers, Charles H. Pearce and Robert Meacham, had engaged in a rivalry that sometimes aired itself in open conflict. By late 1872 Pearce had determined to resolve the situation by undercutting Meacham in his home county. One month after Governor Hart's election, the presiding elder arranged for the transfer of his protégé, George Washington Witherspoon, to a Jefferson County church. The young man possessed a gift for oratory. Of him it would be said that "whenever it was announced that [he] would preach . . . the roads would be full of women, children, horses and wagons."[14] To many of the county's poor rural residents, Witherspoon as a black man likely also offered a desirable contrast to the mulatto Meacham.

Witherspoon's transfer ignited a sometimes-heated struggle for control of Jefferson County's black votes, about 10 percent of the state's total. Well aware of the political threat, Meacham struck at his new rival. The senator's friend, state attorney J. N. Stripling, indicted Witherspoon on a questionable morals charge. An AME district meeting responded by denouncing the prosecution as malicious and demanding Stripling's removal. Witherspoon reacted directly at Meacham. In 1874 the junior man fought the senator's congressional candidacy, aiding that of William J. Purman. He also challenged Meacham's local control with his own successful candidacy for the state house. By late 1875 Representative Witherspoon sought to widen his popular appeal for future installments of the fight. He chose to juxtapose his own militant perspectives with Meacham's moderate approach by aggressively urging Jefferson County blacks to demand wages rather than agreeing to tenant farm or to sharecrop.[15]

The intra–AME church and intra–Jefferson County squabble created ripples locally and statewide. It continued with results that will be discussed later in this chapter, but, already in 1875, it had begun to turn many disenchanted blacks away from political involvement. When white fraud and occasional violence were added to the equation, it led within a decade to Democratic domination of the county's legislative delegation. More important, it helped to fuel resentments present within the Florida church against any involvement by ministers in politics.

The issue of ministers in politics was not a new one. Critics for years had sounded warnings about the corrupting influence of politics upon the ministry. By early 1876 calls for reform had grown so substantial that Pearce felt that he needed to respond. When the annual conference convened, he proposed a resolution "providing that no one be admitted hereafter into the Conference as ministers who were involved in political pursuits."[16] The motion never came to a vote, but the issue remained alive and dampened the enthusiasm of young ministers for political work. Within five years a dramatic change had taken place. "The annual assembling of [the AME church conference] was once closely watched by designing politicians and inducements held out for the influence of the ministers in their respective sections to elevate some unworthy person into office," noted a white Jacksonville editor in 1881, "but those days died with carpet-bagism." He added, "The ministers and delegates now seem to confine themselves to their church work and nothing more, which is gratifying to all christians."[17]

Beyond personality conflicts, lack of AME church unity, and moral questions about political involvement, other dynamics at play within the black leadership community ate away at its ability to combine for effective political action. As suggested in the case of Witherspoon and Meacham, significant divisions appeared between blacks and mulattoes in some areas. "About five years ago," a Jacksonville account noted of the problem in 1879, "the same subject agitated the colored people, and at times they would meet, quarrel and fight over it on the public streets."[18] Because many of the earliest black leaders were mulattoes and many of the emerging leaders in the mid-70s were black, the problem symbolized a generational shift and its political dynamics.

A separate concern related to place of birth. Many early leaders—Charles H. Pearce and Jonathan C. Gibbs, for example—arrived from the North. Of the northern-born group, Civil War veterans and former noncommissioned offices such as Owen B. Armstrong, Josiah Armstrong, Henry S. Harmon, and Richard H. Black predominated. At least some of these men looked down upon southern blacks. "He could at any time excite the negroes to a frenzy," recalled a white carpetbagger of one black carpetbagger, "but being of Northern birth he had a contempt for the Southern negro, and always held him under control."[19] Presumably such attitudes sparked resentments of the northern blacks by the objects of their discrimination and added to the difficulties involved in forging a cohesive voting block.

Costs to officeholders inherent in black leadership also were increasing, depriving the state of many experienced men by the critical mid-1870s. On a basic level the potential cost of an official's own life weighed heavily. At times violent intimidation beset many regions of the state, especially rural areas. The situation claimed the lives of numerous individuals who were politically active, although the violence seldom targeted legislative officeholders directly. Still, attempts were made. Auburn Erwin endured a knife assault in 1870, armed horsemen accosted David Montgomery the same year, and Robert Meacham was shot at on the steps of his Monticello home in 1876. Of his state-representative father who confronted the deadly potential of the Jackson County War, T. Thomas Fortune wrote, "Emanuel Fortune was not afraid of any man or combination of men, but the bravest hesitates when the enemy lurks in the dark or the brush with a rifle in one hand and a torch in the other." He continued, "Every Negro and Southern loyalist and carpet-bagger in Jackson County lived in constant fear of assassination."[20] Emanuel Fortune chose to protect himself and his family by leaving his home and the legislature for a safer existence at Jacksonville. Others did likewise. Many men doubtless refrained from politics for the same reason.[21]

The financial costs of office holding also took their toll. In an area with few nonagricultural jobs, the state offered some employment possibilities through appointments to local office, but payment in scrip limited the rewards. The federal government, on the other hand, paid in hard cash; so patronage positions loomed as very desirable, especially in the customs service and the post office. Many African Americans—among them, Robert Meacham, Nelson F. English, Benjamin F. Livingston, Edward I. Alexander, Sr., and Amos Hargret[t]—became postmasters, some remaining in office during Republican administrations into the 1890s. The accessibility of other postal jobs for blacks particularly was enhanced in 1873 when William G. Stewart became Tallahassee's postmaster, a position that afforded him some supervisory influence statewide. Even then, the expenses of office and living usually outran income. One humorous story in that regard was told about Hernando County commissioner Henry Harper, who transported mail in his county "in an old broken down buggy," while yelling to oncomers, "clear the way for the United States mail." Strapped for cash, Harper supposedly insisted upon and was granted the right to carry merchandise and passengers.[22]

As black officeholders and other race leaders became more dependent upon federal jobs, demands for civil service reform echoed through the country. Broad-based changes came slowly, but as early as 1871 the United States commissioner of internal revenue forbade his employees to hold any county office. Then, during the Hart administration, President Ulysses S. Grant acted more forcefully. He prohibited, effective March 4, 1873, "persons holding any Federal civil office by appointment" from accepting or holding "any office under any State or Territorial government, or under the charter or ordinances of any municipal corporation."[23] The results evidenced themselves immediately. That year William G. Stewart, Zebulon Elijah, Alfred B. Osgood, and John R. Scott, Sr., resigned from the legislature. Conversely, to keep his senate seat, Robert Meacham gave up the lucrative office of register of public lands at Tallahassee. The law affected local officers, as well. For instance, James D. English departed the Monroe County commission in 1875. Cedar Keys lost mayor John G. Williams in 1874, and Riley E. Robinson left office as Fernandina alderman five years later.[24]

All of these factors and many others militated against black political cohesion and effective leadership as the date approached for elections in 1876. Except for Florida, Louisiana, and South Carolina, Democrats had redeemed the former Confederate states from Republican rule. Democrats also had made substantial gains in Congress, and Democrat Samuel J. Tilden seemed likely to capture the presidency. In turn, Florida's Democrats exulted at their own chances for capturing the state, especially after they named

Federal regulations compelled Pensacola's Zebulon Elijah (1838–1910) to resign from the legislature in the 1870s. (Courtesy Historic Pensacola Preservation Board)

popular New Hampshire–born former Republican George F. Drew as their gubernatorial candidate.[25]

As could have been predicted, Republicans split into warring camps. With Charles H. Pearce's assistance, Stearns took the Republican nomination at a boisterous convention. At the insistence of Alfred B. Osgood and other black leaders, he accepted David Montgomery as his running mate for lieutenant governor. During the debates Congressman Purman, John Wallace, and George W. Witherspoon denounced the governor. Joined by Josiah T. Walls, John R. Scott, Sr., and J. Willis Menard, they organized their own convention to designate Senator Simon Conover to oppose Stearns. They named Joseph E. Lee to challenge Montgomery. In August Walls and Scott then squared off to contest a congressional nomination. With black delegates divided, the prize went to white carpetbagger Horatio Bisbee.[26]

The sad state of party affairs appeared to guarantee Florida to the Democrats until national Republican officials forced Conover's withdrawal. The majority of African American leaders thereafter supported Stearns, with important exceptions such as John Wallace and William U. Saunders. Enunciating anger that resonated among many voters, J. Willis Menard declared: "The Ring returned to this state and placed a white ticket in the field to be elected by colored votes! Voting, without being voted for, like 'taxation without representation,' is tyranny; and if the intelligent and thinking colored men in the State have any aspirations and hopes in the future, they will resist this outrage and fraud, and fight for equal representation and common justice."[27]

The political infighting and resentments against the carpetbaggers fed the distaste that growing numbers of African Americans held for the Republican Party. As a result—although violent intimidation played an important role in certain rural areas—some would choose of their own volition not to vote. Others endorsed the Democrat. Alachua County legislator Theodore C. Gass came out for Drew in September. A visitor to Monticello "found the town full of people eager and excited, among many colored Drew and Hull Clubs."[28] At Marianna, Baptist minister Richard Ellis backed the Democrats, insisting that it "[is] as much my duty to support honest government as it is to preach honest principles."[29] Drew later believed that he received about 1,000 black votes in all.[30]

The campaign was conducted amid, as one historian put it, "threatened violence, hostile verbal exchanges, fraud, and subterfuge."[31] Irregularities marked the polling in many counties, with some members of both races and both parties stealing votes and stuffing ballot boxes. A notorious incident occurred in Alachua County where white carpetbagger Leonard G. Dennis and black carpetbagger Richard H. Black allegedly cast several hundred extra votes. Black's efforts eventually brought their reward from national party officials when he received a choice appointment in his hometown of Philadelphia. He quickly left Florida for good.[32]

The balloting ended badly for state Republicans and African Americans. On the bright side, after prolonged political maneuvering, high drama, and constitutional crisis, Florida's four presidential electoral votes were given to Republican Rutherford B. Hayes, permitting him to deny the office to Tilden and the Democrats. Charles H. Pearce and Thomas W. Long enjoyed the honor of casting two of the votes. In the state, though, Democrats triumphed. Drew assumed the governorship, and narrow, but solid, Democratic majorities ruled both houses of the legislature. African American representation slumped. Three senators—Robert Meacham,

Members of the 1885 Florida house of representatives. Thomas Van Renssalaer Gibbs (1855–1898), son of Jonathan C. Gibbs, may be seen peering from the top row (third from the right, immediately left of his colleague with the prominent beard and derby hat). (Courtesy Florida Archives)

Thomas W. Long, and former congressman Josiah T. Walls—sat in the upper chamber, although a fourth, Fuller M. White, did claim Jackson County's seat until ousted in favor of a white Democrat. The house delegation dropped to thirteen, almost half of whom were from Leon and Jefferson Counties.[33]

With Democratic rule came wholesale dismissals of African Americans from county offices. The Democratic governor could name his own men, and conservative whites took up the reins of local government. The change presented itself most tellingly in black-majority counties such as Leon,

Gadsden, Jefferson, and Jackson. Occasionally the governor would place a conservative black on a county commission. Anthony Bellamy, to cite an example, sat on the Jefferson County board in 1877, and Anthony Porter may have served in Franklin as late as 1881. Drew designated a few black justices of the peace, as well. Peter W. Bryant could offer a measure of justice to African Americans in Hillsborough County, while John Wallace for a time did the same in Leon. Yet, for the most part black voices no longer were heard in an official capacity in county courthouses.[34]

Interested in ensuring the permanence of their victories, Democratic legislators adjusted voting rules. They empowered county commissioners to create districts for electoral purposes and required voting within the district of residence. This action took away from rural blacks the protection afforded them by voting together at the county seat and mandated that they exercise their rights in potentially hostile areas away from the eyes of federal officials. It effectively disenfranchised blacks who moved away from their original district without observing the technicalities imposed for re-registration. The law additionally provided for annual revisions of registration lists and directed county commissioners to strike persons believed ineligible. The latitude permitted to Democratic partisans opened the door for manipulation of the rolls. In many counties they took up the challenge with great success. "The elective franchise of the negro . . . has been almost nullified in some portions of the State," J. Willis Menard insisted in 1884. "The system adopted in certain counties of the 'Black Belt' to deprive colored voters of their rights to the registration and manipulations of the voting precincts, was an outrage on the ballot."[35]

The disheartening results of the 1876 election placed black leaders in a predicament even greater than previous ones. Some sought advice and assistance from Washington. William U. Saunders, J. Willis Menard, and Peter W. Bryant called upon President Hayes but left the encounter with little more than soothing words. Duval County men, led by John R. Scott, Sr., and Joseph E. Lee, called for a state convention to foster "an understanding as to our present position, and whither we are drifting," noting that "the colored man is [still] a power in the body politic."[36] When that convention met at Tallahassee in July, though, men such as Scott, Lee, Thomas W. Long, John Wallace, Matthew M. Lewey, Cataline B. Simmons, and Salvador T. Pons stressed basic education, temperance, land ownership, and moderation over calls for aggressive political action. Other voices called out for alliance with Democrats. "Ten years of political slavery to one party has done nothing but produce conflict after conflict," observed John T. Shuften in his 1877 book *A Colored Man's Exposition of the Acts and Doings of the Radical Party South*, "and kept the states in a disordered condition, producing almost general poverty [to blacks]."[37]

From the uncertainty that followed Reconstruction's end, Florida's black political leadership entered a transitional period that saw the emergence of a new and different generation of leaders. First, many of the first generation passed from the scene. Charles H. Pearce turned his attention more toward church duties. His rival Robert Meacham tried once again in 1878 for a congressional nomination but suffered the easy victory of Simon P. Conover. Thereafter the senator's star declined, and he left office for good the following year. David Montgomery emerged from his heartbreaking defeat for lieutenant governor as a sick man. He sought medical relief in Jacksonville before returning to his father's New York home. He died there in April 1878. The next year John R. Scott, Sr., returned to the state house of representatives. He passed away during the legislative session on March 7.[38]

The men who took their places often appeared to be very different from their predecessors. Where first-generation lawmakers tended to be veterans or churchmen with limited educations, the new men often were lawyers, businessmen, and teachers. More than a few possessed formal educations and college degrees. Henry Wilkins Chandler, for example, arrived at Ocala from Maine in 1876, after taking degrees at Bates College and the Howard University law department. He taught and, within two years, achieved admission to the bar. The young man viewed the world pragmatically rather than ideologically, and he benefited politically from what one man described in the early 1880s as "a general distrust among our people against the old time political leaders."[39] Chandler took on longtime senator and AME patriarch Thomas W. Long in 1880, wrenching away Long's senate seat and ending his days as a public official.[40]

Sometimes the second-generation men literally belonged to a second generation. Jonathan C. Gibbs's son, Thomas Van Renssalaer Gibbs, attended Howard University, the United States Military Academy, and Oberlin College before entering the legislature in 1885. A teacher and administrator, he would serve as the first vice president of what became Florida A&M University. John Robert Scott, Jr., took his degree at Wilberforce University and was remembered there as a "great Hebrew scholar." Also a teacher, he sat in the Florida house of representatives in 1889. Peter H. Davidson, Jr., had done the same two years earlier, a decade after his father served in the chamber.[41]

These men and their fellows participated in legislative proceedings until 1889. Pursuant to a Hart administration reform, the assembly met

Marion County state senator and constitutional convention delegate Henry Wilkins Chandler (1852–1938). (Courtesy Florida Archives)

only every second year beginning in 1875. Four senators and fourteen representatives made up the African American complement in 1879. Two years later the numbers had improved to three senators and seventeen representatives. John E. Proctor and Henry W. Chandler sat in the senate in 1883, with eighteen black men in the house. As late as 1885 four senators—Chandler, Proctor, Daniel C. Martin, and Egbert C. Sammis—remained, as did fifteen representatives. These last numbers coincided almost identically with those for 1868. The difference for Republican power: southern Loyalists long had stopped voting for the party, and carpetbaggers almost had disappeared from legislative halls.[42]

These men of the second generation expected little from the legislature. Rather, they invested much of their energies in an issue of morality that had begun to gain real strength in Florida about 1878: the temperance movement. Its power as a political tool first had been displayed that year when George W. Witherspoon took up the cause in a manner that resulted in Robert Meacham's expulsion from his own

Monticello pulpit. At the time, the Florida division of the International Order of Good Templars had begun to thrive under the leadership of Joseph E. Lee, later succeeded by William M. Artrell. Despite racial segregation within parts of the movement, the organization and its officers and adherents worked well and easily with white ministers and legislators who shared a commitment to fight alcohol. As movement leader, Lee exercised tremendous influence. Because he also served in the legislature and later as a federal official, he maintained solid Republican ties. By the 1880s he had become identified, more than any other individual, as the leader of moderate to conservative black Republicans.[43]

Lee's conservative and somewhat accommodationist viewpoints found their counterpoint in the political beliefs of the man who emerged as the other key second-generation black leader, George W. Witherspoon. Rather than accept a working partnership with the remaining carpetbaggers, Witherspoon offered an aggressive agenda keyed to black occupation of high office. Particularly, he offered himself for Congress in 1880 against former state house speaker Malachi Martin. Given little chance of success, Witherspoon grasped the nomination to the glee of his supporters. "The hall was in an uproar at once," one account related, "and all cries of order failed to find a response."[44] The campaign locked Witherspoon into a closely fought and spirited match. Seeking to stir black voters, he advocated "Africanizing" Florida and warned that Democrats sought to "re-enslave" the freedmen. "We colored people will dictate all the nominations [now]," he proclaimed, "and by an exodus from the surrounding States to Florida, will hold it for all time."[45] Democratic fraud afforded his opponent a small majority, but Witherspoon appealed to the United States House of Representatives, where white Republicans ignored him and seated the Democrat. In 1882 delegates turned away the embittered Witherspoon from a second nomination, although he secured a seat from Jefferson County in the state house. By then, as will be seen, he prepared to take his followers on a new political course.[46]

Congressional and state politics had turned hostile to black aspirants by the early 1880s. Florida was then undergoing profound changes, and the path ahead appeared increasingly ominous. In one area, though, the changes had worked for the benefit of black leadership and African Americans generally, as ever greater numbers found a home in Florida's towns.

4

"The negro possesses a controlling influence in our municipal elections"

A Refuge in the Towns

The 1877 Democratic takeover of Florida government signaled the future exclusion of African Americans from most state and county offices, but significant opportunities remained for position in and control of towns and cities. That fact would become critically important in Florida's political life by the mid- and late 1880s. As will be considered in chapter five, it remains central to our understanding of why state laws were changed to erect virtually insurmountable barriers to widespread black voting. Beyond that, by 1890 African Americans already had played a vital role in the development of urban life in what soon became the South's most urban state.

African American involvement in Florida municipal governance was more than a decade old at Reconstruction's end. As discussed in chapter one, black voting in the state can be traced back to the Civil War's close, when freedmen participated in selecting a mayor and council for Fernandina. Two years passed before they again achieved access to the polls. The first of the congressional Reconstruction acts, which set the stage for black enfranchisement, became effective only in early 1867. At Pensacola on April 1, African Americans asserted their suffrage rights, and Jacksonville blacks would have done the same had military authorities not temporarily suspended elections.[1]

Black voting did not mean the same thing as black office holding during these early years. The 1865 Fernandina ticket had been all white, as were the 1867 Pensacola and Jacksonville lists. While available records do not permit a final determination, apparently the first blacks elected to municipal office were Fernandina clerk Samuel Boyd and alderman Charles Knabb, who received their positions on January 4, 1869. Later the same month Joseph Wyer became Pensacola's tax collector, and Heraldo Hernandez joined its council. Jacksonville added Cataline B. Simmons and

Cataline B. Simmons (1806–1883) achieved election to Jacksonville's board of aldermen in March 1869. (Courtesy Florida Archives)

William T. Garvin to its board of aldermen in March, which coincided with Cyrus Charles's election to Tampa's council. By year's end Gainesville and Ocala, among other towns, also included black members on local governing boards.[2]

When these men stepped into municipal offices, Florida remained an overwhelmingly agricultural state, but its towns were growing and taking on substantial commercial and political importance. In 1870 Key West likely was the largest town, with 5,016 residents, despite the fact that a temporary influx of immigrants showed Jacksonville with a population of 6,912. In round numbers, Pensacola boasted 3,400 and was trailed by Tallahassee at 2,000, Fernandina and St. Augustine at 1,700, Gainesville at 1,400, and Apalachicola and the Jacksonville suburb of LaVilla at 1,100. Of these towns, only Tallahassee, Fernandina, Gainesville, and LaVilla had black-majority populations, although Jacksonville temporarily possessed a black majority that year due to a surge of immigrants passing through.[3]

During the 1870s these and most other Florida towns experienced sustained growth. Key West expanded by 97 percent to 9,890; Jacksonville probably doubled; Pensacola ballooned by 105 percent; and Fernandina grew by 49 percent. Some former villages, especially in the St. Johns River area, mushroomed with the arrival of immigrants, many of them from the North. To give one example, the port town of Palatka jumped by 124 percent to a population of 1,616. Present-day metropolises along the lower coasts and in the central and southern interior, if they existed at all, remained villages or isolated outposts.[4]

Increases in the 1880s overshadowed the substantial growth of the 1870s. Railroad development opened up areas previously inaccessible. Tourism dramatically increased, and many visitors returned to make the state their home. In 1880 the census reported 269,493 residents, about 10 percent of whom lived in the four towns of 2,500 or more. Ten years later the total had soared by 45 percent to 391,422. Twelve towns then boasted more than 2,500 inhabitants, and they amounted to 20 percent of the state total. Key West still was the largest city with 18,080, but Jacksonville's 125 percent growth to 17,201 foretold that city's climb to the first rank. Third-place Pensacola became home to 72 percent more residents, while the resort town of Tampa climbed 668 percent from 720 to 5,532 and fourth place. During the period, towns such as Orlando, Green Cove Springs, DeLand, Sanford, Tavares, and Leesburg emerged into prominence.[5]

While Florida's towns flourished in the 1870s and 1880s, they did so partly from the arrival of large numbers of African Americans, many of whom provided the labor and skills for needed construction and commercial and personal services. To offer an example, at Jacksonville individuals such as Emanuel Fortune, Tillman Valentine, Thomas C. Claiborne, Adam White, John E. Onley, M. J. Christophe, May R. Green, W. A. Middleton, W. M. Robinson, and J. A. Pierce conducted businesses ranging from floral and dry goods to contracting and real estate speculation. "Colored people have a fair show in the trades, most of the native mechanics being colored," a resident noted in 1883, "and of this state of affairs the colored people have not been slow to avail themselves."[6] Naturally these men and other black residents paid close attention to their municipal government, many serving it in some official capacity—an accomplishment in which their fellow blacks often took pride. "Of the colored city clerks, marshals, market clerks, Police Justices and other colored functionaries who have held office [at Jacksonville] during the past nineteen years," T. Thomas Fortune wrote in 1889, "we can call to mind but *one* instance in which a colored official defaulted."[7]

Thousands of the African Americans who helped to fill Florida's towns came from other states, especially Georgia and South Carolina, but, just as important, they arrived from within the state. The old cotton plantation belt that lay between the Apalachicola and Suwannee Rivers had been home before the Civil War to the greater part of Florida's wealth and a majority of its slaves. This Middle Florida area included Jackson, Gadsden, Leon, Jefferson, and Madison Counties, although prior to the war its way of life had begun expanding into nearby Suwannee, Columbia, Alachua, Marion, and Hernando Counties.[8]

By the early 1880s poor living and working conditions in Middle Florida, combined with degenerating agricultural prospects, had produced an out-migration. "They go to other sections of this State, and to Louisiana and Texas," noted Governor William D. Bloxham in 1882, "where they find work on the railways under construction."[9] Many of the families eventually settled in the growing towns of East Florida, leaving Middle Florida with population losses, particularly during the period 1880 to 1885. The decreases hurt the chances of Middle Florida blacks for election to the state legislature but made little political difference in county seat towns such as Marianna, Monticello, and Quincy. There local tradition, intimidation, and careful drawing of town boundaries permitted few African Americans to hold city government positions. The situation varied at Madison and Tallahassee. In the former community at least seven blacks sat on the board of aldermen from 1876 to 1896 and one, Thomas McLeary, served as marshal for a term. At the state capital, a Republican ticket took control in 1872, with William G. Stewart as clerk and Henry Sutton as marshal and a council that included Jonathan C. Gibbs, Jonas W. Toer, and Everett C. Jones. Blacks thereafter served in every local office except mayor until all-white government commenced in 1890.[10]

West Florida historically had been sparsely settled with relatively few slaves. Pensacola, Milton, and Apalachicola—the region's three principal municipalities in 1870—had totals of black residents equal, respectively, to 37, 40, and 20 percent of their populations. Still, area residents recognized somewhat more flexible racial attitudes than did their Middle Florida counterparts. "In this city white and colored people protect each other," claimed an African American resident of Apalachicola in 1880. "It is the only city in Florida where white and colored gentlemen shave in the same shop."[11] At Pensacola blacks numbered among respected businessmen, contractors, teachers, and editors. "Pensacola, with its great shipping facilities, its railroads and the contemplated ones, its energetic business men, the rapid progress being made by the colored people, the manner in which it is building up at present give promise of a great city," wrote a local man in 1887. "We are proud always to walk by the light being held by members of our race or read the newspapers published by men of our race."[12]

Conditions in these communities began to change in the 1880s, but by then African Americans had achieved local office in all three towns. With its small black population, Milton saw race representatives on the council only in 1882, with Alexander M. Collins executing responsibilities as tax assessor in 1885. Apalachicola's available records are spotty, but Thomas Clark sat on the council by 1871 and at least four other men followed him by 1890. At Pensacola Republicans took control of local government in 1868 and held it, with a few exceptions, until 1885. No fewer than twenty-one African Americans occupied some position during that time, with Salvador T. Pons presiding as mayor in 1874.[13]

Florida's largest city, Key West, stood isolated on its island from the state's other regions. The cosmopolitan population mix often produced public brawls, but it also created and fostered relatively tolerant patterns of race relations. "The relations existing between the races in Key West has always been a very pleasant one," declared a correspondent of Florida's largest-circulation black newspaper in 1895, "and we know of no other city in the United States where the Negro enjoys his liberty to a greater extent than in Key West."[14] Blacks constituted only 20 percent of the population in 1870, but, beginning no later than 1875, at least one African American and sometimes more served in municipal office until the late 1880s. The representation recommenced by 1897 and continued into the twentieth century.[15]

East Florida, which encompassed the peninsula east and south of the Suwannee River, presented a complicated picture. Even after 1880 the frontier of organized settlement ran roughly from present-day Daytona Beach to Orlando to the headwaters of Peace River and down that stream to the Gulf of Mexico. Railroad development would not foster the birth or transformation of towns such as Fort Pierce, Palm Beach, Fort Lauderdale, and Miami until the 1890s or later. Growth during the 1870s and 1880s did spur new towns, but in good part they were sited in the St. Johns River valley and nearby areas of what now would be called central Florida.[16]

As a general rule of thumb, the older the East Florida town, the greater chance that blacks would hold public office. Some older communities did not incorporate until the 1870s and 1880s, and, when they did, they often included an African American on the first council or two but quickly moved to all-white slates. Such was the case at Live Oak (incorporated 1878) and at Bronson (1885). Strikingly, many new towns that were associated with northern developers and immigrants drew the hardest color lines. For example, neither Sanford (1877) nor DeLand (1882) appears to have elected a black official. The resistance of DeLand whites to a black marshal drew a mocking response from one Tallahassee newspaper in 1885. "Why not a Negro marshal for DeLand as well as Tallahassee?" its editor inquired. He continued: "Tallahassee has not been without one for ten or a dozen years, and as things generally go has not had much to complain of in them. Yet DeLand, the most intensely Northern settlement in Florida, founded by a zealous New York Republican whose name it bears, is startled at the idea of a Negro marshal."[17]

Orange County, as it existed in its larger form during the 1870s and 1880s, seems to have been particularly inhospitable to black officeholders. Clearly the low percentage of African Americans in its population—15 percent in 1880 and 28 percent a decade later—made election extremely difficult. Orlando chose no black officials. When Maitland elected Tony Taylor in its first election (1885), resulting white resentments helped to encourage local blacks to form their own town, which incorporated as Eatonville two years later. Goldsboro, adjacent to Sanford, followed Eatonville's lead in 1891.[18]

The story unfolded quite differently in the older towns. Ocala, Gainesville, Cedar Keys, and Lake City, for instance, witnessed the public service of dozens of African American men. At Ocala, Richard Dinkins joined the council in 1869 and others continued in his footsteps until at least 1893. Marshal Burrell Dawkins lost his life in the performance of his duties in 1881. Merchant and entrepreneur Frank P. Gadson served as treasurer, tax collector, and alderman after 1883. No fewer than seventeen blacks held positions at Gainesville from 1869 to 1891. They included mayor Josiah T. Walls (in 1873) and clerk and treasurer Daniel C. Martin (1880–1885, 1888–1890). Of the fifteen men who served at Cedar Keys, thirteen helped make the local laws as councilmen, John V. Cornell, Sr., worked as clerk, Fred E. Miller became marshal, and John G. Williams oversaw government as mayor (1874). Lake City's experience differed little. During the two decades beginning in 1872 and in the face of Columbia County's reputation for racial violence, ten men served as town councilmen. Romulus Spencer additionally held the position of tax assessor and Harry Drake that of marshal.[19]

The heart of African American municipal office holding could be found in the lower St. Johns River towns and in the cities on the upper Atlantic coast. Over a score of black Palatkans held office from 1870 until

Joseph Newman Clinton (1854–1927) sat as a member of Gainesville's city council during 1883–1885. Clinton also served in the Florida house of representatives from Alachua County and, later, as a federal official at Tampa. (Courtesy Florida Archives)

well past the turn of the century. "The negro possesses a controlling influence in our municipal elections," sputtered an enraged local editor in 1887.[20] Local favorites included Albert N. Doyle, who protected the town as marshal for most of the years from 1870 to 1884. At Green Cove Springs the names of only seven minority officials are known with certainty, but the total likely ran higher. Edward Fells and July Bram were on the council by 1874, and Lewis F. Forrester outlasted the century.[21]

On the coast, St. Augustine and Fernandina stand out as centers of the local power retained by African Americans. Whites ruled in the Ancient City until 1873, but afterward sixteen individuals held a variety of offices for three decades. One, alderman John Papino, was shot by the white city marshal following a dispute at a 1902 council meeting. He survived. The Fernandina record exceeds St. Augustine's and probably that of any other community except LaVilla. Forty-two black men helped mold policy at the town from 1869 to 1902. Turner Duling acted as marshal for ten years beginning in 1871, and Richard L. Denefield [Delafield] continued his work for half the next decade. Peter Bonaud, Samuel Boyd, Port W. King, and George Washington administered town affairs as clerk.[22]

Jacksonville and, particularly, LaVilla likewise constituted fertile grounds for minority office holding. With its black-majority population, LaVilla hosted a minimum of forty-six African Americans in its local government from no later than 1870 to its consolidation with Jacksonville in 1887. Mitchell P. Chappell[e], who also achieved election as tax collector and alderman, presided as mayor from 1874 to 1876. Future banker Sylvanus H. Hart served as clerk during the 1880s, and Handy [Hiram] N. Huggins kept the peace for nearly a decade as marshal. Although a much larger city than LaVilla, Jacksonville boasted fewer black officials, a result of hard-fought partisan politics and a white-majority electorate until after consolidation. Still, a score of African Americans held almost every available kind of local elective office, except mayor, from 1869 until after the century's end. Among the most prominent were clerk James D. Garvin, marshals Emanuel Fortune and George H. Mays, tax assessors Cataline B. Simmons and Thomas Lancaster, and aldermen William T. Garvin, William W. Sampson, and Cato Lee.[23]

Although conditions varied with each municipality, several general observations can be made with respect to black involvement in these local governments. First, levels of municipal office holding varied over time, usually as the Republican Party's fortunes waxed or waned. Beginning in 1869 the magnitude of service slowly increased over several years until reaching a high point during Governor Ossian B. Hart's administration and immediately following—that is to say, during 1873–1875. The African American mayors of Pensacola, Cedar Keys, Gainesville, and LaVilla all served during 1874. The trend reversed after 1875, with towns such as Gainesville, Jacksonville, Palatka, Pensacola, and St. Augustine coming, at least for a time, under the domination of conservative whites. By 1879 a state editor could insist, with a degree of exaggeration, that "There is only one town in the state under Republican sway, and that is Fernandina."[24]

With the new decade, Republican and black fortunes rebounded with the strength of George W. Witherspoon's congressional candidacy and, as will be considered in chapter five, African American involvement in the Independent movement. During the early 1880s Milton gained its first black officers, and Republicans enjoyed big wins at Tallahassee, St. Augustine, Gainesville, and other locales. The optimism dropped along with voter turnouts at mid-decade in a number of municipalities, with frustrated black leaders finding themselves compelled to support moderate whites against more rigid whites. "The ticket elected at the municipal contest [at Lake City] the other day was not the 'White ticket,' " insisted a local correspondent in 1886. "He says it was made by the negroes."[25]

Even when Democrats dominated a town government, some blacks could be serving as a part of it. Mixed tickets that contained white Democrats and conservative African Americans were common. For instance, two black Democrats sat on Marianna's council in 1877, and five years later Thomas Lancaster ran for Jacksonville tax assessor on a Democratic ticket. Numerous other examples could be cited. In addition, local voters routinely opted to elect candidates from both sides of the political divide, reflecting the personal nature of much local politicking. Such was the case at Tallahassee in 1877 when residents endorsed most candidates on the white-controlled "citizen's ticket" but still placed in office a black clerk, tax assessor, and two councilmen. Similarly, that year Ocalans elected five white conservatives and four black Republicans as aldermen.[26]

White attitudes toward black officeholders reflected wide swings. Conservative editors delighted in reporting tumultuous Republican gatherings. "The permanent organization was followed by the wildest excitement," a Jacksonville newspaperman exclaimed in 1885 of one local meeting, "during which a general 'knock down and drag out' fight prevailed."[27] At a time when critics leveled charges of corruption and vote buying, especially in the larger cities, against both races and parties, some whites naturally stressed black participation. Partisan attacks reinforced the rumors. Typically, LaVilla's white "reform" Mayor J. E. T. Bowden declared in 1887: "The majority of the council is composed of drunkards, barroom pimps, and men who have the least regard for their oath of office, and for a drink of whiskey some of them will sell their vote for any purpose."[28]

Yet, when partisan and racial generalizations were set aside, communities often retained sentiments of respect for individual black officeholders. Obituaries, usually published years after an individual left public life, illustrate the point. "Sober, honest, industrious, he stood for all that was praiseworthy to his race," the Madison *New Enterprise* stated of marshal Thomas McLeary in 1904, "and has for years held an enviable position in the community, commanding the respect and emulation of his own people and the esteem of all who knew him."[29] In 1918 the Jacksonville *Metropolis* praised the "spotless integrity, rare executive ability, and safe business judgment" of McLeary's counterpart George H. Mays. His obituary concluded, "A good citizen, model father and husband, an ideal craftsman, and all around good and faithful man has gone."[30] In the same vein, a front-page notice in the Ocala *Evening Star* in 1901 recalled Elias Glasco Smith as a "worthy and much respected colored citizen."[31] As late as 1926 the Madison *Enterprise-Recorder* could acknowledge Oliver J. Coleman's contributions. "During and after reconstruction days," it observed, "he held several political offices until the negroes ceased active participation in politics in this part of the state." The editor concluded, "He was generally liked by the white people, as well as members of his own race."[32]

The popularity and talents of some leaders, when coupled with their Republican Party or church connections, enabled them to transfer easily from power in one jurisdiction to office in another. State legislator Emanuel Fortune, who had represented Jackson County in the 1868 constitutional convention but who fled to Duval County to protect his family from violence, became Jacksonville's marshal in 1873 and served as a councilman as late as 1889. Jeff McQueen sat on the Cedar Keys council, then on its Gainesville counterpart, and by 1885 again held position at Cedar Keys (though in 1878 the town name was changed to Cedar Key). That town's clerk, John V. Cornell, Sr., occupied the same office in Key West. Fernandina marshal Turner Duling began his public career as Wakulla County voter registrar in 1867–1868, while Francis B. Carolina acted as alderman at Lake City and Palatka before becoming an AME leader in Arkansas. Furthermore, some individuals retained significant influence within the Republican Party into the twentieth century in areas far removed from where they held office. Owen B. Armstrong at Punta Gorda and Alexander C. Lightbourn[e], Sr., at Miami offer examples.[33]

As to corrupt practices by African American politicians, the record suggests that they indulged to no greater degree than did white politicians of their time, and perhaps less. Certainly cities such as Jacksonville experienced epidemics of vote buying and influence peddling. For instance, a reporter in 1885 claimed that "last year the price [for a vote in Jacksonville] ranged from 25 cents to $2.50 each; but this year the average was $7.00 per vote, the range being from $5.50 to $12.50 each."[34] Two years later another reporter charged that "In all the wards money was used freely and openly on both sides."[35] Nonetheless, T. Thomas Fortune insisted in 1889 that only one of Jacksonville's black officials had defaulted in office, apparently referring to clerk James D. Garvin's late-1872 departure from the city.[36]

Occasionally state newspapers would record an isolated incident of an African American official's arrest for criminal wrongdoing. Charles H.

AME minister Francis B. Carolina (1837–1911?) held a variety of local offices during the 1870s, including Columbia County tax assessor and city councilman at both Lake City and Palatka. (Courtesy Florida Archives)

Pearce's bribery trial affords the best-known example, although the proceedings' political nature and Pearce's subsequent pardon suggest his innocence. Contemporary critics, state senator John Wallace, and white historian William Watson Davis related tales of bribery and other forms of corruption. Tellingly, though, once in power the Democrats declined to pursue criminal charges against any black legislators, a fact that hints, at the least, of partisan exaggeration or else of equal or greater Democratic culpability.[37]

When newspapers reported arrests, the alleged crime rarely related to official duties. Oliver J. Coleman's 1870 indictment, to offer one incident, was for murdering William Bryan. Authorities quashed it and never pursued the matter, with Madison County voters sending Coleman that year to the legislature. Cedar Keys alderman John G. Williams found himself in court in 1876, but the charge was "for making or causing to be made false claims and receipts with intent to defraud the United States." Apparently he also avoided conviction.[38] When authorities detained one-time Cedar Keys marshal Fred E. Miller in 1878 for stealing, news accounts took pains to note that he was a "man of previously good repute."[39]

Notwithstanding allegations of corruption by some individuals and partisan attacks upon black officials generally, African American leaders persisted in their attempts to provide representation within municipal governments. As already seen, they often did so successfully. That circumstance angered and frustrated many Democrats, leading by 1879 to a legislative attempt to seize control of at least one Republican city, Pensacola. The measure easily passed the senate but failed to clear the house before adjournment. Two years later, in the opening months of Governor William D. Bloxham's first term, legislators renewed the effort, enacting laws that would have dissolved the charters of Pensacola and Fernandina and placed control in the hands of gubernatorial appointees. When Bloxham attempted to exercise his newfound power, Republicans took the issue to the state supreme court. Under the 1868 constitution the justices served for life terms, permitting the court in 1881 to remain in the hands of a Republican majority. The panel that summer found the attempt unconstitutional, and for the remainder of Bloxham's term the controversy simmered.[40]

The situation changed with the inauguration in January 1885 of Governor Edward A. Perry, a former Confederate general and Pensacola resident. That month two Republican-appointed justices resigned from the supreme court, and the new governor designated partisan Democrats to fill the vacancies. Perry's friends then steered through the legislature a special law to abolish Pensacola's city government and to hand Perry the power to appoint its mayor and council, following up the next month with the call of a convention to rewrite the state constitution. Perry signed the Pensacola measure on January 25 and acted with dispatch to place conservative whites in control. The new supreme court upheld his actions. "The Supreme Court has decided that the legislature had a right to take the city charter," reported an AME minister. "Being democrats, this is natural." He added, "Some of the people looked as though they would go crazy."[41]

The legal steps taken in 1885 against Republican rule in Pensacola set a precedent, to which Democratic legislators would return within just a few years. Governor Perry's execution of the new law also marked a turning point for leadership within the black community, for among the men he appointed to the new Pensacola council was George W. Witherspoon. The trails that led Democratic legislators and Witherspoon to those ends provide the context for the eclipse of African American office holding in Florida.

5

"We are in the hands of the devil"

The Road to Disfranchisement

As of the early 1880s, a sizable delegation of African Americans sat in Florida's legislature, but Democratic control forestalled their ability to influence the body's deliberations. Because of experiences such as carpetbagger betrayal of George W. Witherspoon's 1880 congressional race, many black leaders increasingly had begun to seek an alternative political alliance that would permit them some share of power. Tentative steps were taken in 1882 after a voice from the past, Robert Meacham, published a call for a state convention to "join with liberal white men who are determined to have a fair election."[1]

Meacham's initiative referred to a small group of Democrats, the Independents, who were seeking to distance themselves from the conservative "Bourbons" who controlled state politics. Within months of his call, a substantial segment of the state's African American leadership had responded positively. Their actions effectively split the Republican Party into two factions. The "Straightouts" or "Regulars," primarily federal officeholders and their friends, remained loyal to the Republican Party under leaders such as Joseph E. Lee. The Independents were the second faction.[2]

Although the Independent movement failed to conquer Florida in 1882, it produced important results. Enough Independents and Republicans were elected to the house of representatives to delay the chamber's organization by the Democrats in January 1883. That situation provoked some Bourbons to demand a constitutional convention to rewrite the 1868 document that guaranteed black voting rights, called for a public school system, and contained other provisions important to African Americans. Governor William D. Bloxham joined in the cry. Opposition by George W. Witherspoon and others at first kept the measure from

Straightout Republican leader Joseph E. Lee (1849–1920) of Jacksonville. (Courtesy Florida Archives)

approval, but the Democrats finally placed the convention question on the 1884 general election ballot.[3]

After the legislature's adjournment, the idea of black fusion with white Independents received enhanced support. Leading African American editor J. Willis Menard strongly endorsed Independentism while scoring Straightout Republicans. "I need not tell you that the success of the Independent movement is the only salvation for the Negroes of the South," he wrote in April, "and that those Republican leaders who are opposed to this movement are acting in the direct interest of hide-bound Bourbonism and the continued solidity of the South."[4] The following month he returned to the same theme, connecting it with opposition to a constitutional convention. "The remedy of the evils complained of can only be found in the political divisions of the southern whites," he proclaimed, "and in local alliances between the colored people and the liberal white element."[5]

The wedge between black and white Republicans deepened later in 1883 when the Republican-appointed United States Supreme Court issued a series of key opinions. Known as the "Civil Rights Cases," the decisions found unconstitutional important provisions of the Civil Rights Act of 1875, a law that had banned racial discrimination in the enjoyment of public and many private facilities. In one historian's words, the actions "spelled the end to the positive use of federal law to promote equality."[6]

Some of Florida's African American leaders despaired, while the situation enraged others. "[George W. Witherspoon] disclaimed entirely all pretensions to any enforced social equality," one account related. "He asked simply for justice and equality in civil, political and business relations of life." A frustrated Witherspoon had concluded that "[blacks] must utterly renounce the idea that the federal government is going to support their claims." He urged his audiences to "support men, of whatever party, who would best secure them in their just rights."[7] Former congressman Josiah T. Walls angrily resigned from his district Republican committee. "I do not believe that it is to the best interest of the colored voters of the South, from past experience," he declared, "to even dream of holding the Republican organization intact, and to urge it upon them as a duty, would be a crime against their manhood."[8]

In February 1884 the disenchanted leaders clashed with Republican regulars at a "state conference of colored men," held at Gainesville. Walls, Menard, Witherspoon, and others urged Independentism against the opposition of Republican Regulars Joseph E. Lee, Peter W. Bryant, and their allies. The Regulars fought off endorsement of an Independent for Congress, but the Independents showed strength nonetheless. Some shaken white Republicans countered with calls for a whites-only party. "The white Republicans cannot afford to allow the colored people to have any control in the State Government," the editor of the Eustis *New Yorker* exclaimed in May. "It is the duty of the white Republicans to organize at an early day and adopt a platform of principles."[9]

The Independent movement blossomed. At a racially integrated convention in June, delegates nominated Madison's Frank W. Pope, a white Democrat, for governor. In July a split Republican convention also turned to Pope after "angry blacks" shouted down a carpetbagger's attempt to deny Pope the honor.[10] Meanwhile, the Democrats tapped one-time Confederate general Edward A. Perry of Pensacola. Anxious about the potential strength of Pope's coalition, Perry pledged himself to a "government which, honestly and economically administered, shall alike protect the rights and foster the interests of the adopted and native born, the rich and the poor, the white and the black, with equal and exact justice."[11] The words masked a persistent campaign theme. As Thomas V. Gibbs explained, Democrats argued that the failure of their candidates meant "negro supremacy."[12]

The white supremacy appeal of Democratic campaigners, combined with polling-place fraud and Republican divisions over Independentism, decided the hard-fought contest in Perry's favor. His 32,000 votes exceeded Pope's total by 5,000. Democrats won heavy majorities in the state house and senate, while the nation elected its first Democratic president since the Civil War, Grover Cleveland. The call of a constitutional convention also received approval, although voters supporting it numbered about 1,000 fewer than Perry's total.[13]

The 1884 elections set in motion a train of events that were to undermine black political influence and office holding in Florida even further. When in late November William W. Sampson, on behalf of the state's African American population, visited with President-elect Cleveland, he heard assurances that his fellow blacks "need feel no alarm" over the election results.[14] Within two months events had dissipated any comfort gained from the words. Chance enabled Governor Perry in January 1885 to appoint two new justices to the state supreme court. His allies then pushed through the legislature a bill to seize control of Pensacola city government from Republicans, with Perry holding power to appoint the council. The new supreme court upheld the law despite an earlier court decision finding such an action unconstitutional. In February legislators called a constitutional convention for the summer.[15]

The legislative actions found black leaders more divided than ever. Once-fiery George W. Witherspoon, grown bitter at carpetbag Republicans and disappointed at Independentism's failure, had permitted the governor to name him as the sole race representative on Pensacola's new Democratic council. With resignation, the man who had almost served as a Republican congressman in 1881 urged blacks in 1885 "to join the Democrats in all undertakings of reform, particularly in municipal affairs."[16] Many African Americans intensely resented what they saw as his alliance with Bourbon enemies. "Going to the parsonage I met Rev. G. W. Witherspoon and family," a fellow AME minister recorded in February. "We were sorry to find the elder in such low spirits, but, like a host of other colored politicians, he has made a mistake."[17] Witherspoon served out his four-year council term, but his political influence had shattered. In 1889 he relocated to Key West, where he died January 2, 1892.[18]

The year 1885 began badly for African Americans and worsened as it evolved. President Cleveland took office in March, and his Democratic administration began removing most black Republicans from significant federal jobs, including postmasterships. Many race leaders found themselves scrambling to support their families, when the same energies otherwise might have been devoted to politics. On the other hand, the four-year experience dispelled some fears of Democratic rule among the black voting public as a whole, giving further reason for disillusioned voters to withdraw from the polls. A Palatka man, while overstating the case, explained the situation in a letter to the leading black newspaper in New York City. "Four years of Democratic supremacy over the affairs of this great country have totally put to flight every germ of anxiety in the black man's breast as to what disposition that party will make with the subject of re-enslavement," he wrote in 1888. "Do away with lynching practice and the suppression of the Negro's vote," he continued, "and the Negro will not give a snap of his finger which party rules."[19]

In Florida the 1885 constitutional convention marked another step in the slide. May elections had given a large majority of the 108 delegates to the Democrats or, as one historian summarized, "the convention represented a fair cross section of the state's middle-class white voters."[20] The black-majority Middle Florida counties, except Leon, went Democratic, with many African Americans either staying home or supporting, with Witherspoon's example before them, the Democrats. Only seven black representatives would serve: William F. Thompson, John W. Mitchell, and Wallace B. Carr, all of Leon County; Henry W. Chandler of Marion; Thomas V. Gibbs of Duval; Samuel Petty of Nassau; and Amos Hargret[t] of Wakulla. The convention substantially revised the 1868 constitution by decentralizing state government, diluting the governor's powers, making many county offices elective, mandating racial segregation in public education, and authorizing the legislature to impose a poll tax as a prerequisite for voting. The proposed document was placed on the 1886 general election ballot for approval.[21]

Reaction to the convention's outcome varied among black leaders. Some individuals, accustomed to receiving personal respect from old-line Bourbon patricians and experienced at working easily with them in furtherance of the temperance cause, saw no threat to black voting. "The poll-tax was left to the legislature," Thomas V. Gibbs reported to the *New York Freeman*, "which will never impose it."[22] Other leaders searched anew for the possibility of a political alliance. The Republican Party remained deeply divided, and Independentism had vanished from the scene. Then, in late 1885 and early 1886, the searchers found what they had been seeking.

The potential political partner for Florida's blacks appeared in the form of a national labor union, the Knights of Labor. During the summer of 1885, major victories against a northern railroad had catapulted the union into public attention. The union expanded rapidly, including in the South where its policy of admitting blacks on an equal basis with whites appealed to the region's African American artisans and laborers. By May 1886, seven Knights "assemblies" had been organized at Key West, and, four months later, the union's rolls in Florida included thirty-two assemblies and 7,500 members. In September a biracial meeting at Jacksonville organized a state assembly. Active were prominent black leaders including former Monroe County state representative Robert Gabriel and soon-to-be Escambia County legislator Peter H. Davidson, Jr.[23]

African Americans constituted most of the union's Florida membership, and that fact promised a powerful political alliance with national connections other than the major parties. "The Order in the South must of necessity be composed largely of the Negro race," one Knights official recorded. "The great bulk of the labor in this country is performed by colored hands, against whom a cultivated prejudice . . . is most intense."[24] In the major port towns, especially, those "colored hands" quickly asserted themselves under their union guise. In October 1886 a Knights ticket won the municipal elections at Key West, still the state's largest city. In the process they placed African American Frank Adams in office as tax assessor and Charles R. Adams, Roman M. Stevens, and Washington A. Cornell as councilmen. They also fielded a legislative ticket that included Charles A. Shavers for state representative. At Pensacola, where municipal elections no longer were held, the labor men presented Peter H. Davidson, Jr., for the state house from Escambia County.[25]

The 1886 state elections turned out poorly for African Americans but well for the Knights. In the latter case, Shavers and Davidson were elected to the legislature, but they would sit among a diminished black delegation. Many rural voters, always subject to threats of violence or economic intimidation and deeply disturbed by broken political promises and failed campaigns, declined to visit the polls or opted for Democrats. In the house of representatives, counties that long had enjoyed black representation—such as Alachua, Jefferson, and Nassau—now saw white Democrats in office. Of the seven blacks who remained (half the 1885 total), four hailed from Leon, with one each from Duval, Escambia, and Monroe. Two senators, Henry W. Chandler and Daniel C. Martin, would continue in office for another two years, until the expiration of their four-year terms.[26]

Other changes accompanied the 1886 elections. Voters approved the proposed constitution. They did so with some black support, as Joseph E. Lee and J. Willis Menard urged its adoption, at least partly because it permitted counties to elect some of their own officers. Additionally, Demo-

As shown by this photograph taken during the 1887 session, African American representation in Florida's legislature neared its end by the late 1880s. (Courtesy Florida Archives)

cratic voters sent to the legislature a new crop of representatives, many of them younger businessmen and professionals, who openly advocated white supremacy and a tightening of the laws to ensure continued white control. "Nearly all the members of the House are new members," one man observed, "very few of them having had any experience at all in deliberative bodies."[27]

Political confrontation loomed as Floridians entered the new year. In March a Knights of Labor ticket won Jacksonville municipal elections. Its officials soon expanded the city's limits to include heavily black suburbs such as LaVilla, giving Jacksonville an African American majority. Following the Jacksonville victory, the Knights scored gains at Fernandina and Palatka. Meanwhile, the new Democrats in the state legislature perceived a serious threat to their agenda. They reacted by passing a new and stricter voter registration procedure and by permitting reorganization of municipalities into wards that isolated black voters into one or two districts. For Fernandina and Palatka, the solons mandated the ward scheme. In case they had not signaled their intentions firmly enough, the legislators also enacted Florida's first law requiring racial segregation on railroads.[28]

The 1887 legislature's racially punitive measures spurred the Knights and numbers of black Republican leaders to greater efforts. On July 4 the union paraded its clout. Reportedly 1,200–1,500 individuals marched at Pensacola alone, behind men such as former Pensacola and Escambia County official Richard Gagnet. The same month former state representative and constitutional convention delegate Samuel Petty barely lost the Fernandina mayoral election. The Knights enjoyed more luck at Tampa, where a slate including Joseph A. Walker carried the day. A Jacksonville resident described the energized sentiments of many urban blacks. "The colored people realize, as fully as many of them did during the dark days of the war which effected their liberation from chattel slavery, that 'God helps those who help themselves,' " he wrote, "and that to be freed from the control of sharks and Shylocks requires no less exertion than it did to abolish the laws which made them slaves." He added, "They now have the ballot, which is preferable to the bullet."[29] The sentiments were not universally held. That they did not apply to other—and especially rural—residents resounded with an Escambia County man's words. "Too late to talk about the 'suppressed vote' now," he wrote. "We are in the hands of the devil."[30]

Despite conservative opposition and some racial friction within its organization, the Knights of Labor coalition moved ahead. In October it retained control at Key West and two months later elected a ticket at Jacksonville that included five African Americans on the city council. That body, in turn, elected Joseph E. Lee as municipal judge and named a black-majority board of police commissioners. Into 1888 the union expanded its reach, particularly in new and growing towns such as Leesburg and Kissimmee. By May the rolls included 12,000 to 14,000 names.[31]

Knights successes fostered greater opposition. "A hawk watching a brood of chickens," a Milton man explained, "is not more keen than those who are watching us."[32] Prominent African Americans were among the critics. "The race has enemies in all parties, and we are always ready to fire at them," proclaimed editor J. Willis Menard, "whether they be found among Democrats, Republicans, or Knights of Labor."[33] White Republicans also distanced themselves from aggressive black leaders and their Knights allies. As early as January 1887 Menard's *Southern Leader* had reported that "the Carpet-baggers are quietly organizing a Republican party in that State from among the leadership of which colored men are to be carefully excluded."[34] These "Lily White" Republicans spread their message during the year and into 1888, forming influential clubs at Jacksonville, Tampa, and other locations.[35]

The Knights thus faced obstacles at every turn. The union also suffered internally from some white resentments at black influence. Externally, it failed to reach out successfully to rural blacks, who yet made up the large majority of Florida's African American population. Accordingly, the organization could not exert nearly sufficient strength to sway the 1888 elections in the face of Democrats' overtly racist appeals.[36]

Disaster ensued. After counters had tallied the 1888 election results, it became clear that Democrats had voted strongly. To the contrary, disenchanted rural blacks had turned out in ever smaller numbers to support Republicans or Knights candidates. The Knights had posted important wins, but African Americans and Republicans had experienced more setbacks. Henry W. Chandler, the losing Republican secretary of state nominee, received only 135 votes in Leon County to his Democratic opponent's 1,320. African American presence in the General Assembly now stood at two representatives. John R. Scott, Jr., and George A. Lewis won in Duval County, but neither associated directly with the Knights. On the other hand, local elections under the new constitution resulted somewhat more favorably. Duval County elected Joseph E. Lee as its circuit court clerk. Monroe County chose James Dean as Florida's first African American county judge and Charles F. Dupont as the state's first elected black sheriff. Several counties chose African Americans as justices of the peace.[37]

The elections' most significant result manifested itself early in 1889. The new Democrats who pushed approval of racially restrictive legislation in 1887 saw their numbers increased, and they determined to put the threat of black political power behind them once and for all. When, after the 1888 general election, St. Augustine and Palatka came under racially integrated Republican control, they acted. During the 1889 legislative session, the lawmakers attacked black voting directly. They required use of a difficult and confusing "eight ballot-box system." More important, the legislators imposed a poll tax as a prerequisite for voting. Furthermore, they looked back to the precedent set in 1885 in the case of Pensacola and passed laws seizing control of the municipal governments of Jacksonville and Key West. At St. Augustine and some other towns, new charters imposed ward systems that reduced black representation on local councils to a maximum of one or two votes.[38]

Effectively, the 1889 statutes and actions taken in furtherance of their provisions eliminated African Americans from a significant role in Florida politics, while also serving as precursors of Mississippi's heralded constitutional revisions of 1890. When in subsequent years legislators

On the municipal level, some African American representation and influence persisted into the twentieth century. The fact infuriated many white political leaders and newspapermen, who attempted to belittle black leaders by misrepresenting their views or mocking their service. This cartoon, which focuses upon Jacksonville lawyer J. Douglas Wetmore, ran first in the Jacksonville *Florida Sun.* (From Lake City *Florida Index*, March 25, 1904)

mandated a white primary system for selecting Democratic party nominees, the actions merely nailed tighter a lid already firmly in place.[39]

This is not to say that black officeholders disappeared entirely from the scene or that African American men ceased political activity. For another generation persistent leaders would, at least in some locales, attempt to preserve race representation in spite of restrictive laws and a color line drawn increasingly tight within the state's society.

"Where to start?" was the question faced by black leaders in the wake of the electoral and legal disasters of 1888 and 1889. The Knights of Labor organization began to crumble, as failed strikes crippled it nationally and internal dissensions split it in Florida. The Republican Party fared little better. It still could dispense federal patronage when a Republican held the White House, and its representatives could vote in national Republican nominating conventions. Yet, by 1890 it could not influence statewide elections or legislative debates. Additionally, the Republican leadership—with African Americans such as Joseph E. Lee fighting defensively—tilted toward its Lily White factions with relatively few federal jobs going to blacks. "My people comprise about nine-tenths of the republican party," a Jacksonville man asserted, "why are they not recognized by the [Benjamin] Harrison administration?"[40]

Many black Republicans cried out against the party tide and allegations of corrupt bargaining for office. "The negro [will] have nothing to do in the future with the white louse," declared a St. Johns County resident.[41] In Marion County well-regarded former legislator Wesley A. Wilkerson declined to have his name placed on a local slate with white Republicans. "I refused to allow my name to go on the ticket as a candidate for judge of probate," he maintained, "because, as I told the convention, the ticket was reeking with fraud and bribery."[42] Three years later a fellow Marion resident would report, "We are abandoned by the white republicans here and are entirely disregarded as a faction." He added wisely, "United we stand, divided we fall."[43]

Scores of leaders determined to create an independent political organization for African Americans. Meeting at Jacksonville in June 1890, they organized the Colored Man's Political Protective League of the State of Florida. Their expressed goal was captured in a *Florida Times-Union* headline: "No Longer Will They Be Used by a Handful of White Republicans." The men elected Fernandina's Samuel Petty as their president, T. S. Harris of Suwannee County as vice president; Duval's J. E. Sistrunk as secretary; A. J. Cody as corresponding secretary; and H. A. Price as treasurer. The "cheers and greetings" that followed the organization's initial meeting never translated, though, into real political influence.[44]

Other African American leaders continued the difficult quest for trustworthy white allies. Poor economic and social conditions for farmers through the 1880s had resulted late in the decade in the growth of the Farmers' Alliance to pressure legislatures and Congress for helpful new laws and programs. Although the organization technically was for whites only, its backers had aided and encouraged the creation of the Colored Farmers' National Alliance, with which they cooperated closely. In Florida an AME minister, Joseph Leandria Moore, led the black affiliate, but he faced formidable challenges in gaining broad support for the alliance. Meanwhile, the Farmers' Alliance rejected an 1890 overture from the Knights of Labor for a merger of their Florida operations.[45]

The efforts of African American organizers for the Farmers' Alliance suffered from the organization's insistence that it work within the Democratic Party. Probably their major success involved helping to bring the December 1890 national convention to Ocala, a town with a reputation for moderate race relations and where numbers of black merchants, entrepreneurs, and professional men enjoyed community respect. Out of the meeting came the alliance's "Ocala Demands," which established a concrete program for national action in the interests of farmers and other working people.[46]

Unfortunately for alliance men, Democratic Party power brokers declined to adopt the Ocala Demands as their own program, resulting by 1892 in the creation of the People's or Populist Party. J. L. Moore served on its Florida executive committee, and other race leaders including Josiah T. Walls offered counsel. That year the African Americans secured Republican Party endorsement of major Populist candidates, but Democrats used their action as a pretext for demanding support as "the white man's party." Given the impact of poll taxes, confusing election laws, frustration, and intimidation, not enough African Americans voted to make a difference in the election's outcome. The Populists remained a factor in Florida politics for several years thereafter but never came close to taking control away from the Bourbons.[47]

By the mid-1890s the Republican Party offered the only remaining home for politically involved African Americans who chose not to support Democratic candidates. The weak and divided organization scrambled for what support it could find, to the extent that in 1896 its "Lily White" faction nominated one-time Leon County state senator John Wallace for state attorney general. But, practically speaking, party advocates held virtually no electoral influence, although occasionally Florida's votes at national party conventions—Joseph E. Lee's 1912 support for William Howard Taft over Theodore Roosevelt stands out—made some difference. J. Willis Menard summed up the situation in 1898. "The Negro politician of to-day attends Republican National Conventions, helps to nominate the candidate for President, and is thereafter completely lost in the shuffle,"

This editorial cartoon expressed African American disappointment at President Woodrow Wilson, who in 1913 dismissed black federal officials in the South, including Florida's Joseph E. Lee, Joseph N. Clinton, and Henry W. Chandler. (From *New York Age*, August 14, 1913)

he wrote. "If he gets anything at all, it is not on account of his prominence as a politician, but because of the friendship of some prominent white politician."[48]

The national administrations of William McKinley and Theodore Roosevelt, which commenced in 1897, did offer African Americans some prominent federal patronage positions. McKinley tapped Joseph E. Lee as United States collector of internal revenue for the district of Florida, and Roosevelt continued him in the office. Other former public officers benefited as well. At Tampa, for example, Henry W. Chandler, once Marion County state senator, became inspector of customs in 1908. Former Alachua County state representative Joseph N. Clinton served under Lee as deputy collector of internal revenue, also at Tampa. Their tenure abruptly halted in 1913, when Democratic president Woodrow Wilson's administration removed the state's remaining black Republican officials from the federal jobs.[49]

On the municipal level some African American officials still survived in elective office. The larger towns and cities often utilized a ward system that permitted election of one or two blacks to a council. As a result, racially integrated boards continued to make policy in 1896 at Madison, in 1902 at Fernandina, in 1904 at St. Augustine, in 1907 at Jacksonville and Key West (both of which had begun to elect their own officials again in the 1890s), and in 1909 at Cedar Key. In 1912 Booker T. Washington noted the presence of two black aldermen at Ocala, although they have not been identified. As late as 1924 two men, Albert Lewis Browning and Joseph A. Nottage, maintained an African American presence as Palatka councilmen.[50]

White attempts to block black office holding, rather than surrender by black leaders, explains the disappearance of the last race representatives on these city governing authorities. Town and city officials dropped blacks from voter registration lists upon slight pretext; new elections laws made qualification more difficult; informal whites-only mass meetings assumed authority to nominate candidates on "official" slates; at-large elections replaced ward systems; and, eventually, Democratic Party slates nominated by whites-only primaries became common.[51]

Still, African Americans resisted, especially after many men served in World War I and returned with demands for decent treatment. As late as 1921, for example, black candidates challenged white rule in the state's largest city, Jacksonville. George M. Madison and Charles C. Manigault, particularly, ran credible, if unsuccessful, races despite the *Florida Times-Union*'s urgent appeals to white voters. "ALL WHITE DEMOCRATIC ELECTORS URGED TO TURN OUT EN MASSE AND VOTE STRAIGHT WHITE DEMOCRATIC TICKET," one of its headlines screamed. "Failure to Vote May Mean One or More Negro Members of the City Council—Negro Candidates and Supporters are Active."[52]

The previous year had witnessed numerous incidents resulting from African American determination to participate in political affairs. When residents of Ocoee, near Orlando, demanded recourse to the polls, a white "posse" attacked the town, burning homes and churches and killing ten to thirty individuals. July Perry, who had led the demands for voting rights that resulted in the Ocoee riot, paid the penalty of his life, but not before killing two of his white attackers. At about the same time, at Daytona Beach, Mary McLeod Bethune confronted Ku Klux Klansmen angered by her encouragement of black voting.[53]

One national event of 1920 created an interesting situation respecting African American voting rights. The language of many restrictive elections laws seemed not to apply to women, newly enfranchised by amendment to the United States Constitution. In the vacuum thousands of black women registered. One report suggested that 6,500 women had done so in Duval County alone. White politicians responded by urging registration of white women, and police targeted blacks for minor or technical violations of registration laws. The number of arrests in Duval County totaled 500, effectively dampening voting enthusiasm.[54]

By the early 1920s the legal and extralegal manipulations had worked their course. When an all-white council assumed office at Palatka in 1924, a fifty-seven-year era of black office holding ended. Although all-black towns such as Eatonville elected officials thereafter, the opportunity for racially integrated public service would be denied to the state's African Americans for a generation or longer. Yet, black Floridians could look back upon almost three generations of substantial and persistent contributions to Florida's political life and development. Perhaps 1,000 individuals had served, offering lasting legacies such as the state's public education system and leadership for the growth of Florida's cities and urban culture.

Just after the Civil War's end, the Reverend Charles H. Pearce had declared of the freedmen he met, "They must have somebody to guide them; and it is natural that they should get their best informed men to lead them."[55] In Florida African Americans such as Pearce, Jonathan C. Gibbs, Josiah T. Walls, Robert Meacham, William Bradwell, John R. Scott, Sr., Thomas W. Long, David Montgomery, John Wallace, George W. Witherspoon, John Willis Menard, Joseph E. Lee, and hundreds of others stepped forward to assume those responsibilities. Their labors made a difference despite the obstacles mounted against them, and they deserve to be remembered.

BIOGRAPHICAL DIRECTORY

Adams, Charles R.
Born June 1852, Bahama Islands. Carpenter. Died December 20, 1929, Key West, Florida. Key West councilman 1880–1882, 1887–1888.[1]

Adams, Frank.
Born 1852, Key West. Mulatto. Laborer. Died October 12, 1926, Key West, Florida. Key West councilman 1882–1884; Key West tax assessor 1886–1887, 1888–1889.[2]

Adams, George.
Born 1838, Florida. Mulatto. Waiter. Alive in St. Johns County 1885. Died 1901, St. Johns County, Florida? St. Augustine marshal 1880–1883.[3]

Adams, Joseph.
Alachua County constable 1874.

Adams, Joseph A.
Born 1861, Florida. Mulatto. Plasterer. Died February 8, 1921, Palatka, Florida. Palatka councilman 1900–1902, 1908–1912.[4]

Alexander, Edward I., Sr.
Born 1850, South Carolina. Mulatto. Grocer. Died November 29, 1911, Jacksonville, Florida. Florida house of representatives (Madison County, 1877, 1879, 1885); Madison councilman 1882; Madison postmaster 1883–1885. *Madison Recorder*, October 4, 1889: "His success as a merchant is to his credit as a man and speaks well for his dealing with his fellow citizens."[5]

Allen, Robert.
Born 1820, Virginia. Minister. Alive in Suwannee County 1885. Suwannee County justice of the peace 1876–1877.[6]

Alston, Crummie.
Born 1851, South Carolina. Barber. Died 1915, Cedar Key, Florida. Cedar Key councilman 1883–1885, 1898–1909.[7]

Anderson, John H.
Born January 1842, Virginia. Fruit packer and shipper. Died October 25,

1916, Jacksonville, Florida. Florida house of representatives (Duval County, 1887).[8]

Anderson, Peter R.
Born 1830, Georgia. Farmer and minister. Alive in Marion County 1885. Marion County justice of the peace 1872.[9]

Anderson, Samuel.
Born March 10, 1841, Fort Moniac, Baker County, Florida. Thirty-fourth USCI (1864–1866). Farmer. Died September 8, 1909, Philips, Duval County, Florida. Florida house of representatives (Duval County, 1887).[10]

Andrews, Frank.
Born 1815, Florida. Laborer. Died January 14, 1873, Duval County, Florida. LaVilla marshal 1870–1872.[11]

Andrews, George W.
Born 1857, Florida. Mulatto. Butcher. Alive in Jacksonville 1893. LaVilla city clerk 1882–1884.[12]

Andrews [Andreu], James.
Born 1835, Florida. Farmer. Clay County commissioner 1871–1877.[13]

Armstrong, Josiah Haynes.
Born May 30, 1842, Lancaster County, Pennsylvania. Third USCI (1863–1865). AME minister and bishop. Died March 23, 1898, Galveston, Texas. Florida house of representatives (Columbia County, 1871, 1872, 1875). H. T. Kealing, *History of African Methodism in Texas* (1885): "The evidence of his sure success was to be seen in his stern struggle with almost insurmountable difficulties, but with every struggle he strengthened those qualities of hanging-on which mark the secret of his rapid advancement and prosperous termination of all his enterprises."[14]

Josiah Haynes Armstrong (Courtesy Florida Archives)

Armstrong, Owen B.
Born February 12, 1838, Half Moon Township, Centre County, Pennsylvania. Mulatto. Second USCI (1863–1866). Teacher and carpenter. AME. Died July 4, 1914, Punta Gorda, Florida. Delegate, 1868 constitutional convention (Leon and Wakulla Counties); Leon County commissioner 1869–1870. Vernon Peeples, Punta Gorda: "Armstrong hung tenaciously to his political convictions. He partici-

pated in Punta Gorda's first election on December 7, 1887, and remained active in the county Republican Party until at least 1904."[15]

Artrell, William Middleton.
Born 1836, Nassau, Bahama Islands. Mulatto. Teacher. Episcopal. Died March 28, 1903, Key West, Florida. Key West councilman 1875–1876. William M. Artrell, October 1876: "The Southern whites remind me forcibly of Pharaoh of old. He would not let the children of Israel go, notwithstanding the many chastisements he received directly at God's hand. As so it is with the Southern whites; they have been sorely punished for the oppression of my race (God's people), and yet they would not let them go, but continue to persecute them. I hope God is not hardening their hearts, even as He did the heart of Pharaoh, for fearful will be their end."[16]

William Middleton Artrell (Courtesy David M. Fahey)

Atkinson, R. W.
Fernandina councilman 1887–1888.

Baker, Caesar.
Born 1830, Duval County, Florida. Stevedore and farmer. Died September 1907, Fernandina, Florida. Nassau County commissioner 1868–1872.[17]

Baker, Moody.
Born 1844, Florida. Laborer. Died November 22, 1877, Jacksonville, Florida. LaVilla councilman 1870–1871, 1875–1876.[18]

Ballard, Jacob Reed.
Born November 25, 1846, Philadelphia, Pennsylvania. Mulatto. United States Navy (USN) (USS *Florida*, 1861–1862). Teacher and AME Zion minister. Died ca. May 1902, New York City. Fernandina tax assessor 1877–1878.[19]

Ballou, John H.
Born June 1853, Providence, Rhode Island. Lawyer and editor (*Florida Baptist*, 1888). Baptist. Died 1926, Jacksonville, Florida. Duval County justice of the peace 1889–1891.[20]

Baptiste, John W.
Born 1816, New Orleans, Louisiana. Mulatto. Drayman. Died March 5, 1893, Pensacola, Florida. Escambia

County voter registrar 1867–1868; Escambia County justice of the peace 1868–1874?[21]

Barkley, Edward.
Born 1849, Florida. Farmer. Alive in Jackson County 1880. Jackson County justice of the peace 1872–1875.[22]

Barkley, George W.
Born 1844, Florida. Farmer. Alive in Jackson County 1880. Holmes County voter registrar 1867–1868.[23]

Barnes, Alfred.
Born 1842, North Carolina. Farmer. Alive in Jackson County 1885. Jackson County justice of the peace 1874–1877.[24]

Baxter, Daniel R.
Born 1848, South Carolina. Brick mason. Alive in Fernandina 1910. Fernandina councilman 1877–1882.[25]

Beattie, Mitchell H.
Born 1851, South Carolina. Teacher. Alachua County commissioner 1872–1873?[26]

Bell, Cornelius.
Born June 1839, Maryland. Waiter. Died November 8, 1906, Fernandina, Florida. Nassau County tax assessor 1876–1877.[27]

Bell, William.
Born 1824, South Carolina. Mulatto. Baptist minister. Died 1921, Putnam County, Florida. Palatka councilman 1871–1873, 1876, 1879–1881.[28]

Bellamy, Anthony.
Born 1830, Florida. Farmer and AME minister. Alive in Jefferson County 1904. Jefferson County commissioner 1877–1878.[29]

Bellamy, Morris Benjamin, Sr.
Born November 1871, Florida. Farmer. Died 1941, Sarasota County, Florida. Goldsboro mayor 1911.[30]

Benedee, Charles.
Born 1842, Florida. Mulatto. Clerk. Alive in St. Augustine 1885. St. Augustine councilman 1881–1882.[31]

Benjamin, Stacio.
Born 1839, Florida. Carpenter. Alive in St. Augustine 1875. St. Johns County justice of the peace 1870–1871; St. Johns County commissioner 1871–1873.[32]

Benson, Charles H.
Born March 1858, South Carolina. Mulatto. Barber. Died 1924, Alachua County, Florida. Cedar Key councilman 1878–1879, 1882–1884, 1888–1898.[33]

Benton, George W., Sr.
Born July 1870, North Carolina. Painter. Died 1928, St. Lucie County, Florida. Goldsboro councilman 1911; Goldsboro mayor 1911.[34]

Bird [Byrd], William A.
Born June 10, 1848, Decatur County, Georgia. AME minister. Died 1921, Columbia County, Florida. Florida house of representatives (Jefferson County, 1883, 1885).[35]

William A. Bird [Byrd] (Courtesy Florida Archives)

Black, Isaac.
Born 1827, South Carolina. Mulatto. Teacher. Alive in Marion County 1870. Marion County superintendent of schools 1868–1869.[36]

Black, Richard Horatio.
Born August 11, 1839, Philadelphia, Pennsylvania. USN (USS *Daylight*, 1861–1862) and Third USCI (1862–1865). Teacher. Died May 13, 1911, New York City. Volusia County voter registrar 1867–1868; Alachua County justice of the peace 1868–1869; Florida house of representatives (Alachua County, 1869, 1870). Regarding Black's participation in the notorious 1876 Archer election fraud that besmirched Republican reputations in Alachua County and fueled a generation of partisan attacks by Democrats, William Watson Davis noted: "R. H. Black, who helped forge the registration list in Alachua County, [was rewarded with] a position in the custom house, Philadelphia."[37]

Blake, John.
Born February 1854, Florida. Mulatto. Boatman and porter. Alive in St. Augustine 1910. St. Augustine marshal 1888–1889.[38]

Blanchard, Joseph.
Born 1862, Florida. Laborer. St. Augustine councilman 1901–1904.[39]

Boger, Columbus H., Sr.
Born 1858, North Carolina. Teacher, minister, and editor (*Florida Watchman*). Died 1918, Jacksonville, Florida. Eatonville mayor 1887–1888.[40]

Bonaud, Peter.
Born November 12, 1838, Savannah, Georgia. Thirty-fourth USCI (1863–1866) [in service as Bond Garrick]. Stevedore. Died March 21, 1915, Fernandina, Florida. Fernandina clerk and treasurer 1873–1874.[41]

Bonner, Killis B.
Born 1847, North Carolina. Farmer. Alive in Marion County 1885. Florida house of representatives (Marion County, 1877). Ocala *East Florida Banner*, May 1876: "Bonner is a young colored man of good character and is beliked by both white and black in his neighborhood; he is . . . for a colored man a very excellent selection [for state representative]."[42]

Booth, Simon.
Born 1840, Georgia. Mulatto. Lumberman. Alive in Jacksonville 1905. LaVilla councilman 1886–1887.[43]

Boyd, Samuel.
Born July 4, 1847, South Carolina. Mulatto. Public officer. Died August 25, 1872, Fernandina, Florida. Fernandina clerk and treasurer 1869–1871; Nassau County justice of the peace 1870?–1871; Florida house of representatives (Nassau County, 1871, 1872).[44]

Braddock, William P.
LaVilla tax assessor 1871–1872.

Bradham, Anthony.
Born 1837, South Carolina or North Carolina. Farmer. Alive in Wakulla County 1920. Died 1922, Wakulla County? Wakulla County commissioner 1870–1872; Wakulla County justice of the peace 1873–1877.[45]

Bradwell, William.
Born December 1822, Darien, Georgia. Mulatto (son of Judge Asa Holt, Macon, Georgia). AME minister. Died July 16, 1887, Lower Peachtree, Alabama. Delegate, 1868 constitutional convention (Duval, Nassau, and St. Johns Counties); Florida senate (Duval County, 1868, 1869, 1870). Jacksonville *Florida Union*, July 1867: "Rev. Wm. Bradwell of Jacksonville being called upon said that he was born a radical though he never dared to avow it. I am, he said, an uneducated man standing among educated gentlemen, but my father was one of the first representatives to the Legislature of Georgia and I mean to follow in his steps, but to labor for the Republican Party." Florida AME historian Charles Sumner Long: "He seemed to be careful for nothing; all things seemed to work together for his good—for persecutions . . . and the threats and abuse of his enemies tended to replenish his storehouse."[46]

Bram, Henry.
Born 1829, Florida. Laborer. Alive in Green Cove Springs 1893. Clay County commissioner 1876–1877.[47]

Bram, July.
Born 1850, Florida. Brick mason. Died 1892, Green Cove Springs, Florida. Green Cove Springs councilman 1874–1876, 1878–1879, 1881–1882.[48]

Braswell, Robert.
Born 1830, Florida. Mulatto. Farmer. Alive in Wakulla County 1885. Wakulla County commissioner 1876–1877.[49]

Brazell, J. B.
Eatonville tax assessor 1887–1888.

Brazell, L. D.
Eatonville treasurer 1887–1888.

Brazell, Matthew B.
Born 1862, Florida. Laborer. Died 1934, Orange County, Florida. Eatonville councilman 1887–1888; Eatonville mayor 1916–1920.[50]

Broadenax, Joseph.
AME minister (to 1873). Leon County justice of the peace 1873.[51]

Brooks, Benjamin.
Died 1920, Jacksonville, Florida? LaVilla councilman 1873–1874.[52]

Brooks, Henry.
Born November 1835, South Carolina. Farmer. Alive in Sumter County 1900. Sumter County commissioner 1873–1877.[53]

Brothers, Wright.
Brevard County voter registrar 1867–1868.

Brown, Charles.
Born 1842, South Carolina. Merchant. Monroe County constable 1872.[54]

Brown, Henry.
Born 1846, Frederick County, Maryland. Third USCI (1864–1865). AME minister. Died December 6, 1887, Ray's Hill, Bedford County, Pennsylvania. Bradford County voter registrar 1867–1868; Bradford County commissioner 1868–1870, 1873–1875.[55]

Brown, John.
Born February 1835, Florida. Laborer. Died 1928, Putnam County, Florida. Palatka councilman 1881–1882.[56]

Brown, John H.
Born 1833, Pennsylvania. Deputy U.S. marshal and bookkeeper. Alive in Jacksonville 1896. LaVilla councilman 1871–1872; Duval County constable 1871, 1874–1875.[57]

Brown, Richard Lewis, Sr.
Born March 1854, Abbeville District, South Carolina. Printer, carpenter, architect, AME minister. Died August 24, 1948, Jacksonville, Florida. Florida house of representatives (Duval County, 1881, 1883). Inez Nesbitt in February 1995: "He was a kind, gentle person. From a slave beginning, he came to accomplish what he did—an amazement of things."[58]

Brown, Samuel.
Born 1838, South Carolina. Carpenter. Alive in Fernandina 1900. Fernandina councilman 1879–1880.[59]

Brown, William.
Born 1842, Florida. Farmer. Died December 4, 1917, Madison County, Florida. Madison County justice of the peace 1874–1877.[60]

Browning, Albert Lewis.
Born January 1872, South Carolina. Barber. Died 1946, Putnam County, Florida. Palatka councilman 1903–1909, 1912–1914, 1920–1924.[61]

Brumick, Henry.
Born 1850, Florida. Boot and shoe maker. AME. Died March 11, 1898, Tampa, Florida. Tampa city councilman 1876–1877.[62]

Bryan, Homer.
Born 1810, North Carolina. Farmer. Delegate, 1868 constitutional convention (Washington, Calhoun, and Jackson Counties); Jackson County tax collector 1868–1871; Jackson County treasurer 1871–1872.[63]

Bryant, Furney B.
Born 1840, Kinston, Lenore County, North Carolina. Mulatto. Thirty-fifth USCI (1863–1866). Farmer. Died October 22, 1900, Callahan, Nassau County, Florida. Nassau County justice of the peace 1875–1876.[64]

Bryant, Peter W.
Born October 18, 1853, Thomas County, Georgia. Mulatto. Graduate, Howard University. Lawyer. Died July 30, 1912, New York City. Hillsborough County justice of the peace 1877–1881.[65]

Burgess, W. Samuel.
Born 1850, Virginia. Labor foreman. Died 1917, Jacksonville, Florida? Duval County justice of the peace 1873–1874.[66]

Peter W. Bryant (Courtesy University of South Florida Special Collections)

Burroughs, Edmund.
Born 1854, Florida. Mulatto. Laborer. Alive in Jacksonville 1910. Madison councilman 1884.[67]

Bush, James.
Born 1831, Beaufort, South Carolina. Second USCI (1864–1866). Carpenter. Died April 5, 1887, Fernandina, Florida. Fernandina councilman 1884– 1885.[68]

Butler, Robert W.
Born 1844, Bahama Islands. Mulatto. Carpenter and AME minister. Alive in Jacksonville 1910. Monroe County commissioner 1876–1877.[69]

Butterfield, John [Jack].
Born 1839, Florida. Mulatto. Boatman and painter. Died March 9, 1905, Pensacola, Florida. Escambia County commissioner 1873–1875; Pensacola

councilman 1877; Pensacola marshal 1881.[70]

Byrd, Oliver.
Born February 1850, Florida. Minister. Alive in Jacksonville 1908. Calhoun County justice of the peace 1875–1879.[71]

Call, Henry W.
Born 1834, Florida. Mulatto. AME minister. Alive in DeFuniak Springs 1910. Washington County voter registrar 1868; Walton County voter registrar 1868; Walton County justice of the peace 1873–1875; Walton County commissioner 1875–1877.[72]

Campbell, Alexander E.
Born 1850, Florida. Mulatto. Butcher. Alive in Jacksonville 1899. LaVilla councilman 1884–1886.[73]

Campbell, David.
Born 1831, Florida. Mulatto. Farmer. Alive in Jackson County 1896. Jackson County justice of the peace 1874–1877.[74]

Canty, William.
Born February 1852, South Carolina. Mulatto. Laborer. Cedar Key(s) councilman 1874–1875, 1876–1877, 1888–1894, 1898–1902; Levy County commissioner 1876–1877.[75]

Carolina, Evans Charlton.
Born May 1850, Florida. Blacksmith. Died 1921, Lakeland, Florida. Goldsboro councilman 1891–1892.[76]

Carolina, Francis B.
Born December 13, 1837, Columbia, South Carolina. Carpenter and AME minister. Alive in Arkansas 1911. Columbia County tax assessor 1873–1874; Lake City councilman 1874–1875; Palatka councilman 1875–1876.[77]

Carr, Wallace B.
Born June 22, 1853, Leon County, Florida. Mulatto. Farmer. Died 1931, Leon County, Florida. Florida house of representatives (Leon County, 1881, 1887); 1885 constitutional convention delegate (Leon County). Tallahassee *Weekly Floridian*, November 1880: "Wallace B. Carr . . . a shrewd and successful farmer living about ten miles north of town."[78]

Carroll, Phillip.
Born March 1847, Maryland. Farmer. Alive in Tallahassee 1920. Florida house of representatives (Leon County, 1881). Tallahassee *Weekly Floridian*, November 1880: "Phillip Carroll . . . a small tenant farmer living some three miles from town."[79]

Carter, Cato B.
Born February 1848, Georgia. Mulatto. Farmer. Alive in Columbia County 1900. Columbia County commissioner 1871–1873, 1876–1877.[80]

Chaires, James.
Born 1825, Florida. Farmer. Orange County voter registrar 1867–1868.[81]

Chandler, Alexander [Alonzo].
Born 1822, Tennessee. Farmer. Alive in Marion County 1870. Delegate, 1868 constitutional convention (Marion, Putnam, and Levy Counties).[82]

Chandler, Henry Wilkins.
Born September 22, 1852, Bath, Sagadahoc County, Maine. Mulatto. Graduate, Bates College and Howard University law department. Lawyer. Baptist. Died March 27, 1938, Lakeland, Florida. Florida senate (Marion County, 1881, 1883, 1885, 1887); Ocala clerk 1883–1884; 1885 constitutional convention delegate (Marion County); Ocala councilman 1886–1893. Historian Monroe N. Work: "He was delegate to the National Republican Convention 1884–1908. He was Inspector of Customs at Tampa from May 1908 to December 1913."[83]

Chappell[e], Lewis [Louis] H.
Born June 1843, South Carolina. Carpenter. Alive in Jacksonville 1905. LaVilla councilman 1875–1877.[84]

Chappell[e], Mitchell P.
Born April 1846, South Carolina. Grocer. AME. Died September 16, 1884, Jacksonville, Florida. LaVilla tax collector 1873–1874, 1876–1877; Duval County justice of the peace 1874–1877; LaVilla mayor 1874–1876; LaVilla councilman 1877–1878.[85]

Charles, Cyrus.
Born 1823, Georgia. Cedar mill worker. Died January 1878, Hillsborough County, Florida. Hillsborough County commissioner 1868–1871; Tampa councilman 1869.[86]

Chester, W. T.
Born 1858, Florida. Mulatto. Farmer. Died May 1, 1929, Leon County, Florida. Tallahassee clerk and treasurer 1880.[87]

Chestnut, Johnson.
Born 1829, South Carolina. Mulatto. Carpenter. Died January 2, 1898, Alachua County, Florida. Gainesville councilman 1869–1870.[88]

Claiborne, Thomas C.
Born 1852, Tennessee. Mulatto. Grocer and butcher. Alive in Jacksonville 1889. LaVilla tax collector 1881–1887.[89]

Clark, Joseph E.
Born October 1859, Covington, Georgia. Merchant. Died 1916, Seminole County, Florida. Eatonville councilman 1887–1888; Eatonville mayor 1889–1890, 1900–1912.[90]

Clark, Thomas.
Born 1819?, Georgia. Blacksmith. Apalachicola councilman 1871–1874.[91]

Clark, William M.
Born 1870, Florida. Merchant and carpenter. Died 1928, Seminole County, Florida. Goldsboro marshal and tax collector 1891–1892.[92]

Clarke, Washington.
Monroe County voter registrar 1867–1868.

Clinton, Joseph Newman.
Born November 19, 1854, Pittsburgh, Pennsylvania. Graduate, Lincoln University. AME minister and teacher. Died September 6, 1927, Tampa, Florida. Gainesville councilman 1883–1885; Florida house of representatives (Alachua County, 1885). Compiler Clement Richardson in *National Cyclopedia of the Colored Race* (1919): "During his many years of public service, Mr. Clinton conducted himself in a manner that reflected credit on himself and on his people. Always remembering that not only he himself, but through him the Negroes as a race were on trial before the most critical jury in the world, his every action bespoke the studied consideration of a highly trained public servant towards the public he was appointed to serve."[93]

Cobb, Alfred.
Born April 1832, South Carolina. Barber. Alive in Tallahassee 1900. Leon County justice of the peace 1868–1872, 1873–1877; Tallahassee councilman 1882–1883, 1886–1890.[94]

Coleman, George C.
Born January 1851, Ohio. Mulatto. Laborer. Alive in Duval County 1920. Died 1926, Jacksonville, Florida? Florida house of representatives (Nassau County, 1881).[95]

Coleman, Oliver J.
Born 1844, Florida. Mulatto. Merchant and shoemaker. Died May 29, 1926, Madison, Florida. Florida house of representatives (Madison County, 1871, 1872, 1875); Madison County justice of the peace 1873; Florida senate (Madison County, 1874); Madison County commissioner 1874–1877; Madison councilman 1883–1884, 1887–1896. Madison *Enterprise-Recorder*, June 1926: "During and after reconstruction days, he held several political offices until the negroes ceased active participation in politics in this part of the state. He was generally liked by the white people, as well as members of his own race."[96]

Coleman, Robert.
Born 1815, South Carolina. Farmer. Alive in Ocala 1885. Ocala councilman 1880–1881.[97]

Coleman, Singleton.
Born 1825, near Richmond, Virginia. AME minister. Died October 11, 1874,

Singleton Coleman (Courtesy Florida Archives)

Ocala, Florida. Florida house of representatives (Marion County, 1873, 1874). Ocala *East Florida Banner*, October 1874: "He was a man of sound judgment, and was elected by his race to represent their county in the Legislative halls of the State in 1872, and was renominated for a second term. The large funeral procession, consisting of white and colored, is an evidence that he was highly esteemed."[98]

Collier, Benjamin F.
Born 1839, Georgia. Farmer. Hamilton County tax assessor 1872–1873; Hamilton County sheriff 1872–1874.[99]

Collins, Alexander M.
Born 1849, Florida. Mulatto. Carpenter. Milton councilman 1882; Milton tax assessor 1885.[100]

Collins, John B.
Born 1825, South Carolina. Seaman. Franklin County commissioner 1873–1875.[101]

Colson, Jesse.
Born 1802, Georgia. Farmer. Alive in Taylor County 1870. Taylor County voter registrar 1867–1868.[102]

Cooper, Milton.
Born 1855, Florida. Merchant. Died June 17, 1893, Palatka, Florida. Palatka councilman 1882–1883.[103]

Cornell, John V., Sr.
Born March 1852, Key West, Florida. Mulatto. Clerk. Alive in Key West 1900. Cedar Keys clerk 1874–1875; Key West clerk 1875–1876.[104]

Cornell, Washington A.
Born 1858, Key West, Florida. Mulatto. Cigar maker. Died November 17, 1943, Key West, Florida. Key West councilman 1884–1885, 1887–1888.[105]

Cox, Robert.
Born September 12, 1828, Lawrence County, Alabama. Mulatto. Carpenter. Alive in Tallahassee 1900. Florida house of representatives (Leon County, 1868, 1869, 1870).[106]

Crampton, Lloyd.
Born 1842, Maryland. Mulatto. Carpenter. Alive in Jacksonville 1880. Leon County commissioner 1872–1873?; Tallahassee councilman 1873.[107]

Cray, Robert.
Born 1813, Florida. Farmer. Alive in Madison County 1885. Madison County commissioner 1868–1873, 1875–1877.[108]

Crews [Cruse or LaCruse], Joseph C.
Born 1840, South Carolina. AME minister. Alive in Monticello 1878. St. Johns County voter registrar 1867.[109]

Cribb, Romain.
Born 1853, Florida. Mulatto. Barkeeper. Alive in Fernandina 1910. Died 1914, Nassau County, Florida? Fernandina councilman 1880–1881.[110]

Crowell, Archer D.
Born 1852, Florida. Farmer. Tallahassee marshal and tax collector 1880.[111]

Cruse, Harry.
Born 1841, Florida. Mulatto. Farmer and restaurant owner. AME. Alive in Gadsden County 1885. Florida senate (Gadsden County, 1869, 1870); Florida house of representatives (Gadsden County, 1871, 1872, 1873, 1874, 1877).[112]

Daly, Charles F.
Leon County justice of the peace 1872–1873.

Daniels, Joseph T.
Born 1825, Florida. Laborer. Alive in Walton County 1880. Walton County justice of the peace 1872–1873?[113]

Davidson, Green.
Born March 10, 1839, Charlotte, North Carolina. Barber. Delegate, 1868 constitutional convention (Leon and Wakulla Counties).[114]

Davidson, Peter H., Sr.
Born 1813, Monroe County, Alabama. Laborer. Died September 12, 1903, Pensacola, Florida. Florida house of representatives (Escambia County, 1877).[115]

Davidson, Peter H., Jr.
Born 1851, Conecuh County, Alabama. Laborer. Died 1919, Pensacola, Florida. Florida house of representatives (Escambia County, 1887). *New York Freeman*, February 1887: "Hon. P. H. Davidson, Assemblyman-elect, is one of Florida's most prominent Knights of Labor."[116]

Davis, Alfred.
Born May 1835, Virginia. Mulatto. Blacksmith. Alive in Ocala 1900. Ocala councilman 1874–1877, 1879–1883.[117]

Davis, Alfred [Alford].
Born 1827, South Carolina. Fruit grower. Alive in Putnam County 1885. Putnam County justice of the peace 1868–1873?, 1875–1877.[118]

Davis, Henry Mack.
Born September 18, 1851, Thomasville, Georgia. Baptist minister. Florida house of representatives (Leon County, 1883).[119]

Davis, Wesley.
Born April 1832, Florida. Domestic servant. AME. Died 1902, Leon County, Florida. Tallahassee councilman 1880.[120]

Dawkins, Burrell.
Born 1843, South Carolina. Mulatto. Farmer. Died March 1, 1881, Ocala, Florida (killed in performance of duties as marshal). Ocala marshal 1873–1876, 1880–1881.[121]

Dawkins, Wallace D.
Born 1843, South Carolina. Mechanic. Died November 18, 1890, Ocala,

Florida. Ocala councilman 1882–1883.[122]

Dean, James.
Born February 14, 1858, Ocala, Florida. Graduate, Howard University law department. Lawyer and AME minister. Died December 18, 1914, Jacksonville, Florida. Monroe County judge 1889. *New York Globe*, February 1884: "Your correspondent cannot speak too highly of the ability and promise of the chairman [of the Florida Negro Convention], James Dean, Esq., a young lawyer just from Howard Law Department, and yet in his twenties. Courteous, thoroughly posted in parliamentary law, and eloquent withal, he made a friend of every man in the convention."[123]

James Dean (Courtesy P. K. Yonge Library of Florida History, University of Florida)

DeCourcey [DeCoursey], Andrew.
Born 1841, Florida. Mulatto. Brick mason. Died February 21, 1875, Tallahassee, Florida. Tallahassee councilman 1874.[124]

DeCourcey [DeCoursey], Benjamin.
Born 1840, Florida. Mulatto. Mail contractor and vegetable dealer. Alive in Jacksonville 1890. Tallahassee councilman 1875, 1878, 1880–1881.[125]

DeCourcey [DeCoursey], Philip L.
Born 1846, Florida. Mulatto. Clerk. Died November 12, 1875, Tallahassee, Florida. Tallahassee tax assessor 1874–1875; Leon County sheriff 1875.[126]

Delaney, Ray S.
Born May 29, 1846, Georgia. Mulatto. Brick mason. Died May 28, 1896, Fernandina, Florida. Fernandina councilman 1870–1871, 1880–1881.[127]

Delaney, Thomas S.
Born March 15, 1810, Fernandina, Florida. Mulatto. AME minister and ship carpenter. Died August 6, 1890, Fernandina, Florida. Nassau County voter registrar 1867; Florida house of representatives (Nassau County, 1868, 1869, 1870).[128]

Denefield [Delafield], Richard L.
Born January 1860, Florida. Laborer. Died August 3, 1930, Palm Beach County, Florida. Fernandina marshal 1881–1883, 1884–1886; Fernandina councilman 1894–1902.[129]

Denegal, Romeo.
Born 1808, Georgia. Mulatto. Carpenter. Died by 1895, Fernandina, Florida. Fernandina councilman 1873–1875.[130]

Denham, Tully C.
Born 1851, Florida. Mulatto. Carpenter and AME minister. Died 1907, Texas. Suwannee County commissioner 1875–1876.[131]

Dennis, Robert H., Sr.
Born 1846, Philadelphia, Pennsylvania. Teacher. Died April 17, 1900, Pensacola, Florida. Florida house of representatives (Jackson County, 1875).[132]

Dennis, Samuel Maxwell.
Born October 12, 1857, Pablo Beach, Duval County, Florida. Brick mason. Baptist. Died November 12, 1909, Jacksonville, Florida. Jacksonville councilman 1888–1889.[133]

Samuel Maxwell Dennis (Courtesy Florida Archives)

DeVaughn, Herbert B.
Born 1842, Florida. AME minister. Alive in Leon County 1882. Leon County justice of the peace 1873–1874.[134]

Dilworth, Benjamin Franklin, Sr.
Born 1845, Florida. Mulatto. Methodist Episcopal minister and carpenter. Died December 1, 1900, Jacksonville, Florida. Jefferson County commissioner 1870–1872, 1873–1877.[135]

Dinkins, Richard.
Born 1841, South Carolina. Mulatto. Farmer and drayman. Alive in Ocala 1885. Ocala councilman 1869–1870.[136]

Dixon, Stepney Blount.
Born 1840, Georgia. Farmer. Alive in Hillsborough County 1880. Polk County voter registrar 1867–1868.[137]

Dorsey, Willoughby.
Born 1845, South Carolina. Mulatto. Porter and messenger. Died 1918, Nassau County, Florida. Fernandina councilman 1873–1875, 1876–1877, 1884–1887.[138]

Douglass, Henry.
Born 1847, Jefferson County, Florida. Mulatto. Farmer. Died May 6, 1912, Tallahassee, Florida. Tallahassee marshal and tax collector 1881–1882, 1884; Tallahassee marshal 1885–1886.[139]

Douglas[s], Henry N.
Born 1847, Florida. Carpenter. Alive in Tallahassee 1920. Tallahassee marshal and tax collector 1883; Tallahassee councilman 1884, 1888–1889.[140]

Doyle, Albert N.
Born 1840, South Carolina. Mulatto. Thirty-fourth USCI (1865–1866) [in

service as Albert Dows]. Shoemaker and carpenter. AME. Died April 8, 1893, Palatka, Florida. Putnam County commissioner 1868–1877; Palatka marshal and tax collector 1870–1874; Palatka marshal 1876, 1880–1881, 1882–1884; Palatka councilman 1889–1890.[141]

Drake, Harry.
Born 1825, North Carolina. Laborer. Lake City marshal 1873–1874.[142]

Dryer, Edward.
Born 1813, Georgia. Carpenter and AME minister. Died May 1880, Alachua County, Florida. Gainesville councilman 1873–1874.[143]

Duling, Turner.
Born March 1840, Georgia. Railroad laborer and shoemaker. Methodist Episcopal. Alive in Fernandina 1900. Wakulla County voter registrar 1867–1868; Fernandina marshal and tax collector 1871–1881; Nassau County justice of the peace 1871–1877.[144]

Dupont, Augustus.
Born 1830, South Carolina. Drayman. Died 1888, Escambia County, Florida. Pensacola councilman 1870–1872, 1874, 1877, 1885; Escambia County commissioner 1876–1877. Historian Charlene A. Hunter: "Augustus Dupont I was a highly educated man who came to Pensacola from Washington, D.C. He helped form the first public school. Whitfield Dupont, the son of Augustus DuPont I, was an interpreter of seven languages."[145]

Dupont, Charles F.
Born September 3, 1861, Tampa, Florida. Mulatto. Carpenter. Died September 29, 1938, Key West, Florida. Monroe County sheriff 1889–1893.[146]

Eckles [Eckels], William H.
Born 1837, Virginia. Mulatto. Farmer. Alive in Gadsden County 1910. Dead by 1916. Gadsden County commissioner 1873–1877.[147]

Eddin, Richard E.
Born 1845, New Providence, Bahama Islands. Junk dealer. Fernandina tax assessor 1880–1881; Fernandina councilman 1890–1892.[148]

Edwards, John.
Born 1842, Georgia. Laborer. Lake City councilman 1872–1873.[149]

Elijah, Zebulon.
Born 1838, Santa Rosa County, Florida. Salesman. Episcopal. Died December 3, 1910, Pensacola, Florida. Florida house of representatives (Escambia County, 1871, 1872, 1873); Escambia County commissioner 1872–1873; Pensacola postmaster 1874–1878; Pensacola tax assessor 1881–1882. Andrew F. Warren of Pensacola, December 1910: "For nearly twenty-five years 'Zeb,' as he has been known to almost all the older residents of Pensacola, has been in the service of the business with which I am connected. During all that time he has commended himself to all with whom

he came in contact, as a gentleman. His rank has not been exalted, but his honesty, faithfulness, and courtesy endeared him to us all."[150]

Elliott, James F.
Born December 1854, New Providence, Bahama Islands. Methodist Episcopal minister. Died 1921, Jacksonville, Florida. LaVilla clerk 1881–1882.[151]

Emmerly, Henry M.
Born 1840, South Carolina. Mulatto. Carpenter. Died 1904, St. Johns County, Florida. St. Johns County justice of the peace 1873–1875; St. Johns County commissioner 1875–1877.[152]

English, James D.
Born 1816, St. Augustine, Florida. Mulatto. Barber and grocer. Roman Catholic. Died by 1897, Key West, Florida. Monroe County commissioner 1868–1875.[153]

English, Nelson Francis deSales.
Born April 15, 1847, St. Augustine, Florida. Mulatto. Storekeeper. Roman Catholic. Died 1914, Key West, Florida. Dade County voter registrar 1867–1868; Key West postmaster 1882–1886.[154]

Epps, William Frank.
Born 1848, Mississippi. Brakeman. Died September 30, 1914, Jacksonville, Florida. LaVilla councilman 1884–1886.[155]

Nelson Francis deSales English (Courtesy Monroe County May Hill Russell Library)

Erwin, Auburn H.
Born November 1834, Pennsylvania. AME minister and teacher. Alive in Bradenton 1900. Delegate, 1868 constitutional convention (Columbia and Baker Counties); Florida house of representatives (Columbia County, 1868, 1869, 1870); Duval County justice of the peace 1873–1874; Duval constable 1872, 1877–1878.[156]

Evans, Jefferson J.
Born 1847, South Carolina. Farmer. Alive in Madison County 1910. Madison County justice of the peace 1872–1873?[157]

Evans, Reddish.
LaVilla councilman 1874–1875.

Everett, William.
Alive in Jackson County 1880. Died September 16, 1888, Jackson County,

Florida? Marianna councilman 1877–1878.[158]

Fells, Edward.
Born 1852, Florida or Georgia. Painter. Alive in Green Cove Springs 1920. Green Cove Springs councilman 1874–1876.[159]

Feltner, Jennings.
Born March 1857, South Carolina. Teamster. Died January 8, 1914, Alachua County, Florida. Gainesville tax collector 1881–1882; Gainesville tax assessor 1882–1885, 1886–1887, 1888–1890.[160]

Fields, Lewis.
Born 1828, Georgia. Mulatto. Farmer. Suwannee County commissioner 1870–1873.[161]

Figueroa, José Juan.
Born 1855, Cuba. Laborer. Alive in Key West 1880. Key West councilman 1875–1876.[162]

Fisher, Lucien.
Born 1837, Florida. Mulatto. Farmer. Alive in Leon County 1880. Florida house of representatives (Leon County, 1875).[163]

Fitzgiles, George S.
Born 1844, Maryland. Drayman. Tallahassee councilman 1875, 1878, 1880–1882, 1885–1886.[164]

Fitzgiles, Henry.
Born February 1841, Florida. Mulatto. Waiter. Alive in Tallahassee 1900. Tallahassee marshal and tax collector 1876, 1878.[165]

Forbes, James J.
Born 1841, New Providence, Bahama Islands. Mulatto. Carpenter. Alive in Jacksonville 1887. Duval County constable 1873–1875.[166]

Ford, William Henry.
Born June 2, 1840, Prince Georges County, Maryland. Mulatto. Second USCI (1863–1866). Farmer. Baptist. Died January 30, 1925, Tallahassee, Florida. Leon County constable 1870, 1873–1874; Florida house of representatives (Leon County, 1877, 1879).[167]

Forrester, Lewis F.
Born May 1856, Florida. Mulatto. Head waiter. Died 1936, Clay County, Florida. Green Cove Springs councilman 1896–1900.[168]

Forrester, Samuel.
Born October 1848, Florida. Farmer. Died 1930, Jacksonville, Florida. Cedar Keys councilman 1876–1877.[169]

Fortune, Emanuel.
Born January 3, 1832, Marianna, Florida. Mulatto. Merchant. AME. Died January 27, 1897, Jacksonville, Florida. Jackson County voter registrar 1867; 1868 constitutional convention delegate (Washington, Calhoun, and Jackson Counties); Florida house

of representatives (Jackson County, 1868, 1869, 1870); Florida house of representatives sergeant at arms 1872; Duval County commissioner 1873–1877; Jacksonville marshal 1873–1875; Jacksonville councilman 1888–1889. Cleveland (Ohio) *Gazette*, February 1897: "For 30 years Mr. Fortune had been a prominent figure in the political affairs of the state of Florida, and he had served his state, county, and city in the capacities of legislator, election officer, delegate to national conventions, sergeant-at-arms, city marshal, county commissioner of Duval county and member of the city board of health. Perhaps there is not a man in the state who was more generally known."[170]

Emanuel Fortune (In possession of the author, courtesy of Richard J. Ferry)

Foxworth, Bristow.
Born 1827, South Carolina. Mulatto. Mill worker. Alive in Jacksonville 1880. Madison County constable 1872.[171]

Francis, Edward S.
Born 1839, Charleston, South Carolina. Mulatto. Carpenter. AME. Died July 28, 1883, Jacksonville, Florida. Palatka councilman 1870?–1873; Putnam County justice of the peace 1873–1875.[172]

Francis, Paul.
Born September 1834, Florida. Stevedore. Alive in Fernandina 1910. Fernandina councilman 1870–1871, 1878–1880, 1881–1882.[173]

Franklin, Frank.
Born 1840, Florida. Mulatto. Grocer. Methodist Episcopal. Died June 23, 1886, Jacksonville, Florida. Jacksonville councilman 1871–1872.[174]

Franklin, Henry.
Born 1853, Florida. Laborer. Died ca. December 1898, Fernandina, Florida. Fernandina councilman 1898.[175]

Franklin, William [Frank].
Born 1839, Bedford County, Pennsylvania. Third USCI (1863–1865). Carpenter. CME. Died August 29, 1906, Tallahassee, Florida. Tallahassee councilman 1876.[176]

Frazier, Samuel W.
Born 1851, Georgia. Farmer. Alive in Leon County 1900. Leon County justice of the peace 1872–1873; Florida

house of representatives (Leon County, 1879, 1885, 1887).[177]

Freeman, Anthony E.
Born January 1848, Georgia. Mulatto. Laborer. Died 1917, Volusia County, Florida. Volusia County justice of the peace 1876–1880.[178]

Gabriel, Robert.
Born May 1854, Key West, Florida. Blacksmith. Died October 18, 1922, Key West, Florida. Key West councilman 1876–1880, 1897–1898, 1901–1907; Florida house of representatives (Monroe County, 1879). Jacksonville *Florida Times-Union*, December 1897: "The only colored man who is a member of the [Key West] City Council, is Robert Gabriel. He was at one time a member of the State Legislature, and has consequently had some experience in public life before. He is a respected member of his race and manifests a desire to co-operate with those who seek to establish a good and wholesome code of laws for the government of the city."[179]

Robert Gabriel (Courtesy Monroe County May Hill Russell Library)

Gadson, Frank P.
Born 1861, Charleston, South Carolina.

Frank P. Gadson (Courtesy Florida Archives)

Merchant and banker. AME. Died February 6, 1941, Ocala, Florida. Ocala treasurer 1884–1886; Ocala councilman 1886–1888; Ocala tax collector 1888–1890; Ocala treasurer and tax collector 1890–1892. *Florida Bureau of Immigration Monthly Bulletin*, February 1891: "The young colored merchant, Frank P. Gadson, of Ocala, has been re-elected collector of revenue for the city of Ocala. The Ocala Banner, in referring to his election, says: 'Mr. F. P. Gadson, one of our most highly respected colored citizens and prosperous merchants, was re-elected collector and treasurer by the president of the council casting one vote as the unanimous choice of the council. Mr. Gadson has been a faithful and capable official and we are pleased at this recognition of his merits.' "[180]

Gagnet, Richard.
Born 1827, Pensacola, Florida. Mulatto. Tailor. Died August 19, 1893, Pensacola, Florida. Pensacola councilman 1872, 1882; Escambia County tax assessor 1873–1874; Escambia County commissioner 1874–1876; Pensacola marshal 1878–1880, 1883–1884.[181]

Gallaway, Charles B.
Born 1857, South Carolina. Waiter. LaVilla clerk 1877–1878.[182]

Gambia, John C.
Born 1841, New York. Teacher. Alive in Putnam County 1885. Madison County tax assessor 1870–1872; Madison County clerk 1871–1874.[183]

Gardner, Berry M.
Born August 1844, Georgia. Farmer. Died 1928, Hernando County, Florida. Suwannee County commissioner 1873–1877.[184]

Garnett, Henry.
Born January 1838, Florida. Mulatto. Painter. Alive in Tallahassee 1900. Tallahassee councilman 1876.[185]

Garvin, James D.
Born 1847, New Providence, Bahama Islands. Mulatto. Market clerk. Alive in Jacksonville 1887. Jacksonville clerk 1871–1873; Duval County constable 1872.[186]

Garvin, William T.
Born 1822, Florida. Mulatto. Carpenter and builder. Died September 8, 1900, Jacksonville, Florida. Jacksonville councilman 1869–1871, 1873–1874; Duval County commissioner 1871; Duval County tax assessor 1871–1874.[187]

Gass, Theodore C.
Born 1833, South Carolina. Mulatto. Carpenter. Alachua County voter registrar 1868; Alachua County commissioner 1868–1870, 1872–1873?; Florida house of representatives (Alachua County, 1871, 1872, 1873, 1874, 1875); Gainesville councilman 1878–1879, 1881–1885.[188]

Gavin, Isaac.
Born March 1842, Florida. Carpenter. Alive in Crawfordville, Wakulla County, 1910. Died 1921, Jacksonville,

Florida? Wakulla County commissioner 1870–1871, 1873–1875.[189]

Geiger, George W.
Hernando County justice of the peace 1876–1877.

Gibbs, Burton C.
Born July 1854, Florida. Teacher and AME minister. Alive in Tallahassee 1902. Florida house of representatives (Jefferson County, 1881, 1885).[190]

Gibbs, Jonathan C.
Born 1827, Philadelphia, Pennsylvania. Graduate, Dartmouth College. Studied at Princeton Theological Seminary. Carpenter and Presbyterian minister. Died August 14, 1874, Tallahassee, Florida. Delegate, 1868 constitutional convention (Nassau, Duval, and St. Johns Counties); Florida secretary of state 1868–1873; Tallahassee councilman 1872; Florida superintendent of public instruction 1873–1874. *New York Daily Tribune*, February 1868: "Rev. J. C. Gibbs [was] a Presbyterian missionary in South Carolina, who came to Jacksonville just before the election [for constitutional convention delegates in 1867], probably for the purpose of getting into the Convention. . . . He is about 25 years old, pure African, rather undersized, active in body and intellect, well educated, and an orator by nature, not a roarer but a convincing, argumentative, pleasant speaker; in this respect, the most talented man in the Convention."[191]

Gibbs, Thomas Van Renssalaer.
Born September 16, 1855, Troy, New York. Mulatto. Attended Howard University, the United States Military Academy, and Oberlin College. Teacher and administrator. Died October 31, 1898, Tallahassee, Florida. Florida house of representatives (Duval County, 1885, 1887); 1885 constitutional convention delegate (Duval County); professor and vice president, State Normal College for Colored Students [predecessor of Florida Agricultural and Mechanical University], 1887–1898. James Weldon Johnson, 1933: "He was a slender, indeed delicate looking, light brown young man, who was a frequent visitor at our house. . . . Tom Gibbs had spent a year at West Point. He used to talk about his cadet days, and assigned his physical condition rather than race

Thomas Van Renssalaer Gibbs (Courtesy Florida Archives)

prejudice as the reason for having to leave the Academy. This young man, despite his quiet, reserved, soft-spoken manner, always carried himself like a soldier. He impressed me as an exemplar more than anyone else that I used to see at our house."[192]

Gibson, Birch.
Born 1828, Alabama. Carpenter. Baptist. Died September 10, 1895, Ocala, Florida. Florida house of representatives (Marion County, 1872); Marion County justice of the peace 1873–1875; Ocala councilman 1877–1878, 1881–1883. Jacksonville *Florida Times-Union*, September 1895: "It was next to impossible to suppress 'Birch' in a political gathering. . . . In many instances he was permitted to keep the floor for the amusement of the audience, for 'Birch' was possessed of considerable shrewdness and invariably got in a word or two that, figuratively speaking, brought down the house."[193]

Gibson, John A.
Born March 1837, Nassau, Bahama Islands. Teacher. Died October 3, 1906, Pensacola, Florida. Pensacola councilman 1879, 1882–1883, 1885.[194]

Gilchrist, Sir Sidney.
Born 1829, Florida. Farmer and laborer. Alive in Gadsden County 1894. Gadsden County justice of the peace 1868–1871.[195]

Goodbread, James.
Born October 1840, Georgia. Laborer. Alive in Nassau County 1900. Nassau County justice of the peace 1876–1877.[196]

Goodman, Nathaniel.
Born May 1830, North Carolina. Farmer. Alive in Suwannee County 1910. Suwannee County commissioner 1870.[197]

Gordon, John.
Born 1830, Tennessee. Baptist minister. Alive in Fernandina 1893. Nassau County commissioner 1875–1877. Jacksonville *Florida Union*, November 1867: "John Gordon is one of the smartest colored men in Nassau County. He is a local preacher of the Baptist Church, and, to his credit, be it said,—thinks and acts for himself in political matters. Led away by no man's vagaries, he is intelligent enough to be guided by reason and judgment."[198]

Gowens, Primus.
Born January 1841, South Carolina. AME minister. Died August 13, 1913, Ocala, Florida. Marion County commissioner 1868–1870?[199]

Graham, Noah.
Born 1815, Washington County, Georgia. Carpenter, machinist, AME minister. Died May 1885, Jefferson County, Florida. Florida house of representatives (Leon County, 1868, 1869, 1870, 1871, 1872); Leon County commissioner 1868.[200]

Granberry, Oscar.
Assassinated October 2, 1869, Marianna, Florida. Jackson County voter registrar 1868.[201]

Grant, Abram [Abraham].
Born August 25, 1848, Lake City, Florida. Mulatto. AME minister and bishop. Died January 22, 1911, Kansas City, Kansas. Duval County commissioner 1876–1877.[202]

Abram [Abraham] Grant (Courtesy Florida Archives)

Grant, Alfred.
Born 1840, Alabama. Clerk. Died March 24, 1883, Chattahoochee, Florida. LaVilla councilman 1871–1872, 1874–1875; Florida house of representatives (Duval County, 1875, 1877); LaVilla mayor 1876–1877; LaVilla tax assessor 1878–1879.[203]

Green, Robert.
Born 1825, Florida. Laborer. Died October 21, 1899, Duval County, Florida. LaVilla councilman 1873–1876, 1881–1887.[204]

Green, T. T.
Born 1866, South Carolina. Mulatto. Laborer. Alive in Sanford 1920. Goldsboro clerk 1911.[205]

Griffin, Henry.
Born 1832, Georgia. Carpenter. Alive in Jacksonville 1899. LaVilla councilman 1876–1877.[206]

Hadley, George.
Born 1829, Georgia. Carpenter. AME. Alive in Jefferson County 1885. Jefferson County justice of the peace 1871–1877.[207]

Hall, Anthony.
Born 1838, Georgia. Farmer. Died 1920, Madison County, Florida. Madison County justice of the peace 1870–1872, 1874–1878.[208]

Hall, Edward.
Born 1835, Georgia. Mulatto. Farmer. Alive in Columbia County 1880. Lake City tax assessor 1873–1874, 1876–1877; Columbia County commissioner 1874–1877.[209]

Hall, Esau W.
Born 1857, Florida. Laborer. Alive in

Tallahassee 1900. Tallahassee tax assessor 1889.[210]

Hall, Robert.
Born 1839, Georgia. Mulatto. Liquor dealer. Alive in Jacksonville 1900. Died 1914, Jacksonville, Florida? LaVilla councilman 1870–1871.[211]

Hannahan, Henry.
Born January 7, 1833, near St. Johns River, Florida. Twenty-first USCI (1863–1866). Laborer. Died October 1, 1910, Fernandina, Florida. Fernandina marshal and tax collector 1870–1871.[212]

Hargret[t], Amos.
Born September 14, 1833, Miccosukee, Jefferson County, Florida. Farmer. Baptist. Died November 1905, Wakulla County, Florida. Wakulla County commissioner 1868–1870; commissioner of pilotage, St. Marks, 1874–1877; Wakulla County justice of the peace 1876–1877; 1885 constitutional convention delegate (Wakulla County); St. Marks postmaster 1892–1894. Tallahassee *True Democrat*, December 1905: "He was a consistent Christian and deacon of the Missionary Baptist Church for thirty years. He was known to be a devoted husband and a loving father and was highly respected by white and colored. Our loss is heaven's gain."[213]

Hargrett, Richard H.
Born June 1841, Florida. Farmer. Alive in Crawfordville, Wakulla County, 1910. Died April 2, 1919, Wakulla County, Florida? Wakulla County commissioner 1873–1875.[214]

Harmon, Henry S.
Born 1839, Pennsylvania. Third USCI. Lawyer, editor, cabinetmaker. Died December 24, 1889, Tallahassee, Florida. Alachua County voter registrar 1867; Florida house of representatives (Alachua County, 1868, 1869, 1870); Gainesville councilman 1869–1870; chief clerk of the Florida house of representatives 1873, 1874, 1875. T. Thomas Fortune (1927): "Harry S. Harmon of Alachua county was the dandy, the lady's man, very intelligent and alert and a very ready speaker."[215]

Harper, Henry.
Born December 1818, Georgia. Farmer and Baptist minister. Alive in Hillsborough County 1900. Hernando County commissioner 1871–1875?[216]

Harris, Charles.
Florida house of representatives (Jefferson County, 1875).

Harrison, Primus.
Born 1826, Florida. Farmer. Alive in Duval County 1880. Columbia County commissioner 1869–1870.[217]

Harrison, Stanford.
Born April 1842, Florida. Mulatto. Carpenter. Died 1923, Tallahassee, Florida. Tallahassee councilman 1879–1880.[218]

Harrod, Thomas.
Born 1844, Pennsylvania. Watchman. Died September 20, 1873, Pensacola, Florida. Escambia County commissioner 1871–1873.[219]

Hart, Peter.
Born 1849, Georgia. Laborer. Levy County justice of the peace 1874; Cedar Keys councilman 1874–1876.[220]

Hart, Reuben.
Born 1831, Georgia. Farmer. Died October 14, 1871, Lake City, Florida. Columbia County commissioner 1870–1871.[221]

Hart, Sylvanus H.
Born August 1860, Darlington County, South Carolina. Contractor and banker. Alive in Jacksonville 1935. LaVilla clerk 1884–1887.[222]

Sylvanus H. Hart (Courtesy University of North Florida Special Collections)

Hawkins, Alexander B.
Born 1833, North Carolina. Mulatto. Methodist minister. Died November 1875, Calhoun County, Florida. Calhoun County voter registrar 1867–1868; Leon County commissioner 1868–1870; Calhoun County superintendent of schools 1873–1875; Calhoun County commissioner 1874–1875.[223]

Hawthorne, Anthony.
Born 1850, Alabama. Merchant. Died 1929, Escambia County. Milton councilman 1882.[224]

Haynes, John D.
AME minister. Alive in Gadsden County 1876. Leon County justice of the peace 1872–1873.[225]

Headsby [Headcopy or Headspey], Anthony.
Born 1836, Alabama. Stevedore. Died November 10, 1898, Pensacola, Florida. Pensacola councilman 1874.[226]

Hearn, James.
Born 1835, Florida. Laborer. Cedar Keys councilman 1875–1876.[227]

Henderson, Bristow.
Born 1854, South Carolina. Sawmill worker. Alive in Brevard County 1900. LaVilla councilman 1886–1887.[228]

Henderson, Noah.
Born 1830, Georgia or South Carolina. Grocery clerk and carpenter. Alive in Jacksonville 1892. LaVilla councilman 1870–1871, 1873–1874.[229]

Henderson, Tanner.
Born 1840, South Carolina. Farmer. Alive in Sumter County 1885. Sumter County commissioner 1868–1870.[230]

Hernandez, Heraldo.
Born 1838, Florida. Mulatto. Shoemaker. Alive in Pensacola 1886. Died 1888 in Escambia County? Pensacola councilman 1869, 1871, 1884–1885; Escambia County commissioner 1873–1874.[231]

Herndon, Calvin.
Born 1827, North Carolina. Laborer. Alive in Apalachicola 1885. Franklin County commissioner 1872–1877.[232]

Hicks, Henry.
Born 1817, Florida. Mechanic. Died January 4, 1876, Tallahassee, Florida. Tallahassee councilman 1875.[233]

Hicks, Moses.
Born 1840, Georgia. Teamster. Alive in Jacksonville 1887. Duval County constable 1868–1870.[234]

Hicks, William B.
Born 1824, South Carolina. Laborer and painter. Died January 22, 1901, St. Johns County, Florida. St. Augustine tax assessor 1873–1874; St. Augustine councilman 1878.[235]

Hill, Frederick [Frederick Stephens until 1867].
Born 1833, North Carolina. Farmer. AME. Alive in Gadsden County 1878. Died before 1893. Delegate, 1868 constitutional convention (Gadsden County); Florida house of representatives (Gadsden County, 1868, 1869, 1870); Quincy postmaster 1869–1875; Gadsden County commissioner 1870; Florida senate (Gadsden County, 1871, 1872, 1873, 1874, 1875, 1877). *New York Daily Tribune*, February 1868: "Frederick Hill, an intelligent, full-blood African." Tallahassee *Weekly Floridian*, August 1875: "[Quincy postmaster] Hill is very much respected by all classes."[236]

Holder, Joseph.
Born 1843, Newnansville, Alachua County, Florida. Mulatto. Thirty-third USCI (1862–1866). Carpenter. Baptist. Died January 21, 1917, Jacksonville, Florida. LaVilla councilman 1871–1872.[237]

Hollingsworth, Mack.
LaVilla clerk 1878–1879.

Holloman, Adam.
Born August 14, 1838, Florida. Mulatto. Farmer. Died July 25, 1905, Hillsborough County, Florida. Hillsborough County commissioner 1873–1877.[238]

Holloman, Mills.
Born 1795, Virginia. Mulatto. Farmer. Died January 6, 1882, Hillsborough County, Florida. Hillsborough County commissioner 1868–1870, 1870–1871.[239]

Holmes, Elbert T.
Born August 1862, Georgia. Teacher. Died February 13, 1926, Palatka, Florida. Lake City councilman 1890–1892; Palatka councilman 1904–1908.[240]

Horn, E. L.
Eatonville councilman 1887–1888.

Houston, Edward J.
Born 1846, Georgia. Mulatto. Laborer. Alive in St. Augustine 1918. St. Augustine tax collector 1882–1883, 1884–1885.[241]

Huggins, Handy [Hiram] N.
Born 1847, South Carolina. Mulatto. Policeman. Died January 22, 1889, Jacksonville, Florida. LaVilla marshal 1876–1879, 1881–1887.[242]

Hughes, John.
Born January 1865, Florida. Laborer. Alive in Jacksonville 1907. LaVilla councilman 1887.[243]

Hurston, John.
Born January 1861, Alabama. Baptist minister. Died May 1918, Memphis, Tennessee. Eatonville mayor 1912–1916. On Zora Neale Hurston's father, the *Sanford Herald*, November 1910: "Rev. John Hurston has been pastor of the [Zion Hope Baptist Church] for seventeen years. . . . He is beloved by his church and has a membership of some two hundred. A favorite greeting of Rev. Hurston's is 'Welcome, ye lovers of Jesus. Our doors are open—Come.' "[244]

John Hurston (In possession of author, from *Sanford Herald*, November 25, 1910)

Hutchinson, Henry.
Born April 1842, Virginia. Mulatto. Stevedore. AME. Alive in Apalachicola 1900. Franklin County sheriff 1874–1877; Apalachicola councilman 1886–1890.[245]

Hutchinson, Samuel.
Born 1852, Alabama. Mulatto. Laborer. Franklin County justice of the peace 1873–1876?[246]

Jackson, Lee.
Born 1848, Florida. Laborer. LaVilla councilman 1873–1876.[247]

Jacobs, David E.
Born 1842, Georgia. Farmer and Methodist Episcopal minister. Alive in Fernandina 1894. Marion County commissioner 1875–1876; Florida house of representatives (Marion County, 1877). Ocala *East Florida Banner*, May 1876: "Jacobs is a member of a very prosperous family of colored people, and before his removal from the Board of County Commissioners stood square up to Mr. [Jesse H.] Goss [a local, white Republican leader]. . . . If he fights corruption and dishonesty as usefully in the legislature as he did while a member of the Board of County Commissioners the people of the county will have no cause to complain."[248]

James, Henry.
Born 1808, South Carolina. Mulatto. Carpenter. Died September 24, 1889, Alachua County, Florida. Alachua County commissioner 1873–1877.[249]

James, William.
Born 1840, Florida. Farmer. Florida House of Representatives (Duval County, 1885).

Jasper, T. Scipio.
Born 1815, South Carolina. Farmer. Alive in Marion County 1885. Florida house of representatives (Marion County, 1871, 1872). *The Struggle for Survival: A Partial History of the Negroes of Marion County* (1977): "If ever there was a politician who loved humanity, it was T. Jasper. The love he had for people was in large measure responsible for his representing Marion County in the house of representatives, Tallahassee."[250]

Jefferson, James W.
Born 1832, Florida. Mail carrier. Died November 25, 1895, Tallahassee, Florida. Tallahassee councilman 1873; Leon County commissioner 1875–1877; Tallahassee tax assessor 1877, 1879, 1881–1883, 1886, 1888.[251]

Jenkins, Isaac.
Born August 10, 1846, Leon County, Florida. Clerk and painter. Baptist. Died November 30, 1911, Leon County, Florida. Tallahassee councilman 1876; Florida house of representatives (Leon County, 1881, 1883). Legislative biographer J. V. Drake (1883): "Isaac Jenkins, of Leon, was born in the county he represents, August 10, 1846, and was raised on the farm of his owner, General Robert Butler, where he lived until the civil war in 1861; went then as cook with his young master, Robert Patten, into the Confederate service, and so continued until 1863, when he became free by virtue of the emancipation proclamation; came then to Tallahassee, and worked at the tinner's trade under W. P. Slusher, now of the City Hotel, for two years; was then clerk in a store for a time; was married in 1860, to Miss Mary Adkerson, worked for two or three years at the painter's trade; then was clerk again for a time; was sexton of the city cemetery for

three years; was elected in 1880 to the Legislature, and again in 1882 to the same position."[252]

Jewett, Hubbard [Herbert].
Born September 1862, Georgia. Laborer. Alive in Goldsboro 1900. Goldsboro councilman 1891–1892.[253]

Johnson, Anthony.
Born 1838, Georgia. Mulatto. Farmer. Madison councilman 1876–1877.[254]

Johnson, Elias.
Born 1847, Alabama or Georgia. Merchant. Alive in Pensacola 1916. Pensacola councilman 1883.[255]

Johnson, Harry.
Born 1826, Florida. Mulatto. Blacksmith. Alive in Nassau County 1895. Fernandina councilman 1871–1873.[256]

Johnson, J. R.
Eatonville clerk 1887–1888.

Johnson, James.
Born August 26, 1830, Richmond, Virginia. Head waiter. Baptist. Died June 1912, Jacksonville, Florida. LaVilla councilman 1871–1872; LaVilla clerk 1876–1877. His son, James Weldon Johnson (1933): "My father was a quiet, unpretentious man. He was naturally conservative and cautious, and generally displayed common sense in what he said and did. He never went to school; such education as he had was self-acquired. Later in life, I appreciated the fact that his self-development was little less than remarkable. . . . The quality in my father that impressed me most was his high and rigid sense of honesty. I simply could not conceive of him as a party to any monetary transaction that was questionable to him."[257]

Johnson, Lewis.
Born January 1843, Florida or Georgia. Farmer and AME minister. Died March 17, 1904, Live Oak, Florida. Columbia County commissioner 1873–1875.[258]

Johnson, Major.
Born 1840, South Carolina. AME minister. Alive in Marion County 1890. Delegate, 1868 constitutional convention (Madison County).[259]

Johnson, Robert.
Born 1841, North Carolina. Minister. Hillsborough County commissioner 1871–1873.[260]

Johnson, Simon A.
Born 1857, Florida. Laborer. Died June 23, 1938, Fernandina, Florida. Fernandina councilman 1899–1900.[261]

Johnson, Willis.
Born 1812, Georgia. Farmer. Alive in Walton County 1870. Walton County voter registrar 1867–1868.[262]

Jones, Allen, Sr.
Born 1813, Queen Anne's County, Maryland. AME minister and farmer. Died February 28, 1888, Quincy, Florida. Gadsden County commissioner 1870–1874. Quincy correspondent of the Jack-

sonville *Florida Times-Union*, March 1888: "Uncle Allen Jones, the oldest colored minister in this county, died on Thursday night. He was the best colored minister here, and was highly thought of by both white and blacks." Jacksonville *Evening Telegram*, February 1894: "the late venerable Rev. Allen Jones, probably the greatest minister Florida ever had."[263]

Jones, Benjamin.
Born 1810, North Carolina. Farmer. Alive in Leon County 1885. Leon County commissioner 1873.[264]

Jones, Everett C.
Born 1844, Tennessee. Schoolteacher and Baptist minister. Alive in Orlando 1900. Tallahassee councilman 1872–1873; Tallahassee clerk and treasurer 1876–1877; Florida senate (Leon County, 1879—unseated). *Miami Metropolis*, September 1899: "Dr. E. C. Jones is a man worthy of compliment. He has done more to advance the Baptist society in South and East Florida than any living man."[265]

Jones, Henry.
AME. Died March 12, 1883, Monroe County, Florida. Tallahassee councilman 1879, 1881.[266]

Jones, Richard.
Born 1856, Florida. Domestic servant. Fernandina tax assessor 1883–1884.[267]

Jones, Richard L.
Born 1835, South Carolina. Brick mason. Died September 4, 1882, Jacksonville, Florida. Duval County commissioner 1873, 1874–1876; Jacksonville councilman 1873–1874, 1879–1880.[268]

Jones, Wiley.
Born September 1850, Florida. Laborer. Alive in Jacksonville 1910. LaVilla councilman 1887.[269]

Jordan, Jacob Clarence.
Born 1857, Georgia. Teacher and letter carrier. Died 1922, St. Johns County, Florida. St. Augustine tax collector 1882; St. Augustine councilman 1885–1886.[270]

Jordan, Morris.
Cedar Keys councilman 1875–1876.

Joseph, William.
Born January 1825, Florida. Carpenter. Alive in Fernandina 1900. Fernandina councilman 1881–1882.[271]

Jourdan, Sampson.
Born 1815, Alabama. Farmer. Hernando County commissioner 1873–1875.[272]

Junius, Andrew Jackson.
Born May 1844, North Carolina. Farmer. Died 1917, Jefferson County, Florida. Florida house of representatives (Jefferson County, 1879).

Kelker, John.
Born 1812, Escambia County, Florida. Mulatto. Farmer, mechanic, and Baptist minister. Died 1893, Santa Rosa

John Kelker (Courtesy University of West Florida Special Collections)

County, Florida. Santa Rosa County voter registrar 1867–1868. His descendant Del E. Jupiter (1992): "[John Kelker was] a free person of color. . . . Born about 1812, Kelker was too old to have participated in the Civil War and his sons were too young. By the time those boys reached adulthood, John was the pastor of New Providence Baptist Church at Bagdad. According to family tradition, he and his sons—along with other artisans of the black community—built the church using timber from Santa Rosa's forests. The church also served the community as a one-room schoolhouse."[273]

Kent, Robert.
Born 1821, Georgia. Carpenter. Leon County commissioner 1871–1874?[274]

Kerby, Nelson M.
Born 1832, South Carolina. Laborer. Alive in Lake City 1900. Suwannee County commissioner 1868–1869.[275]

Kilby, Thomas.
Born December 1850, Florida. Sawmill worker and AME minister. Alive in Apalachicola 1910. Apalachicola councilman 1887–1889.[276]

King, David.
Born 1813, Georgia. Farmer. Alive in Madison 1885. Madison County commissioner 1868–1873.[277]

King, Jesse F.
Born 1833, Florida. Farmer. Alive in Gadsden County 1874. Gadsden County justice of the peace 1872–1873.[278]

King, Port W.
Born 1851, Florida. Carpenter and brick mason. Died 1903, Nassau County, Florida. Fernandina clerk and treasurer 1875–1876; Fernandina tax assessor 1878–1879; Fernandina councilman 1883–1885.[279]

Knabb, Charles.
Born 1817, Darien, Georgia. Twenty-first USCI (1863–1864). Farmer. Died July 7, 1883, Fernandina, Florida. Fernandina councilman 1869–1870; Nassau County commissioner 1872–1874.[280]

Lancaster, Thomas.
Born 1835, Florida. Mechanic, carpenter, and Baptist minister. Alive in Jacksonville 1902. Jacksonville councilman 1871–1874; Jacksonville tax assessor 1874–1876, 1880–1881, 1882–1883.[281]

Lane, James.
Born 1842, Florida. Drayman. Died July 27, 1879, Duval County, Florida. Duval County constable 1873–1875.[282]

Lang, James H.
Born 1842, St. Augustine, Florida. Thirty-third USCI (1863–1865). Fisherman. Died December 14, 1894, Key West, Florida. St. Johns County commissioner 1868–1871.[283]

Langley, Edward Francis.
Born December 27, 1833, St. Augustine, Florida. Mulatto. Twenty-first USCI (1863–1866). Carpenter. Died July 13, 1902, Fernandina, Florida. Fernandina councilman 1870–1871, 1875–1876.[284]

Lee, Cato.
Born 1837, Fernandina, Florida. Stevedore. Died September 20, 1891, Jacksonville, Florida. Jacksonville councilman 1872–1873.[285]

Lee, Daniel F.
Born 1839, Florida. Farmer. Alive in Hamilton County 1885. Hamilton County commissioner 1873–1877.[286]

Lee, Joseph E.
Born September 15, 1849, Philadelphia, Pennsylvania. Graduate, Howard University law department. Lawyer and AME minister. Died March 25, 1920, Jacksonville, Florida. Florida house of representatives (Duval County, 1875, 1877, 1879); Florida senate (Duval County, 1881); Jacksonville municipal judge 1888; Duval County clerk of the circuit court 1889?; United States collector of the port of Jacksonville 1890–1894; United States collector of internal revenue, district of Florida, 1897–1913. Jacksonville *Evening Telegram*, February 1892: "Joseph E. Lee holds one of the most honorable federal positions in the country, and also owns considerable property, but he is one gentleman that never lets these things make him egotistic or get above himself, as a good many do. He goes through the woods and country preaching Jesus Christ and Him crucified, and treats his fellow-man properly, hence he is much thought of by everybody, both white and black." African American lawyer J. D. Wetmore, April 1926: "Judge Lee was a 'carpet bagger' . . . and was probably one of the first colored men in the State to be admitted to practice law. He also was an A. M. E. minister, and combined these two professions with politics. He was very successful as a politician, but ultra conservative as a lawyer, as he was careful never to take any case in which he might give offense to white people. . . . As the result of his conservatism, the leading white men of the community never made any objections when

he was appointed collector of customs and collector of internal revenue. . . . I never saw his superior as a presiding officer in a deliberative body, and he was one of the shrewdest, brightest, coolest, and best read men I ever knew."[287]

LeGrand [LeGrant], Thomas.
LaVilla councilman 1870–1872, 1876–1877.

Lester, Hyrum N.
Born 1881, Georgia. Laborer. Died 1925, Orange County, Florida. Eatonville mayor 1922–1924.[288]

Lewey, Matthew M.
Born December 1848, Baltimore, Maryland. Fifty–fifth Massachusetts Infantry (1863–1865). Teacher, editor, lawyer. Presbyterian. Died August 12, 1935, Jacksonville, Florida. Newnansville mayor 1875–1877; Alachua County justice of the peace 1875–1876; Florida house of representatives (Alachua County, 1883); Gainesville councilman 1886–1890, 1891; editor, *Florida Sentinel*, 1887–1927. Matthew M. Lewey (ca. 1889): "Douglass, Langston and Bruce, have obtained recognition among white men, Democrats as well as Republicans, North and South, by reason of their indomitable self-perseverance in their peculiar field of labor; and other colored men, through pluck and energy, will obtain similar respect and recognition in their peculiar fields of labor, . . . whether it be in the cotton fields, work-shop, school-room, or the grocery store. The sooner we rely entirely upon ourselves in the development of manly character, aspire to excel in everything, work hard day and night, get money, educate our children, don't beg but depend upon our own brain and muscles—in the very nature of things, white men will soon recognize seven millions of Douglasses, Langstons and Bruces."[289]

Lewis, George A.
Born 1861, Columbia, South Carolina. Postal worker and teacher. AME. Died July 1, 1910, Jacksonville, Florida. Florida house of representatives (Duval County, 1889). Jacksonville *Metropolis*, July 1910: "At the time of his death, Mr. Lewis was a letter carrier, which position he had held for a number of years. . . . [He] was a Freemason, a member of Pythagoras Lodge, No. 25, and also a Royal Mason, and Knight-Templar. He was the president and foremost promoter of the Lincoln Memorial Association, and in all public moves he was no silent factor. Friends from all sides bow in sorrow with the bereaved family."[290]

Lightbourn[e], Alexander C., Sr.
Born 1846, Nassau, Bahama Islands. Teacher. AME. Died October 1908, Miami, Florida. Florida house of representatives sergeant at arms 1869, 1870; Gadsden County commissioner 1871–1873; Gadsden County justice of the peace 1871–1874.[291]

Lindsley, George W.
Escambia County superintendent of schools 1873–1875.

Little, Gilbert.
Born January 1831, Florida. Farmer. Alive in Marion County 1900. Marion County commissioner 1873–1877.[292]

Livingston, Benjamin F.
Born April 1841, Florida. Mulatto. Grocer and brick mason. Alive in Jackson County 1902. Jackson County commissioner 1868–1870, 1874–1877; Florida house of representatives (Jackson County, 1871, 1872, 1873, 1874, 1875); Marianna postmaster 1880–1885; Marianna councilman 1882–1884? Philadelphia *Christian Recorder*, December 1880: "Benjamin F. Livingston, the Postmaster of Marianna, Florida, is a man who reflects credit upon his race by his upright character and attention to official duty."[293]

Livingston, James.
Hamilton County voter registrar 1868.

Livingston, John.
Born May 1830, Florida. Brick mason. Died 1926, Jackson County, Florida. Marianna councilman 1876–1877.[294]

Livingston, Robert.
Born 1835, Leon County, Florida. Carpenter. Died ca. December 10, 1868, Leon County, Florida. Florida house of representatives (Leon County, 1868). Resolution, Florida house of representatives, January 1869: "Whereas . . . Hon. Robert Livingston, of Leon, was summoned from earth by an All-Wise Providence, we, as his associates, would tender in a public manner, a testimonial of our respect and esteem for his modest demeanor, his honesty of purpose, and many virtues, which, during his connection with us in this body, won our affection and confidence."[295]

Logan, Ephraim.
Born 1827, Florida. Farmer. Alive in Jefferson County 1880. Florida house of representatives (Jefferson County, 1871, 1872).

Lomans, John.
Born 1840, District of Columbia. Farmer. Died 1899, DeSoto County, Florida. Manatee County voter registrar 1868. Grand jury minutes: "Personally appeared before the Grand Jury for Manatee County and State of Florida this 18th day of April 1871 William H. Hollingsworth who being duly sworn deposes and says that he did not see any one put a Rope around the neck of John Lomans [but Lomans was held] with a Rope around his neck, and William Allen had holt of the other end of it, that he saw four other men with him."[296]

Long, Thomas Warren.
Born January 10, 1839, Jacksonville, Florida. Thirty-third USCI (1862–1865). AME minister. Died October 25, 1917, Jacksonville, Florida. Madison County superintendent of schools

Thomas Warren Long (Courtesy Florida Archives)

1868–1869; Florida senate (Marion County, 1873, 1874, 1875, 1877, 1879). Long's white Civil War commanding officer, Thomas Wentworth Higginson, quoting him in the vernacular on the liberating effect of becoming a soldier and how the experience had prepared him for citizenship (ca. 1862–1863): "If we hadn't become sojers, all might have gone back as it was before; our freedom might have slipped through two houses of Congress and President Linkum's four years might have passed by and notin' been done for us. But now tings can neber go back, because we have showed our energy and our courage and our naturally manhood. Another ting is, suppose you had kep your freedom without enlisting in dis army; your children might have growed up free and been well cultivated . . . but it would have been always flung in dere faces—'Your fader never fought for he own freedom'—and what could day answer? Never can say dat to dis African Race no more."[297]

Long, William Ryal.
Born 1833, Georgia. Blacksmith. Alive in Jefferson County 1896. Jefferson County tax assessor 1869–1870; Jefferson County commissioner 1870–1874; Florida house of representatives (Jefferson County, 1873, 1874, 1877). Tallahassee *Weekly Floridian*, October 1874: "Ryal Long was a member of the last legislature, was better pleased with the labor of framing laws than horse shoes, plows, &C., and is very anxious to try it again. He is a very clever colored man, was a zealous Democrat soon after emancipation, but the pressure was too heavy, and he sunk in the whirlpool of Radicalism."[298]

Lumpkin, Charles.
Born March 1847, Georgia. Farmer. Alive in White Springs, Hamilton County, 1910. Hamilton County commissioner 1872.[299]

McCardy, Moses W. C.
Born May 1, 1853, Beasley, Jefferson County, Florida. Mulatto. Farmer and Baptist minister. Alive in Jacksonville 1900. Jefferson County justice of the peace 1874–1876; Florida house of representatives (Jefferson County, 1883).[300]

McCaslin, James.
Born 1833, South Carolina. Farmer. Died 1920, Alachua County, Florida. Florida house of representatives (Alachua County, 1885).[301]

McCoy, Thomas.
Born 1850, North Carolina. Mulatto. Laborer. Died 1927, Columbia County, Florida. Lake City councilman 1876–1877.[302]

McCray, Lafayette Napoleon Bonaparte.
AME minister. Died February 16, 1885, Jefferson County, Florida. Jefferson County sheriff 1876; Florida house of representatives (Jefferson County, 1881).[303]

McDonald, Obit.
Born 1830, Jacksonville, Florida. Mulatto. Laborer. Died 1885, Fernandina, Florida. Fernandina councilman 1872–1874.[304]

McDonald, Robert.
Born March 1848, Georgia. Mulatto. Laborer. Died 1904, Nassau County, Florida. Fernandina councilman 1882–1884, 1885–1887, 1900–1902.[305]

McDyer, John A.
Born 1860, Georgia. Merchant. Died November 2, 1924, Fernandina, Florida. Fernandina councilman 1896–1898.[306]

McGovern, Ed.
Born June 1858, Florida. Stevedore. Alive in Pensacola 1893. Died 1905, Pensacola, Florida? Pensacola councilman 1883.[307]

McGriff, Austin [Mack].
AME minister. Gadsden County justice of the peace 1873–1874.[308]

McInnis, Daniel M.
Born 1843, Charleston, South Carolina. Mulatto. Tailor. Died April 4, 1897, Jacksonville, Florida. Florida house of representatives (Duval County, 1871, 1872, 1873, 1874). Black state senator John Wallace (1888): "Some days after the [1870 Republican state] convention, while [white Republican William H.] Christy was incidentally in the place of business of Dan McInnis, W. M. Ledwith, who was at that time friendly with [carpetbagger United States Senator Thomas W.] Osborn, came in, and said: 'McInnis, I am authorized by Colonel Osborn to say to you that if you will simply withdraw from your place on the Legislative ticket and let [white Republican Horatio] Jenkins go in your place, he will give you five thousand dollars, and give you also the regular pay; we do not ask you to take an active part in his favor.' McInnis replied, 'Ledwith, tell Osborn to go to——with his money; I have my trade to make my living from.' "[309]

McIntyre, Henry.
Born 1826, North Carolina. Mulatto. Thirty-third USCI (1862–1866). Mechanic and carpenter. Died Febru-

ary 20, 1901, Montague, Marion County, Florida. Duval County constable 1868–1870.[310]

McIver, Samuel.
Born 1843, Georgia. Farmer. Alive in Suwannee County 1885. Suwannee County commissioner 1873–1875.[311]

McLain, Jesse.
Born July 1856, Florida. Merchant. Alive in Palatka 1910. St. Augustine councilman 1897–1902.[312]

McLeary, Thomas.
Born 1843, Florida. Mulatto. Died December 14, 1904, Madison, Florida. Madison marshal 1876–1877. Madison *New Enterprise*, December 1904: "Sober, honest, industrious, he stood for all that was praiseworthy to his race, and has for years held an enviable position in the community, commanding the respect and emulation of his own people and the esteem of all who knew him. . . . He died a comparatively wealthy man."[313]

McMillan, John.
Born July 1865, South Carolina. Merchant. Died 1926, Putnam County, Florida. Palatka councilman 1902–1904.[314]

McMullen [McMillen], Edward.
Born March 1835, Georgia. Mulatto. Farmer. Alive in Sumter County 1900. Sumter County voter registrar 1867–1868.[315]

McQueen, Jeff.
Born 1852, Virginia. Mulatto. Carpenter. Alive in Cedar Key 1900. Cedar Key councilman 1874–1875, 1885–1889; Gainesville councilman 1879–1880.[316]

Mallett, Duncan H. [Dank].
Born October 1850, Alabama. Carpenter. Alive in Pensacola 1910. Pensacola marshal 1885.[317]

Manigault, Charles C.
Born October 1869, Alachua County, Florida. Mulatto. Porter. Died 1940, Palm Beach County, Florida. Jacksonville councilman 1899–1901.[318]

Manker, George.
Suwannee County voter registrar 1867–1868; Suwannee County commissioner 1869–1870.

Manley, Clement.
Leon County justice of the peace 1875–1877.

Martin, Boston P.
Born 1859, Florida. Laborer. Alive in Jacksonville 1930. Cedar Key councilman 1893–1895, 1909.[319]

Martin, Daniel C.
Born 1856, South Carolina. Mulatto. Printer. Died June 29, 1890, Gainesville, Florida. Gainesville clerk and treasurer 1880–1885, 1888–1890; Florida senate (Alachua County, 1885, 1887). *Palatka Daily News*, May 1887: "It was this Negro Senator, Martin, who so stoutly opposed Mr. McKinne's

amendment to reduce the appropriation for the East Florida Seminary, and who, like most of the more intelligent sons of his race, appears to think no sum extravagant which is devoted to the cause of education. When it is remembered that from the institution in question Negroes are excluded, the breadth of purpose animating its Negro champion may be appreciated. Throughout the session Senator Martin has proved himself a warm and intelligent friend of his county's best interests, and a sensible and consistent advocate of the cause of education. He has not forgotten his own race in urging the location of a Normal School for Negroes at Gainesville, and, while the paper which claims the highest rank in the State was boasting of the political victory of its white editor gained by wholesale purchase of votes, this Negro was quietly and thoughtfully framing a law to protect the ballot and guard the voter against the temptations of corruption."[320]

Martin, Edward.
Born September 1857, South Carolina. Printer. Died 1927, Alachua County, Florida. Gainesville councilman 1889–1891.[321]

Matthews, Henry.
Born 1820, Maryland. Mulatto. Shoemaker. Tallahassee councilman 1875, 1877.[322]

Matthews, William.
Born 1846, Florida. Brick mason. Alive in Jacksonville 1892. Tallahassee tax assessor 1880.[323]

Mayo, Andrew D.
Born 1845, North Carolina. Mulatto. Carpenter. Alachua County treasurer 1873–1875; Gainesville councilman 1873–1874, 1876–1880, 1882–1883.[324]

Mays, George H.
Born August 2, 1849, Edgefield, South Carolina. Mulatto. Mail carrier. Presbyterian. Died December 25, 1918, Jacksonville, Florida. Duval County constable 1873–1875, 1878–1880?; Jacksonville marshal 1878–1882.[325]

Mays, John.
Born 1838, South Carolina. Mulatto. Carpenter. Jefferson County commissioner 1870–1872, 1873–1877.[326]

Mays, John B.
Born 1833, South Carolina. Mulatto. Shoemaker. Alive in Madison 1885. Madison County justice of the peace 1870–1879?[327]

Meacham, Robert.
Born spring 1835, Gadsden County, Florida. Mulatto. AME and AME Zion minister. Died February 27, 1902, Tampa, Florida. Jefferson County voter registrar 1867–1868; 1868 constitutional convention delegate (Jefferson County); Florida senate (Jefferson County, 1868, 1869, 1870, 1871, 1872, 1873, 1874, 1875, 1877, 1879); Jefferson County clerk 1868; Jefferson County superintendent of schools 1868–1872,

1873–1877; Monticello postmaster 1869–1870, 1870–1871; Punta Gorda postmaster 1889–1891. Robert Meacham, July 1867: "As politics have become the news of the day, I must say something about them. The most exciting question is, what party shall we vote for, but the answer from all quarters of the State is the Republican Party. There will be a Republican State convention on the 11th of this month at Tallahassee, Florida, and it is thought that delegates will be sent from all parts of the State to the Convention, at which time I expect to be there myself." *Punta Gorda Herald*, March 1902: "[Robert Meacham] was prominent as a preacher but more as a Republican politician; but notwithstanding his color and his politics, he stood high in the esteem of the white people. . . . Meacham's death is regretted both in Tampa and Punta Gorda."[328]

Robert Meacham (Courtesy Florida Archives)

Menard, John Willis.

Born April 3, 1838, Kaskaskia, Illinois. Mulatto. Editor and poet. AME. Author, *Lays in Summer Lands* (1879); editor, *Florida News* and *Southern Leader*, 1882–1888. Died October 8, 1893, Washington, D.C. United States representative-elect (Louisiana, 1868—not seated); Duval County justice of the peace 1874, 1877; Florida house of representatives (Duval County 1874). James Weldon Johnson (1933): "I have a very clear recollection of J. [W.] Menard, looking a good deal like the pictures of Alexandre Dumas; he was the first Negro elected to Congress, and, when I knew him, was running a weekly newspaper in Jacksonville." John Willis Menard, September 1876: "The [white carpetbaggers] have succeeded in getting the whole hog by ignoring the colored people and Southern loyalists, and also by committing daring frauds upon the party. Every intelligent colored man knows these are the facts. This ring does not represent Republican principles, neither does it care anything for the colored man except his vote."[329]

Mickens, Richard.

Born 1836, Florida. Mulatto. Farmer. Died November 1882, Leon County, Florida. Leon County commissioner 1873–1874.[330]

Middleton, Peter B.
Born 1845, South Carolina. Teacher. Fernandina councilman 1879–1881.[331]

Miller, Bird.
Born 1820, Florida. Domestic servant. Died August 1879, Jacksonville, Florida. Clay County commissioner 1871–1873.[332]

Miller, Fred E.
Alive in Cedar Key 1878. Cedar Keys marshal 1874–1876; Levy County commissioner 1876–1877.[333]

Mills, Anthony.
Born 1828, Georgia. Carpenter. AME. Died November 5, 1907, Monticello, Florida. Delegate, 1868 constitutional convention (Jefferson County); Florida house of representatives (Jefferson County, 1868, 1869, 1870); Jefferson County commissioner 1872–1873? *Savannah Morning News*, July 1874: "At a Radical meeting in Monticello the other day, one of the members, a negro named Anthony Mills, made a speech which was loudly applauded. He denounced the carpetbaggers in round terms, and advised his race to support no man for office hereafter who was not born and raised in Florida."[334]

Mills, Joseph.
Born December 1830, South Carolina. Farmer. Alive in Brooksville, Hernando County, 1900. Hernando County commissioner 1876–1877.[335]

Mitchell, John W.
Born 1856, Gadsden County, Florida. Lawyer. Died March 26, 1901, Chattahoochee, Florida. Leon County justice of the peace 1877–1879; 1885 constitutional convention delegate (Leon County); Florida house of representatives (Leon County, 1887). Future Florida supreme court justice James B. Whitfield (1885): "His educational advantages were very limited, but he studied privately while a youth. Afterwards he read law, and was admitted to the bar of the Second Judicial Circuit in 1872. . . . Being a ready and forcible speaker[,] he wielded much influence among his political friends."[336]

Mitchell, Reuben S.
Born 1855, Florida. Mulatto. Mail clerk. Died December 19, 1924, Marion County, Florida. Ocala clerk, tax assessor, and tax collector 1877–1878.[337]

Mizell, York.
Born 1845, Georgia. Mulatto. Carpenter. Alive in Lake City 1900. Lake City councilman 1878–1879.[338]

Monroe, Claiborne.
Born December 28, 1848, Quincy, Florida. Farmer and blacksmith. AME. Alive in Gadsden County 1900. Florida house of representatives (Gadsden County, 1879, 1883). Legislative biographer J. V. Drake (1883): "Being a slave, [Monroe] was a house servant to his

owner, William Monroe, of [Quincy], until the civil war, when he served as cook for a mess, of which one was his young master, William Monroe, Jr., in the Confederate army; being free after the war, he engaged in farming and working in a blacksmith's shop."[339]

Monroe, George W.
Born December 1841, Florida. Mulatto. Laborer. Died ca. 1910, Jefferson County, Florida. Jefferson County sheriff 1876–1877.[340]

Montgomery, David.
Born 1836, New York. Mulatto. Mason, bricklayer, and plasterer. Died April 23, 1878, Hempstead, Long Island, New York. Madison County sheriff 1868–1873; Madison County tax collector 1868–1869, 1872–1877; Florida senate sergeant at arms 1871; Florida house of representatives (Madison County 1873, 1874, 1875); Madison County commissioner 1873–1874. *Quitman* (Ga.) *Reporter*, June 1876: "David Montgomery, the Radical candidate for Lieutenant Governor of Florida, will probably put on a more dignified air and quit playing base ball. He is quite an expert with the bat and ball, and has been 'pitcher' for the Madison club." *Tallahassee Sentinel*, November 1870: "On Tuesday, the 1st instant, as Mr. D. Montgomery, sheriff of Madison county, was on his way from Madison to his residence, about four miles distant, he was stopped on the road by ten or twelve mounted desperadoes, and escaped being murdered by them in a very miraculous manner."[341]

Month, John J.
Born 1825, South Carolina. Mulatto. Laborer. Duval County tax collector 1871–1873.[342]

Mordecai, Edward.
Born July 4, 1837, Georgia. Mulatto. Drayman and surveyor. Died February 26, 1905, Fernandina, Florida. Fernandina councilman 1873–1874.[343]

Morehead, Zack H.
Born 1843, Florida. Farmer. Alive in Leon County 1885. Leon County justice of the peace 1874; Florida house of representatives (Leon County, 1875).[344]

Morris, George W.
Gadsden County voter registrar 1867–1868.

Morris, Stephen.
Born 1831, Florida. Mulatto. Revenue cutter captain. Fernandina marshal 1886–1887.[345]

Morrison, Peter W.
Born 1836, Georgia. Laborer. Alive in Jacksonville 1880. LaVilla councilman 1870–1872, 1873–1875, 1876–1878.[346]

Moseley, Samuel M.
Born March 1860, Florida. Farm manager. Died 1933, Orange County, Florida. Eatonville mayor 1920–1922.[347]

Mosely, James.
Born 1832, North Carolina. Mulatto. Blacksmith. Died 1886, Madison, Florida. Madison councilman 1878, 1885–1886.[348]

Moss, John.
Born 1844, Virginia or North Carolina. Barber. Alive in Madison County 1906. Quincy councilman 1877?–1878?[349]

Murphy, Watson.
Born 1841, South Carolina. Mulatto. Carpenter. Ocala councilman 1875–1876, 1877–1880, 1883–1885; Ocala marshal 1876–1877.[350]

Murray, Edmund.
Born May 1834, South Carolina. Mulatto. Carpenter. Died ca. 1910, Madison County, Florida. Madison County commissioner 1873–1875.[351]

Newberry, Frederick D.
Hillsborough County voter registrar 1867–1868; Hillsborough County justice of the peace 1868–1869?

Niblack, Archibald.
Born 1817, Georgia. Farmer. Alive in Columbia County 1880. Columbia County commissioner 1868–1870.[352]

Nixon, George.
Born 1821, North Carolina. Mulatto. Farmer. Died September 28, 1875, Gadsden County, Florida. Gadsden County commissioner 1869–1872; Florida house of representatives (Gadsden County, 1875). *Quincy Journal*, October 1875: "George Nixon . . . was one of the best, and most liked both by white and black, of any of the colored men in the county.—Though he was not educated, he had good common sense, and desired to do right. He served as deputy sheriff and county commissioner of this county some years back. Peace to his ashes."[353]

Nixon, Ulysses Grant.
Born November 1867, Florida. Merchant. Alive in Madison County 1920. Died 1929, Madison County, Florida? Madison councilman 1890–1891.[354]

Nottage, Joseph A.
Born February 1879, Florida. Grocer. Died 1925, Putnam County, Florida. Palatka councilman 1917–1920, 1922–1924.[355]

Oates, Joseph E.
Born 1839 or 1840, Sumter County, Georgia. Mulatto. Carpenter and mechanic. Alive in Galveston, Texas, 1871. Delegate, 1868 constitutional convention (Leon and Wakulla Counties). Historian William Watson Davis: "Joe Oates, a mulatto of intelligence, of rascally practice, and of suave tongue."[356]

Osgood, Alfred Brown.
Born July 16, 1843, Madison, Florida. Mulatto. Shoemaker, merchant, AME minister. Died ca. 1911, Madison,

Florida. Florida house of representatives (Madison County, 1868, 1869, 1870, 1871, 1872, 1873, 1874, 1879, 1883, 1885); Madison postmaster 1869–1871, 1891, 1892–1893; Florida senate (Madison County, 1875, 1877). Editor T. Thomas Fortune (1927): "a real gentleman."[357]

Oxendine, Jesse H.
Born 1851, Florida. Farmer. Alive in Jacksonville 1900. Duval County constable 1877–1878.[358]

Page, James.
Born 1808, Richmond, Virginia. Baptist minister. Died March 14, 1883, Tallahassee, Florida. Leon County voter registrar 1867–1868; Leon County commissioner 1868–1870?; Leon County justice of the peace 1872–1877. Tallahassee *Weekly Floridian*, March 1883: "Rev. James Page, the aged and venerable pastor of the colored Missionary Baptist Church, last Friday evening quietly and peacefully passed from the scenes of his earthly labors to that rest prepared for those who doeth the Master's will. For more than a half a century he had been a faithful laborer in the Master's vineyard, was a man who had great influence with his race, which was always exerted for their well being, and was respected alike by white and colored people. . . . The funeral took place from his church on Sunday morning, and his remains were followed to the grave by . . . a large concourse of colored and white citizens, aggregating about three thousand persons."[359]

Papino, John.
Born December 1854, Florida. Mason. Alive in St. Augustine 1914. St. Augustine marshal 1884–1886; St. Augustine councilman 1891–1897, 1899–1901, 1902–1903.[360]

Papy, Alfonso A.
Born January 1852, Florida. Mulatto. Barber. Alive in St. Augustine 1900. St. Augustine tax assessor 1885–1886; St. Augustine tax collector 1888–1889.[361]

Papy, Antonio.
Mulatto. Alive in St. Augustine January 1891. St. Johns County commissioner 1868–1871.[362]

Papy, Domingo M.
Born 1849 or 1850, Florida. Mulatto. Gardener and grocer. Died 1936, St. Augustine, Florida. St. Johns County commissioner 1873–1875; St. Johns County tax assessor 1876–1877; St. Augustine councilman 1877–1878, 1884–1886, 1888–1890; St. Augustine tax assessor 1880–1881.[363]

Papy, Frank A.
Mulatto. Twenty-first USCI. Died before January 1891. St. Augustine tax assessor 1881–1882.[364]

Parker, Julius A.
Physician and druggist. Died Novem-

ber 5, 1898, North Carolina. Gainesville councilman 1886–1888.[365]

Parrish, Charles, Sr.
Born 1816, North Carolina. Jailer. Died November 13, 1894, Jefferson County, Florida. Jefferson County commissioner 1868–1869.[366]

Parrish, Jackson.
Born 1835, South Carolina. Laborer. Died April 24, 1875, Cedar Keys, Florida. Levy County commissioner 1873–1875.[367]

Parsons, George A.
Born 1854, Florida. Mulatto. Merchant. Died 1910, Pensacola, Florida. Pensacola tax assessor 1883–1884.[368]

Patterson, Samuel M.
Born 1863, Georgia. Mulatto. Carpenter. Alive in Green Cove Springs 1920. Green Cove Springs councilman 1887–1891.[369]

Peaden, Robert.
Born March 1844, Florida. Mulatto. Farmer. Alive in Hamilton County 1900. Hamilton County commissioner 1875–1877.[370]

Pearce, Charles H.
Born February 14, 1820, Queen Anne County, Maryland. Mulatto. AME minister. Died ca. October 25, 1887, Jacksonville, Florida. Delegate, 1868 constitutional convention (Leon and Wakulla Counties); Florida senate (Leon County, 1868, 1869, 1870, 1871, 1872, 1873, 1874); Leon County commissioner 1868; Leon County superintendent of schools 1868–1872; Tallahassee councilman 1876; Leon County tax assessor 1876–1877. Charles H. Pearce, April 1868: "I have been since 1849 a minister of the African Methodist Episcopal Church of America; was born and brought up in the State of Maryland, a free man; moved from there in 1852 at the age of 35 to Connecticut; in the year 1855 was appointed by Bishop D. A. Payne, then presiding over the New England Conference, to a missionary field in Canada. . . . In 1865 I was recalled by the same Bishop, the Right Reverend D. A. Payne, and ordered to report to the Baltimore Conference where I received my appointment to Florida. I arrived here on the 22nd of February 1866 and have remained here until now." *New York Daily Tribune*, February 1868: "Rev. C. H. Pearce of Tallahassee, the bishop, or controlling power of the African Methodist Church. He is a remarkable fine-looking, middle-aged, yellow-colored man, a good Christian minister, who would claim respect in any community."[371]

Pembroke, Daniel M.
Born 1827, Virginia. Teacher. Died January 26, 1887, Monticello, Florida. Jefferson County voter registrar 1868; Jefferson County justice of the peace 1868–1869?, 1876–1877; Jefferson County commissioner 1869–1870.[372]

Peterson, James.
Born 1826, South Carolina. Farmer.

Alive in Hamilton County 1885. Hamilton County justice of the peace 1870–1872; Hamilton County commissioner 1872–1875.[373]

Peterson, John H.
AME minister. Leon County justice of the peace 1872.[374]

Petty, David.
Born 1815, Florida. Carpenter. Died August 26, 1889, Duval County, Florida. Jacksonville councilman 1875–1876.[375]

Petty, Samuel.
Born March 15, 1842, Duval County, Florida. Carpenter. Alive in Nassau County 1896. Fernandina councilman 1870–1871, 1875–1879, 1881–1882, 1888–1889; Florida house of representatives (Nassau County, 1873, 1874, 1875); 1885 constitutional convention delegate (Nassau County). *Fernandina Observer*, August 1874: "The work of demolition fell to Hon. Samuel Petty the present representative from this county, and that young man did himself great credit by his plain and his earnest and indignant denial of the charges circulated by [carpetbagger Liberty] Billings. We should judge, leaving out those who were indifferent, that the audience stood four to one for Petty and against Billings."[376]

Pittman, Anderson A.
Born 1813, Georgia. Mulatto. Farmer. Walton County justice of the peace 1875–1879.

Plater, Lewis.
Born 1834, Maryland. Mulatto. Mechanic. Alive in Marion County 1885. Leon County commissioner 1873.[377]

Ponder, March.
Born 1847, Georgia. Carpenter. Died May 3, 1915, Jacksonville, Florida. LaVilla councilman 1874–1875.[378]

Pons, John.
Born August 18, 1837, Florida. Mulatto. Barber. Died December 21, 1912, Pensacola, Florida. Escambia County commissioner 1868–1870; Escambia County tax assessor 1874–1875.[379]

Pons, Salvador T.
Born December 23, 1835, Mexico. Mulatto. Bricklayer. Roman Catholic. Died March 21, 1890, Pensacola, Florida. Florida house of representatives (Escambia County, 1868, 1869, 1870, 1875); Pensacola councilman 1869–1870, 1874; Pensacola mayor 1874; Pensacola clerk 1877–1880, 1882–1884. Former Confederate secretary of the navy Stephen R. Mallory, August 1868: "Pons was the honest, honorable and fit representative of Escambia County." Editor T. Thomas Fortune (1927): "Little Pons of Escambia County was . . . little larger than Tom Thumb."[380]

Poole, Joseph.
Born 1840, North Carolina. Farmer. Alive in Crawfordville, Wakulla County, 1900. Died 1918, Wakulla County?

Wakulla County commissioner 1873–1877.[381]

Pope, Washington.
Born 1826, Florida. Mulatto. Farmer. Alive in Jackson County 1880. Jackson County commissioner 1870–1872; Florida senate (Jackson County, 1873, 1874, 1875).[382]

Porter, Anthony.
Born 1820, Georgia. Mulatto. Laborer. Alive in Apalachicola 1885. Franklin County commissioner 1875–1881?[383]

Porter, William.
Born May 1830, South Carolina. Alive in Ocala 1900. Gainesville councilman 1878–1879.[384]

John A. Potter (Courtesy Florida Archives)

Potter, John A.
Born 1832, South Carolina. Baptist minister. Alive in Jefferson County 1892. Jefferson County treasurer 1874–1876.[385]

Pousser, Richard.
Born 1831, Orangeburg District, South Carolina. Mulatto. Farmer. Jackson County constable 1870.[386]

Price, Andrew.
Born May 1848, Virginia. Farmer. Alive in Miami 1900. Dade County commissioner 1869–1873, 1874–1876.[387]

Proctor, George Willis.
Born August 8, 1848, Tallahassee, Florida. Farmer. Methodist. Alive in Tallahassee 1920. Florida house of representatives (Jefferson County, 1883). Historian Lee Warner (1992): "Although George would serve one term in the Florida house of representatives and run for election to the 1885 constitutional convention from Jefferson County, his course was clear: no town life and political speculation was in his future. He rejected his older brother's, his father's, and his grandfather's professions in favor of husbandry and by 1900 would own 180 acres free and clear from mortgage."[388]

Proctor, John Elias.
Born January 13, 1844, Tallahassee, Florida. Bricklayer and teacher. Methodist, later Episcopal. Died December 15, 1944, Tallahassee, Florida. Florida

house of representatives (Leon County, 1873, 1874, 1875, 1879); Florida senate (Leon County, 1883, 1885). Historian Lee Warner (1992): "John's first job after freedom was in Wakulla County, immediately south of Leon, where he led a crew of men cutting palm trees for shipment to Texas. Soon, however, he appeared as a waiter at the City Hotel. Sometime in the next four years he became a schoolteacher, and he also did farm labor when necessary. . . . Before 1870, John must have made a conscious decision to go into politics. He, unlike his brothers, stayed in or close to Tallahassee and, like his father and grandfather, did not start the land acquisition process that led to agriculture. He had the advantages that came from being George's and Antonio's heir. He was literate, he had been raised partially by upper class whites, he had experience in town life, and he, obviously, felt at home with both races and moved easily between them."[389]

Purcell, Isaac L.
Born 1857, South Carolina. Lawyer. Died July 15, 1930, Jacksonville, Florida. Palatka councilman 1885–1887, 1891–1893. *Florida Bureau of Immigration Monthly Bulletin*, February 1891: "The Gainesville Sentinel, (colored), . . . has the following item from its Tallahassee correspondent: 'Our ambitious young men, and our hopeful old men, were cheered by the appearance of I. L. Purcell, Esq., in the supreme court this week. Palatka is justly proud of this rising young attorney, and the entire state can unite in the boast.' "[390]

Purcell, Joseph W.
Born March 1857, South Carolina. Carpenter. Died 1915, Putnam County, Florida. Palatka clerk 1888–1890.[391]

Quarterman, Dernard E.
Born 1852, Florida. AME minister. Died May 1887, Bel Air, Leon County, Florida. Leon County constable 1873–1874; Florida house of representatives (Leon County, 1877).

Rafe, William.
Born 1826, North Carolina or Virginia. Merchant. Alive in Lake City 1900. Columbia County commissioner 1873–1875.[392]

Ramsey, Andrew.
Born 1830, North Carolina. Mulatto. Teamster. Tallahassee councilman 1874.[393]

Ramsey, Richard.
Born 1808, Georgia. Liveryman. Died September 1877, Pensacola, Florida. Pensacola councilman 1874.[394]

Redding, Benjamin.
Born 1845, Florida. Laborer. Died October 28, 1887, Jacksonville, Florida. LaVilla marshal 1874–1876.[395]

Redmon, C. T.
Born 1849, Georgia. Laborer. Alive in Nassau County 1895. Nassau County commissioner 1874; Florida house of representatives (Nassau County, 1879).[396]

Redmon, Farley W.
Born February 1832, Virginia. Mulatto. Sawmill worker. Died September 15, 1908, Nassau County, Florida. Nassau County voter registrar 1868; Nassau County justice of the peace 1873–1875, 1876–1877.[397]

Redmond, Richard W.
Born 1860, Georgia. Drayman. Died 1928, Clay County, Florida. Green Cove Springs councilman 1890–1892.[398]

Reynolds, Albert S.
Born December 1862, Florida. Mulatto. Laborer and manufacturer. Alive in Fernandina 1920. Fernandina councilman 1892–1896.[399]

Richard, Asa.
Born 1832, Georgia. Laborer. Died 1920, Columbia County, Florida. Lake City councilman 1873–1874.[400]

Richardson, Robert.
Born 1838, South Carolina. Mulatto. Alive in Madison 1885. Madison councilman 1876–1878.[401]

Rivers, George Brash.
Born 1806, Florida or South Carolina. Laborer. Alive in Putnam County 1885. Putnam County voter registrar 1867–1868.[402]

Roberts, Alfred.
Born 1826, Georgia. Farmer. Alive in Sanderson, Baker County, 1910. Baker County commissioner 1870.[403]

Roberts, Benjamin W.
Born July 26, 1852, Monticello, Florida. Graduate, Wilberforce University. AME minister. Died February 1, 1904, Texas. Monroe County commissioner 1875–1876; Key West councilman 1875–1876, 1877–1878. AME minister A. J. Kershaw, April 1880: "Elder B. W. Roberts [is a man] upon whose trumpeting voice thousands have hung with ecstasy until the man was lost sight of in the subject which he was handling with the hands of a

Benjamin W. Roberts (Courtesy Florida Archives)

master." Key West collector of customs F. N. Wicker to the United States secretary of the treasury, March 1879: "I have the honor to submit the nomination of Peter W. Bryant (colored) to be Night Watchman at this port, at a compensation of $730 per annum, vice B. W. Roberts (colored) to be removed. Roberts is a Methodist preacher and devotes so much time to his professional calling as to impair somewhat his efficiency as a Customs officer."[404]

Roberts, James A.
Born February 25, 1845, Key West, Florida. Thirty-fourth USCI (1863–1866). Laborer and cigar maker. Died April 30, 1921, Tampa, Florida. Monroe County constable 1872–1874; Monroe County sheriff 1874–1877; Key West councilman 1875–1876. Jacksonville *Daily Florida Union*, February 1876: "The Key West cornet band, which has been in our city for a week past, and which has rendered excellent music on the Fair Grounds, as well as in the city, was organized at Key West, Fla., on the 22d February, 1872, (Washington's birthday,) under the auspices of Ramon Savelle, Nelson F. English, and James A. Roberts, who are three of its prominent members." Rosalie M. Roberts to United States commissioner of pensions, May 1921: "This will inform you of the Death of my dear Husband James A. Roberts who departed this life Saturday morning April 30, at Tampa Fla. His pension is due to day. I know that I can not receive it, which I am indeed very sorry as I am very much in need of the money to pay his funeral expenses and Doctors bill. Sirs I do hope that you will consider me as early as possible."[405]

Robinson, Bradley.
Born 1847, Alabama. Domestic servant. Leon County constable 1875–1877.[406]

Robinson, George B.
Born 1837, Florida. Mulatto. Farmer. Alive in Jackson County 1885. Jackson County justice of the peace 1872–1875.[407]

Robinson, James K.
Born 1855, Virginia. Died January 23, 1899, Duval County, Florida. Duval County constable 1879–1880.[408]

Robinson, Jesse.
Born 1828, Florida. Mulatto. Died ca. 1880, Jackson County, Florida. Washington County voter registrar 1867–1868; Florida house of representatives (Jackson County, 1868, 1869, 1870, 1873, 1874); Jackson County justice of the peace 1876–1880. Tallahassee *Weekly Floridian*, June 1874: "The man Robinson, at work at the Pensacola navy yard, has returned to his home in Marianna, really through fear from those colored men who wanted the place for one of their friends. It was a clear case of intimidation from pursuing his business."[409]

Robinson, John.
Born 1832, Virginia. Thirty-fourth USCI (1864–1866). Drayman. Died

March 27, 1895, St. Augustine, Florida. St. Johns County voter registrar 1868.[410]

Robinson, Lee N.
Born August 1854, Alabama. Baptist minister. Died 1919, Putnam County, Florida. Palatka councilman 1896–1898, 1909–1917.[411]

Robinson, Louis.
Born 1850, Florida. Laborer. Died January–February 1889, Franklin County, Florida. Apalachicola councilman 1885–1886.[412]

Robinson, Riley Edward.
Born November 4, 1847, Lincoln County, Tennessee. Mulatto. Carpenter and Methodist Episcopal minister. Died February 1921, Fernandina, Florida. Fernandina councilman 1875–1876, 1877–1879, 1883–1890, 1892–1894; Florida house of representatives (Nassau County, 1883, 1885). Legislative biographer J. V. Drake (1883): "[Robinson was] born a slave, he had no advantage of any early education; moved to Alachua County, Florida, in 1858, and remained there until the close of the war; then moved to Duval County, and served five years as an apprentice to the carpenter's trade; moved again to Nassau County in 1870, and served three years as Inspector in the Custom House. . . . After emancipation he received such instruction as he could obtain in a night school and by self-culture."[413]

Robinson, William K.
Born 1846, Florida. Mulatto. Farmer. Alive in Jackson County 1880. Florida house of representatives (Jackson County, 1872).[414]

Rogers, Calvin.
Born ca. 1832, Florida. Farmer. Murdered near Marianna January 26, 1870. Jackson County constable 1869–1870.[415]

Rollins, Charles H.
Born December 2, 1832, Tallahassee, Florida. Mulatto. Carpenter and shoemaker. Baptist. Died August 23, 1919, Tallahassee, Florida. Leon County commissioner 1874–1877; Florida house of representatives (Leon County, 1883).[416]

Ross, Benjamin.
Born 1826, Florida. Farmer and Baptist minister. Alive in Leon County 1910. Died 1919, Leon County, Florida? Leon County commissioner 1872.[417]

Ross, George Eugene.
Born December 1869, Florida. Lawyer and cigar maker. Died January 1966, Jacksonville, Florida. Jacksonville councilman 1901–1907.[418]

Roundtree, Warren.
Born May 1841, South Carolina or North Carolina. Farmer. Alive in Olustee, Baker County, Florida, 1900. Baker County voter registrar 1867–1868.[419]

Rouse, Charles.
Born 1837, North Carolina. Laborer. Died 1891, Escambia County, Florida.

Florida house of representatives (Escambia County, 1874); Escambia County commissioner 1874–1875. Pensacola *Daily News*, November 1906: "Escambia sent for her [house member,] a negro named Charlie Rouse, who lived at Molino, and at that time was getting out hewn timber for Epping, Barrs & Co."[420]

Sammis, Edmund G.
Born 1836, Florida. Mulatto. Farmer. Alive in Duval County 1881. Died November 1892, Duval County, Florida? Duval County justice of the peace 1877–1881?[421]

Sammis, Egbert C.
Born 1848, Florida. Mulatto. Farmer. Alive in Jacksonville 1889. Florida senate (Duval County, 1885).[422]

Sammis, George K.
Duval County voter registrar 1867.

Sampson, Morris M.
Born 1834, North Carolina. Laborer. Died ca. 1886, Madison County, Florida. Lafayette County voter registrar 1867–1868; Madison County justice of the peace 1874–1877.[423]

Sampson, William W.
Born 1821, North Carolina. Mulatto. AME minister. Died September 30, 1888, Jacksonville, Florida. Duval County justice of the peace 1871–1875?; Jacksonville councilman 1872–1873, 1879–1880. Philadelphia *Christian Recorder*, December 1872: "Next in point of influence and intelligence is Rev. Judge W. W. Sampson, justice of the peace and Alderman of the city. Like his biblical namesake, he is powerful; and reflects credit not only upon his race, but on the legal profession. He has been highly commended by the County judge for his discretion and economy in the discharge of his duties."[424]

William W. Sampson (Courtesy Florida Archives)

Sanders, Walter.
Born 1833, Florida. Farmer. Alive in Liberty County 1885. Liberty County commissioner 1876–1877.[425]

Saunders, William U.
Born 1835, Baltimore, Maryland. Mulatto. Seventh USCI (1863–1866). Bar-

ber and lawyer. Died September 1, 1883, Clinton, Kentucky. Delegate, 1868 constitutional convention (Gadsden County). Jacksonville *Florida Union*, November 1867: "The Colonel, to do him credit, is a good looking man, indeed, we have heard him called handsome. He is gentlemanly in his manners, neat in his dress, and with a not too perceptible dash of self conceit in his carriage, makes a very creditable appearance. He is a fluent speaker, strong in oratorical display, but weak in argument; happy in the use of language, but unfortunate in the selection of topics; excellent in appeals to passion or prejudice, but utterly useless in appeals to the understanding." Historian William Watson Davis (1913) of Saunders at the 1868 constitutional convention: "one of the shrewdest and withal most dangerous men there."[426]

Joseph J. Sawyer (Courtesy Florida Archives)

Sawyer, Joseph J.
Born August 1839, North Carolina. Shoemaker and AME minister. Alive in Jacksonville 1907. Palatka clerk and tax assessor 1882–1884.[427]

Scott, Charles M.
Born 1850, Virginia. Farmer. Alive in Marion County 1910. Marion County justice of the peace 1875–1879.[428]

Scott, James A.
LaVilla councilman 1874–1875.

Scott, James E. Gardener.
LaVilla councilman 1878–1879, 1883–1885.[429]

Scott, John Robert, Sr.
Born 1840, Virginia. AME minister. Died March 7, 1879, Jacksonville, Florida. Florida house of representatives (Duval County, 1868, 1869, 1870, 1871, 1872, 1873, 1879); United States collector, port of Jacksonville, 1873–1878; LaVilla councilman 1877–1879. The Reverend J. C. Waters, February 1877: "Hon. John R. Scott, Collector of the Port of Jacksonville, former pastor of the A. M. E. Church in [Jacksonville], is a prominent member of the [Florida AME] conference. Though a little man in statu[r]e, he is evidently a big man in heart and brain. At the last State [Republican] convention, he came within one or two votes for securing the nomi-

nation for Congress. He has done good work for both church and state, since the close of the war, and is a man of acknowledged ability and influence." Philadelphia *Christian Recorder*, December 1872: "Mr. Scott will likely be the next Speaker [of the Florida house of representatives]. He is a good parliamentarian, and gives great promise of becoming a power in the state."[430]

Scott, John Robert, Jr.
Born September 19, 1862, Columbia, South Carolina. Graduate, Wilberforce University. Teacher and AME minister. Died February 18, 1929, Jacksonville, Florida. Florida house of representatives (Duval County, 1889); Jacksonville councilman 1897–1899. AME minister W. P. Ross (1884): "Rev. Scott, the great Hebrew scholar of our Church and one of the strongest young men Wilberforce has ever sent from her walls, is a successful teacher." Jacksonville *Florida Times-Union*, February 1889: "For four years he was principal of the Divinity High School in Jacksonville; he has been prominently known as an advocate of prohibition, and introduced in the Republican Congressional Convention in 1884 a resolution on temperance which served almost to break up the convention."[431]

John Robert Scott, Jr. (In possession of author, from Indianapolis *Freeman*, May 20, 1893)

Sevilly, Samuel.
Born June 1850, Florida. Alive in St. Augustine 1900. St. Johns County justice of the peace 1868–1877?[432]

Shanks, Jasper.
Born 1847, Alabama. Mulatto. Drayman. Died 1892, Escambia County, Florida. Pensacola councilman 1877.[433]

Shavers, Charles A.
Born January 1860, Key West, Florida. Cigar maker. Died August 27, 1915, Key West, Florida. Florida house of representatives (Monroe County, 1887); Key West councilman 1898–1901. White Democrat Peter O. Knight on the 1886 Monroe County legislative election (1943): "The Republicans and Knights of Labor parties nominated Charlie Shaver, a colored man. Being afraid that the colored man might beat me because the Knights of Labor parties and republicans were very strong, I withdrew from the race and asked my friends to support [another white man called] Captain Lilly. At the election Charlie beat Captain Lilly very badly. Captain Lilly

was a proud, dignified gentleman and was humiliated very much by the defeat."[434]

Shepard, Aren T.
Born 1859, North Carolina. Railroad engineer. Alive in Goldsboro 1910. Goldsboro councilman 1891–1892.[435]

Sheppard, John.
Born 1840, Florida. Bricklayer. Alive in Leon County 1910. Tallahassee councilman 1877; Tallahassee tax assessor 1878.[436]

Shines, E. J.
Born 1858, Georgia. Alive in Ormond Beach 1910. Eatonville councilman 1887–1888.[437]

Shivery, Richard E.
Born 1824, South Carolina. Mulatto. Tailor and minister (Baptist and AME). Died February 20, 1892, Gainesville, Florida. Alachua County justice of the peace 1873–1875; Gainesville councilman 1875–1876, 1882–1884.[438]

Shuler, Andrew.
Born 1815, Florida. Farmer. Alive in Suwannee County 1885? Hamilton County voter registrar 1867; 1868 constitutional convention delegate (Hamilton and Suwannee Counties).[439]

Shuler, Israel.
Liberty County voter registrar 1867–1868.

Simmons, Arthur.
Born December 1845, Alabama. Carpenter. Alive in Gainesville 1910. Cedar Keys councilman 1873–1874; Gainesville councilman 1877–1878, 1881–1886.[440]

Simmons, Cataline B.
Born 1806, Beaufort, South Carolina. Baptist minister. Died July 13, 1883, Jacksonville, Florida. Duval County voter registrar 1868; Duval County commissioner 1868–1870, 1872–1874; Jacksonville councilman 1869–1871; Jacksonville tax assessor 1872–1874. *New York Globe*, August 1883: "Rev. C. B. Simmons, who was the oldest divine in this city and State at his death, [passed away] at his residence Friday morning, July [13], at 3 o'clock. He was buried from Bethel Baptist Church, of which he was organizer and for ten years pastor. . . . When young [he was] brought to Florida. He was first taken to Key West as a slave, but being among that heroic few who struggled with the adversities and cruelties of slavery, yet had that craving of spirit, that greatness of soul and nobleness of ambition, by his own exertions freed himself, paying in gold for what the laws of his country should have secured to him. Soon after he moved to Jacksonville, then in its infancy; he purchased a home in the wilderness and with others helped to hew out the metropolis of the State, and of which he lived to be twice alderman, and twice tax assessor, and at his death was one of the wealthiest colored men in the city."[441]

Simpkins, Caleb.
Born July 1833, South Carolina. Carpenter. Alive in Live Oak, Suwannee County, 1900. Suwannee County commissioner 1876–1877.[442]

Simpson, Benjamin.
Born 1820, Florida or Georgia. Farmer. Alive in Lake City 1880. Lake City councilman 1873–1874, 1876–1877, 1878–1879.[443]

Simpson, John.
Born 1837, North Carolina. Mulatto. Gunsmith. Alive in Marion County 1870. Florida house of representatives (Marion County, 1868, 1869, 1870). The Black Historical Organization of Marion County (1977): "He believed that a position did not make him greater than anyone else in the sight of God."[444]

Small, John Wesley.
Goldsboro clerk and tax assessor 1891–1892.

Small, Samuel.
Born 1827, South Carolina. Baptist minister and farmer. Died October 16, 1883, Ocala, Florida. Marion County voter registrar 1867–1868; Marion County commissioner 1868–1872?; Florida house of representatives (Marion County, 1873, 1874, 1875). Ocala *East Florida Banner*, October 1883: "Rev. Samuel Small, pastor of Mt. Moriah Baptist Church, colored, died at his residence in this place on Tuesday night, in his fifty-sixth year. He came from South Carolina when a boy, and became pastor of this church soon after emancipation, which position he held until his death. He was much respected by both white and black."[445]

Smith, Edwin.
Born 1835, Georgia. Alive in Duval County 1880. Madison County justice of the peace 1874.[446]

Smith, Elias Glasco.
Born 1849, South Carolina. Merchant. Died January 22, 1901, Ocala, Florida. Ocala councilman 1875–1880, 1882–1883, 1885–1887, 1888–1890. Ocala *Evening Star*, January 1901: "He was a member of the city council for several terms years ago and has always been a worthy and much respected colored citizen."[447]

Smith, Emanuel.
Born 1833, North Carolina. Government employee. AME. Died September 1886, Apalachicola, Florida. Franklin County voter registrar 1867–1868; Franklin County commissioner 1869–1872; Franklin County justice of the peace 1872–1881?; Apalachicola postmaster 1881–1885.[448]

Smith, George W.
Born 1859, Florida. Blacksmith. Alive in Apalachicola 1888. Apalachicola councilman 1882–1883.[449]

Smith, Henry.
Born 1830, North Carolina. Cook and mason. Alive in Jacksonville 1880. LaVilla councilman 1878–1879.[450]

Smith, Joseph.
Born 1842, Georgia. Policeman. Duval County constable 1873–1875.[451]

Smith, Robert Friday.
Born January 8, 1846, St. Marys, Georgia. USN (1864–1865). Laborer. Methodist. Died May 7, 1913, Fernandina, Florida. Fernandina marshal 1883–1884.[452]

Snead, Clinton.
Born 1855, Florida. Laborer. Alive in Leon County 1910. Died 1914, Seminole County, Florida? Florida house of representatives (Leon County, 1885, 1887).[453]

Snowden, Samuel.
Born 1843, Maryland. Farmer. Leon County justice of the peace 1873–1874.[454]

Spearing, John E.
Born 1855, Florida. Blacksmith. Alive in Jacksonville 1932. LaVilla councilman 1881–1887; Jacksonville councilman 1888–1889.[455]

John E. Spearing (Courtesy Florida Archives)

Spearing, Samuel.
Born 1824, South Carolina. Grocer. Baptist. Alive in Jacksonville 1887. Duval County justice of the peace 1868–1870?; LaVilla tax collector 1871–1872; LaVilla councilman 1873–1875; Florida senate (Duval County, 1874); LaVilla treasurer 1882–1887. Jacksonville *New South*, December 1874: "Mr. Samuel Spearing, better known as 'Uncle Sam,' with two other colored men, purchased the grocery store of Mr. George Fuller, on Bay street. This is the first colored firm which has opened a respectable business of this kind in the city, and the colored people should feel it their duty to encourage this firm by their patronage."[456]

Spencer, Romulus L.
Born 1840, North Carolina. AME minister. Alive in 1898. Died Crescent City before 1900. Columbia County voter registrar 1867–1868; Columbia County justice of the peace 1876; Lake City councilman 1876–1877; Lake City tax assessor 1877–1879.[457]

Squire, November.
Born 1830, South Carolina. Mason

and plasterer. Alive in Jacksonville 1889. LaVilla councilman 1876–1877.[458]

St. Clair, Arthur W.
Born 1837, Alabama. Mulatto. Farmer and Baptist minister. Assassinated June 26, 1877, Hernando County, Florida. Hernando County voter registrar 1867–1868; Hernando County commissioner 1875–1877.[459]

Stays, John H.
Born 1854, Virginia. Mulatto. Railroad employee. Methodist. Died February 19, 1937, Fernandina, Florida. Fernandina tax assessor 1884–1887; Nassau County justice of the peace 1889–1901.[460]

John H. Stays (In possession of the author, courtesy of Willie Mae Ashley, Fernandina)

Sterrett, Norman Bascom.
Born September 28, 1841, Maryland. AME minister. Alive in Charleston, South Carolina, 1919. Duval County justice of the peace 1875–1876.[461]

Stevens, Roman M.
Born February 1838, Florida. Mulatto. Carpenter. Alive in Key West 1900. Key West councilman 1887–1888.[462]

Stewart, Milton.
Born 1846, South Carolina. Farmer and blacksmith. Died 1923, Alachua County, Florida. Gainesville councilman 1877–1878.[463]

Stewart, William G.
Born December 15, 1839, Decatur County, Georgia. AME minister. Died May 13, 1911, Tallahassee, Florida. Gadsden County commissioner 1870–1872; Tallahassee clerk and treasurer 1872; Florida house of representatives (Leon County, 1873); Tallahassee councilman 1873; Tallahassee postmaster 1873–1886. Philadelphia *Christian Recorder*, December 1872: "Hon. John R. Scott and Wm. G. Stewart hold the balance of power in the [Florida] House [of representatives]." Tallahassee *Weekly True Democrat*, June 1911: "[Stewart] began to assist in the organization of the A. M. E. Church in the State in 1865. He served in the government service fourteen years as postmaster at Tallahassee. He was Presiding Elder [in the AME church] twenty-seven years. He was an exceptable and progressive pastor and an able

preacher for fifty years. He was of unusual high moral character. He died at his post of duty."[464]

William G. Stewart (Courtesy Florida Archives)

Stidum, Edward B.
Born 1845, Pennsylvania. AME minister and teacher. Levy County commissioner 1870–1872; Levy County justice of the peace 1871–1872; Marion County justice of the peace 1872–1876.[465]

Stockton, Frank.
Born 1831, Florida. Farmer. Alive in Suwannee County 1885. Suwannee County commissioner 1870–1873.[466]

Stokes, John N.
Born August 1838, Virginia. Blacksmith and Baptist minister. Died ca. December 1905, Live Oak, Florida. Florida house of representatives (Leon County, 1874); Tallahassee councilman 1878, 1881–1882. Tallahassee *Weekly Floridian*, February 1880: "That gang of 'processionists,' Wednesday night, after washing down the 'eloquence' of their 'orators' with mean whiskey, proceeded to the house of John N. Stokes, a worthy colored man and the most level-headed among them, and began brickbatting it. Boldly facing them and demanding desistence, they were induced to cease their lawless demonstrations. Their animus toward him grew out of his support for the [conservative] Citizens' ticket [in the recent Tallahassee election], on which he ran as candidate for marshal."[467]

John N. Stokes (Courtesy Florida Archives)

Summers, Ephraim.
Born 1824, South Carolina. Farmer.

Alive in Liberty County 1880. Liberty County commissioner 1871–1876; Liberty County justice of the peace 1876–1877.[468]

Sunday, John, Jr.

Born March 20, 1838, Escambia County, Florida. Seventy-eighth USCI (1863–1865). Merchant and carpenter. Roman Catholic. Died January 7, 1925, Pensacola, Florida. Florida house of representatives (Escambia County, 1874); Pensacola councilman 1878?–1885. *Bliss' Quarterly*, January 1897: "The name of John Sunday is familiar to Pensacola people. . . . He entered the army in 1863, was a courageous soldier and was promoted to the position of first sergeant soon afterward, in which position he had the entire respect of his company and the trust and confidence of his superior officers. After the war he worked as a mechanic in the Pensacola navy yard, receiving full mechanic's pay. Later he was a custom inspector for the port of Pensacola. . . . His business career has been a most successful one and he enjoyed a well established credit. In 1892 he, with other war comrades, organized the B. F. Stephenson post of the department of Florida [Grand Army of the Republic], of which he has served as commander for several years. He has several children, three of whom are being educated in Nashville, Tenn., two are attending the Fisk University and another is a student of medicine in the Meharry medical college. He is one of the wealthiest men in the state and is beloved of his people."[469]

John Sunday, Jr. (Courtesy University of South Florida Special Collections)

Sutton, Henry.

Tallahassee marshal 1872–1875; Tallahassee marshal and tax collector 1877.

Taylor, Howard.

Born 1840, Florida. Hotel servant. Alive in Green Cove Springs 1880. Green Cove Springs councilman 1875–1876.[470]

Taylor, Joseph.

Born 1842, Florida. Farmer. Alive in Jefferson County 1885. Jefferson County commissioner 1876–1877.[471]

Taylor, Robert.

Manatee County voter registrar 1867.

Taylor, Tony.
Born 1852, Florida. Laborer. AME. Alive in Eatonville 1887. Maitland councilman 1885–1886.[472]

Thomas, James Benjamin.
Born 1852, Florida. Mulatto. Waiter and merchant. Died 1922, St. Johns County, Florida. St. Augustine councilman 1882–1884.[473]

Thomas, John.
Born 1839, South Carolina. AME minister. Died June 20, 1892, Enterprise, Florida. Hillsborough County commissioner 1871–1873.[474]

Thomas, Walter T.
Born 1862, Florida. Laborer. Died 1923, Orange County, Florida. Eatonville marshal 1887–1888.[475]

Thompson, Benjamin W.
Born 1823, Virginia. Mulatto. Lawyer and farmer. Alive in Jefferson County 1879. Florida house of representatives (Jefferson County, 1868, 1869, 1870). Monticello *Advertiser*, June 1872: "About the middle of last week, a party of disguised men attacked Hon. B. W. Thompson, . . . on the railroad between his house and the Junction, Station 3, and severely beat him with clubs, ducked him in the water, and threw him under the trestle, leaving him in such a disabled condition that he was unable to go home, and attracted by his cries for help a few hours afterwards he was taken home by some good Samaritans. We do not think that politics was at the bottom of this dastardly and brutal affair, but it is a verita-Ku Klux attack nevertheless."[476]

Thompson, Charles H.
Born 1843, South Carolina. Baptist minister. Alive in Lake City 1900. Florida house of representatives (Columbia County, 1873, 1874, 1875); Columbia County tax assessor 1874–1875; Columbia County commissioner 1875–1877.[477]

Thompson, J. G.
Minister. Jacksonville councilman 1871–1872.[478]

Thompson, James D.
Born August 1842, Florida. Mulatto. Teacher and lawyer. AME. Alive in Tallahassee 1900. Leon County justice of the peace 1872–1874; Florida house of representatives sergeant at arms 1875.[479]

Thompson, Lemuel W.
Born June 18, 1850, North Alabama. Farmer and Baptist minister. Florida house of representatives (Duval County, 1883). Legislative biographer J. V. Drake (1883): "Lemuel W. Thompson . . . was brought to Ocala, Florida, in 1852, by his owner, Stephen Bryant, where he lived for nine years; successively moved to Orange Park, Newnansville, then back to Orange Park, where he was taught the rudiments of an education by D. W.

Gibson; went next to Jacksonville, for three years; then was employed as Orderly, by Quartermaster Johnson, for three years; then was employed by Moody & Brother, saw mill men, to mark lumber, for six years; in 1871, was married to Miss Effina Kingsley, and soon after settled at Mandarin, where he now resides, engaged in orange culture and vegetable growing."[480]

Thompson, Thomas T.
Born 1841, Centreville, Maryland. AME minister. Died June 15, 1896, St. Augustine, Florida. Live Oak councilman 1878–1879.[481]

Thompson, Washington.
Born 1830, Florida. Farmer. Florida house of representatives (Jefferson County, 1871, 1872, 1873, 1874).[482]

Thompson, William F.
Born October 15, 1852, Thomas County, Georgia. Teacher and lawyer. AME. Alive in Tallahassee 1891. Leon County justice of the peace 1872–1873, 1874; Florida house of representatives (Leon County, 1877); Tallahassee tax assessor 1884, 1887; 1885 constitutional convention delegate (Leon County). Future Florida supreme court justice James B. Whitfield (1885): "Hon. William F. Thompson . . . is a self-made man, having attended only the common schools. By perseverance and application he has won distinction among his race."[483]

Tilghman [Tillman], Augustus.
Born November 1850, Florida. Minister. Alive in Jefferson County 1900. Florida house of representatives (Jefferson County, 1875).[484]

Tillman, Green B.
Born July 1848, South Carolina. Minister. Alive in Jefferson County 1910. Florida house of representatives (Jefferson County, 1877).[485]

Tillman, Henry [Harry].
Born 1841, Fernandina, Florida. Thirty-third USCI (1863–1866). Businessman. Died 1903, Jacksonville, Florida. Clay County voter registrar 1867–1868.[486]

Tillman, Samuel E.
Born 1843, South Carolina. Farmer and minister. Alive in Madison County 1885. Died 1917, Gadsden County, Florida? Madison County justice of the peace 1874–1877.[487]

Tillman, Smart.
Born 1833, Fernandina, Florida. Thirty-third USCI (1863–1866). Foreman. Died January 2, 1889, Duval County, Florida. LaVilla marshal 1873–1874; LaVilla councilman 1878–1879, 1881–1884.[488]

Tison, Henry C.
Born July 17, 1823, Georgia. Mulatto. Farmer. Died April 23, 1892, Duval County, Florida. Duval County justice of the peace 1869–1871, 1873–1877.[489]

Toer, Jonas W.
Born 1812, Augusta, Georgia. Baptist

minister. Died May 21, 1872, Tallahassee, Florida. Leon County justice of the peace 1868–1870; Leon County commissioner 1870–1872; Tallahassee councilman 1872. *Tallahassee Sentinel*, May 1872: "Judge Toer was one of Nature's noblemen. He was the very pink of propriety in his manner and personal appearance, and was a good type of the old school Southern gentleman carved in ebony."[490]

Tooley, Alfred.
Born May 1836, North Carolina. Farmer. Alive in Marion County 1900. Marion County commissioner 1872–1875.[491]

Trapp, Littleton Louis.
Born June 1866, South Carolina. Mulatto. Farmer. Died 1932, Putnam County, Florida. Palatka councilman 1916–1920.[492]

Trapp, Milton A.
Born 1842, Georgia. AME minister. Died September 21, 1907, Jackson County, Florida. Leon County justice of the peace 1876.[493]

Trapp, William.
Born October 24, 1841, Camden, South Carolina. Mulatto. Farmer. AME. Died April 2, 1903, Alachua County, Florida. Alachua County commissioner 1873–1874; Florida house of representatives (Alachua County, 1879, 1883).[494]

Triay [Traeye], Julius.
Born 1845, Fernandina, Florida. Mulatto. Carpenter. Alive in Fernandina 1875. Fernandina councilman 1872–1874.[495]

Tucker, John.
Butcher. Alive in Jacksonville 1892. LaVilla councilman 1885–1887.[496]

Turner, George.
Born 1831, Georgia. Sawmill worker and blacksmith. Alive in Jacksonville 1907. LaVilla councilman 1877–1878.[497]

Turner, W. H.
Escambia County justice of the peace 1874–1875.

Valentine, Joseph.
Born 1845, Florida. Farmer. Alive in Alachua County 1876. Alachua County commissioner 1870–1871; Alachua County justice of the peace 1874–1875.[498]

Valentine, Tillman.
Born 1836, Philadelphia, Pennsylvania. Mulatto. Third USCI (1863–1865). Carpenter. Methodist Episcopal. Died March 12, 1895, Jacksonville, Florida. Levy County voter registrar 1867–1868. Jacksonville *Florida Times-Union*, January 1884: "The Grand Lodge of colored Masons, which has been in session in this city during the week, has adjourned, after a very harmonious and pleasant session. The officers elected and installed for the ensuing

year are: M[ost] W[orshipful] G[rand] M[aster]—T. Valentine."[499]

Vandyke, William.
Born March 1846, Florida. Mulatto. Butcher and carpenter. Roman Catholic. Alive in St. Johns County 1910. St. Johns County commissioner 1872–1874; St. Augustine marshal and tax collector 1873–1874; St. Augustine marshal 1877–1878.[500]

Vaughn, Daniel.
Born 1830, Virginia. Mulatto. Ice cream maker. Died July 29, 1889, Tallahassee, Florida. Tallahassee councilman 1875.[501]

Vaught, Capers Michael, Sr.

Capers Michael Vaught, Sr. (Courtesy Florida Archives)

Born August 1857, South Carolina. Grocer and Baptist minister. Died November 22, 1928, Jacksonville, Florida. Jacksonville councilman 1888–1889.[502]

Vester [Vesta], Warren Calway.
Born October 1839, Georgia or Alabama. AME Zion minister. Died 1923, Tampa, Florida. Pensacola tax assessor 1885.[503]

Walker, Joseph A.
Born May 18, 1853, Mississippi. Carpenter and merchant. Died January 7, 1918, Tampa, Florida. Tampa councilman 1887–1888.[504]

Walker, Reuben.
Born 1857, Florida or Georgia. Laborer. Alive in Fernandina 1910. Fernandina councilman 1885–1887.[505]

Wallace, John.
Born 1842, Gates County, North Carolina. Second USCI (1863–1866). Teacher and lawyer. Author, *Carpetbag Rule in Florida: The Inside Workings of the Reconstruction of Civil Government in Florida After the Close of the Civil War* (1888). Died November 25, 1908, Jacksonville, Florida. Florida house of representatives (Leon County, 1871, 1872, 1873, 1874); Florida senate (Leon County, 1875, 1877, 1879, 1881); Leon County justice of the peace 1877. Carpetbagger Hamilton Jay in the Philadelphia *Times*, December 1883: "Wallace was tall, straight as an arrow and as

John Wallace (Courtesy Florida Archives)

plucky a negro as I ever saw. When he left the army he could neither read nor write, but he had plenty of brains, went manfully to work, educated himself and became the most prominent and powerful colored man in the district. He was a fine speaker, clear and argumentative, adroit in his measures, perfectly self-possessed and ready in repartee and his people at first were very proud of him." Fernandina *Florida Mirror*, December 1879: "John N. Stokes and J. Wallace, colored politicians of Leon county, have issued an address 'to the people of the U. S. of America' setting forth their grievances of low wages and short rations, and announce their intentions to emigrate to the Western States. This announcement will start a cold sweat on the people of the whole State."[506]

Waller, Jesse.
Died February 8, 1894, Jackson County, Florida. Jackson County commissioner 1871–1872, 1873–1875; Marianna councilman 1876–1877.[507]

Walls, Josiah Thomas.
Born December 30, 1842, near Winchester, Frederick County, Virginia. Third USCI (1863–1864); Thirty-fifth USCI (1864–1865). Teacher, planter, lawyer, and editor. Died May 15, 1905, Tallahassee, Florida. Delegate, 1868 constitutional convention (Alachua County); Florida house of representatives (Alachua County, 1868); Florida senate (Alachua County, 1869, 1870, 1877, 1879); United States House of Representatives 1871–1873, 1873–1876; Gainesville mayor 1873; Alachua County commissioner 1876–1877. Philadelphia *Christian Recorder*, May 1872: "He is slight in stature, of rather light complexion, close curly hair, dresses well, and wears gay neckties. He has rather the airs and manners of a legislator." Josiah T. Walls, January 1884: "I do not believe that it is to the best interest of the colored voters of the South, from past experience, to even dream of holding the Republican organization intact, and to urge it upon them as a duty, would be a crime against their manhood. I say this because I see them deprived of their natural liberties by the effects of all ill-timed decision of a Republican Supreme Court; because I see them shamefully ignored by the leaders of the Republican organization; because I believe it is to the best interest of the laboring classes generally to free themselves from either of the old par-

ties in the State; and because I believe to hold the Republican organization intact in Florida is to elect a Democratic Governor, and to keep in the most important Federal offices, unprincipled men. Can you, being guided by the light of the past, discourage them, while seeking better friends and more manly positions." Biographer Peter D. Klingman (1976): "During the last twenty years of his life, Walls encountered personal tragedy, financial misfortune, and the afflictions of old age. No doubt the impact of the first two hastened the coming of the latter."[508]

Ward, Frank.
Born 1807, North Carolina. Minister. Alive in Marion County 1885. Marion County justice of the peace 1871–1875?[509]

Warren, William.
Born 1838, Florida. Mulatto. Boatman. Died August 18, 1916, Pensacola, Florida. Pensacola marshal 1874.[510]

Washington, George.
Alachua County commissioner 1868–1871, 1872; Florida house of representatives (Alachua County, 1873, 1874, 1875). Tallahassee *Weekly Floridian*, May 1880, on the Republican state convention of 1880: "Mr. Washington roared like a crocodile in spring, though no one ever found out the point he was continually going to make. The house also roared responsive from the time he got up until he was seated, perhaps an hour and a half. The frequently repeated calls to a 'p'int of order' only served to lend fuel to the flames—volume to his voice. There *might* be some there who considered themselves better informed than he—he wasn't certain about that, but he intended to given them his views whether they wanted to hear him or not. Another gentleman would request him to yield the floor for a moment. With a withering glance he would wave a dirty handkerchief and thunder 'No! no!! no!!!'—didn't propose to yield to any man in the house! . . . Mr. [Sherman] Conant kept insisting that 'Mr. Washington speak louder—louder Mr. Washington.' But there was little necessity for it, for Mr. Washington got louder every minute. When called to order by the chair he said of course he would submit to the ruling of the chair *provided* the chair ruled right!—Roars of laughter followed. . . . The whole house was in an uproar and confusion, the band, occupying a portion of the grand stand . . . struck up a lively air, splinters flew from the gavel in the desperate efforts made by the chairman to restore order, and he, infuriated, turning to the band yelled, 'stop!—STOP!!—G——d d——m that band!—STOP! every d——m one of you!' "[511]

Washington, George.
Fernandina clerk and treasurer 1874–1875; Nassau County commissioner 1874–1875.

Washington, George.
Brick molder. LaVilla councilman 1877–1878.[512]

Washington, George.
Born 1836, Georgia. AME minister. Alive in Jefferson County 1890. Bronson councilman 1885–1886.[513]

Washington, Jerry.
Born 1822, Virginia. Laborer. Died 1895, Escambia County, Florida. Pensacola councilman 1874.[514]

Washington, Randolph W.
Born 1852, Florida. Mulatto. Teacher. Alive in Jefferson County 1886. Florida house of representatives (Jefferson County, 1885).[515]

Watkins, Samuel Crawford.
Born 1842, Virginia. Mulatto. Carpenter. Leon County commissioner 1873–1874; Tallahassee councilman 1876, 1880.[516]

Watson, Hugh.
Born 1840, South Carolina. Laborer. Lake City councilman 1876–1877.[517]

Watson, John N.
Born October 1854, Georgia. Laborer. Alive in Orange County 1910. Eatonville tax collector 1887–1888.[518]

Watts, William A.
Born September 1859, South Carolina. Laborer. Died 1920, Jacksonville, Florida. St. Augustine councilman 1888–1889.[519]

Wells, Richard H.
Born 1831, Smithfield, Virginia. Teacher. Died March 12, 1896, Leon County, Florida. Delegate, 1868 constitutional convention (Leon and Wakulla Counties); Florida house of representatives (Leon County, 1868, 1869, 1870, 1871, 1872).[520]

Wetmore, George Walter.
Born December 10, 1848, Tallahassee, Florida. Mulatto. Clerk, policeman, and postal carrier. Episcopal. Died January 5, 1920, Jacksonville, Florida. Florida house of representatives (Duval County, 1883, 1885). Thomas V. Gibbs, April 1883, in the *New York Globe:* "Out of the house of Rev. W. W. Sampson, father of one of your publishers, have gone within one year, four brides to lighten the way and brighten the course of as many young aspirants for fortune and fame. First, went Miss Bessie P. Alston, formerly of Cleveland, Ohio, and niece of the Reverend gentleman, to the heart, and home of Hon. Geo. W. Wetmore, member of the Legislature from this city. Then Miss Alice J. Menard, daughter of Hon. J. Willis Menard, Ex-Member of Congress, married T. V. Gibbs, son of the late Jonathan C. Gibbs, Secretary of State. Next, Miss Annie C. Alston, sister of the first mentioned lady, carried captive our gallant young steamboat captain, J. W. Floyd; and now it is my pleasant duty to record the marriage of Miss Carrie B. Garvin, daughter of Mr. Sampson, to John H. Ballou, Esq., a prominent lawyer, of Providence, R.I."[521]

Wheaton, Hilliard.
Born 1855, South Carolina. Drayman. LaVilla councilman 1886–1887.[522]

White, Fuller M.
Born 1823, Florida. Mulatto. AME minister. Alive in Marianna 1885. Dead by 1890. Jackson County commissioner 1872, 1873–1875; Marianna councilman 1877–1878. Tallahassee *Weekly Floridian*, August 1876: "Rev. Fuller White advises the negroes of Jackson county to throw off the white carpetbaggers and organize a colored man's party."[523]

White, Isham, Sr.
Born 1839, Florida. Mulatto. Farmer. Died April 20, 1918, Marianna, Florida. Jackson County commissioner 1875–1877.[524]

White, Joseph.
Goldsboro treasurer 1891–1892.

White, Mark S.
Born December 12, 1851, Montgomery, Alabama. Mulatto. Teacher. Baptist. Alive in Pensacola 1912. Florida house of representatives (Escambia County, 1883). Jacksonville *Florida Times-Union*, September 1891: "There was no meeting of the delegates of the Knights of Labor to-day. No national delegates have been elected. The convention has adjourned. M. S. White of Pensacola, and A. C. Lightbourne of Jacksonville, were made a committee to appoint a commission to meet with them at Toledo, O., to examine and report on condition of affairs in Florida to the national convention."[525]

Wiles, Andrew.
Born June 1852, Florida. Gardener and minister. Alive in Green Cove Springs 1900. Green Cove Springs tax assessor 1886–1887; Green Cove Springs councilman 1891–1893.[526]

Wiley, Bulley William.
Born 1855, Georgia. AME minister. Died January 7, 1909, Plant City, Florida. Cedar Key councilman 1878–1879.[527]

Bulley William Wiley (Courtesy Florida Archives)

Wilkerson, Wesley Asbury.
Born February 13, 1844, Anderson District, South Carolina. Teacher and Baptist minister. Died August 8, 1915, Marion County, Florida. Marion County justice of the peace 1873–1877; Florida house of representatives (Marion County, 1881, 1883, 1885). Jacksonville *Florida Times-Union*, May 1890: "W. A. Wilkerson, who had long served his party as a zealous republican, when nominated on [the Marion County Republican] ticket,

refused to serve, declaring the ticket, in a speech in the convention, to be a disgrace to any party. 'I refused to allow my name to go on the ticket as a candidate for judge of probate, because, as I told the convention, the ticket was reeking with fraud and bribery. Such a ticket could not have been elected under the most favorable auspices, but when it is considered that the majority of the persons nominated on this ticket had never cast a vote in the state of Florida, were totally ignorant of the state election laws, and never discovered until two days before the election that a change of residence disqualified a voter unless the registration officer were notified of such change, you can easily perceive what beat the ticket.' "[528]

Wilkinson, John.
Born September 2, 1848, Savannah, Georgia. Policeman and coachman. Baptist. Died July 6, 1891, Fernandina, Florida. Fernandina councilman 1871–1872; Nassau County constable 1874; Florida house of representatives (Nassau County, 1883, 1885). Legislative biographer J. V. Drake (1883): "John Wilkinson . . . came to Florida with his owner, Mrs. Henrietta Harris, afterward the wife of Governor [James C.] Broome, in 1853; was house-servant and carriage driver up to his seventeenth year, when he labored on the farm; in 1865–6 was employed at Fort Clinch, near Fernandina, in the Government Concrete Works; was in the employment of Judge J. C. McGee, of Fernandina, until 1868; then was employed in the freight depot for two years."[529]

Wilkinson, Richard.
Born 1845, Georgia. Teamster. Alive in Nassau County 1895. Fernandina councilman 1872–1873, 1874–1875, 1885–1887.[530]

Williams, A. J.
Palatka councilman 1883.

Williams, Benjamin.
Born 1850, Florida. Laborer. Alive in Jackson County 1885. Jackson County justice of the peace 1868–1873?[531]

Williams, Daniel.
Palatka councilman 1883–1885.

Williams, Edward.
Born 1843, South Carolina. Shoemaker. Columbia County commissioner 1870.[532]

Williams, Elijah L.
Born 1820, North Carolina. Mulatto. Carpenter and inventor. Alive in Jackson County 1880. Jackson County justice of the peace 1868–1870?; Jackson County commissioner 1868–1872. Historian Jerrell H. Shofner (1985): "Elijah Williams was then [1865] working on an application for patent for his invention of a propeller for boats used in shallow water such as that of the Apalachicola River upon which he had worked for years as a slave. Not only was Williams intelligent enough to see advantages of his invention, but he was astute enough

to keep quiet about it until after he was made free. The patent was issued in April, 1867."[533]

Williams, Hampton [Hamilton].
Born 1837, Florida. Carpenter. Died 1918, Jefferson County, Florida. Jefferson County commissioner 1872–1873?[534]

Williams, Henry.
Born 1843, Virginia. Printer. Tallahassee councilman 1876.[535]

Williams, John.
Marion County commissioner 1873.

Williams, John G.
Born 1844, Georgia. Mulatto. Clerk and minister. Alive in Savannah, Georgia, 1880. Levy County justice of the peace 1871–1874, 1876–1877; Cedar Keys councilman 1873–1874, 1876–1877; Cedar Keys mayor 1874.[536]

Williams, Joseph A.
Goldsboro councilman 1891–1892.

Williams, Noah.
Born 1833, Georgia. Farmer. Leon County justice of the peace 1873–1876.[537]

Williams, Peter.
Born 1835, Alabama. Mulatto. Carpenter. Died April 1902, Fernandina, Florida. Fernandina councilman 1875–1876, 1881–1884.[538]

Williams, Robert.
Died July–August 1873, Leon County, Florida. Leon County commissioner 1868–1871.[539]

Williams, Samuel B.
Bradford County justice of the peace 1874–1878.

Williams, Walter.
Died 1918, Orange County, Florida. Goldsboro mayor 1891–1892.[540]

Williamson, James C.
Born 1826, Charleston, South Carolina. Mulatto. Carpenter. Died August 20, 1888, Jacksonville, Florida. LaVilla councilman 1879–1880, 1882–1884.[541]

Wilson, David.
Born 1855, Florida. Laborer. Goldsboro councilman 1891–1892.[542]

Wilson, Samuel.
Born 1858, Florida. Mulatto. Laborer. Alive in Palatka 1885. Palatka councilman 1882–1883.[543]

Wilson, Sanders.
Born September 1846, North Carolina. AME minister. Alive in Jacksonville 1910. Duval County constable 1873–1874.[544]

Wilson, Thomas N.
Born September 1854, Georgia. Carpenter. Died July 28, 1930, Palatka, Florida. Palatka councilman 1887–1889.[545]

Wise, Edward.
Born 1812, South Carolina. Barber. Wakulla County commissioner 1868–1872.[546]

Witherspoon, George Washington.
Born December 15, 1845, Sumter District, South Carolina. Shoemaker and AME minister. Died January 2, 1892, Key West, Florida. Florida house of representatives (Jefferson County, 1875, 1877, 1879, 1883); Pensacola councilman 1885–1889. Historian William Watson Davis (1913): "Deep-chested, jet-black, full-throated, and darkly imposing in manner—[Witherspoon] claimed to be the 'silver-tongued orator of the South' and really did partly make up in a certain eloquent and sonorous cadence of sound what he lacked in knowledge." AME minister Benjamin W. Roberts, May 1885: "The Supreme Court has decided that the legislature had a right to take the [Pensacola] city charter. Being democrats, this is natural. Some of the people looked as though they would go crazy; they came to me, some crying and some cursing their pastor [Witherspoon], charging him with being largely to blame, owing to his course in politics. The Apostle Paul said, 'If eating meat will offend my brother, I will eat no more meat.' I think our preachers had better adhere in this doctrine strictly." Jacksonville *Evening Telegram*, January 1892: "Mr. Witherspoon was the most popular colored man in the country districts in the state, and whenever it was announced that Witherspoon would preach anywhere in the state, the roads would be full of women, children, horses and wagons."[547]

Witsell, Francis E.
Born 1844, South Carolina. Mulatto. Carpenter. Roman Catholic. St. Augustine councilman 1873–1874, 1877–1878, 1880–1881, 1889–1891; St. Johns County justice of the peace 1875–1877?; St. Augustine tax collector 1881–1882.[548]

Wood, Dennis.
Born 1830, North Carolina. AME minister. Died April 18, 1893, Palatka, Florida. Putnam County justice of the peace 1868–1873?; Palatka councilman 1870–1871, 1873–1874, 1877–1878.[549]

Woodward [Woodard], Charles.
Born 1818, Georgia. Mulatto. Farmer. Alive in Madison County 1880. Madison County justice of the peace 1872–1873.[550]

Woodward, Charles M.
Born 1825, South Carolina. Mulatto. Farmer. Alive in Marion County 1880. Marion County commissioner 1869–1873?[551]

Wright, Benjamin.
Bricklayer and Baptist minister. Alive in Jacksonville 1904. Jacksonville councilman 1888–1889.[552]

Wright, Floyd.
Born 1855, Georgia. Mulatto. Alive in Fernandina 1880. Died 1915, Nassau County, Florida? Fernandina tax assessor 1879–1880.[553]

Wright, Peter.
Born 1812, South Carolina. Farmer. Alive in Madison County 1870. Madison County voter registrar 1867–1868.[554]

Wyatt, John W.
Born 1832, Georgetown, South Carolina. USCI. AME minister. Died April 16, 1878, Pensacola, Florida. Delegate, 1868 constitutional convention (Leon and Wakulla Counties); Florida house of representatives (Leon County, 1871, 1872); Leon County commissioner 1872; Leon County justice of the peace 1872–1874. Carpetbagger Hamilton Jay, November 1883: "John Wallace and John Wyatt . . . were coal black, both from the North and both ex-Union soldiers. . . . Wyatt was very illiterate, but the most magnetic speaker of all the negroes. He could mold the country negroes just as he saw fit by his wild and empassioned eloquence."[555]

Wyer, Joseph.
Born 1821, Florida. Mulatto. Baker. Died September–December 1884, Pensacola, Florida. Pensacola tax collector 1869; Escambia County commissioner 1869–1871.[556]

Wynans, Anderson [Anson Wynns].
Born 1846, Florida. Mulatto. Farmer. Alive in Jefferson County 1885. Jackson County commissioner 1870–1871.[557]

Yelder, David.
Born 1848, Alabama. Laborer. AME. Eatonville councilman 1887–1888.[558]

Yellowhair, Edward W.
Born March 1852, Florida. Printer. AME. Died 1926, Leon County, Florida. Tallahassee councilman 1883–1884; Tallahassee tax assessor 1885.[559]

Young, William.
Born 1840, Virginia. Mulatto. Fisherman. Cedar Key councilman 1889–1891.[560]

Appendix

Officials by Political Subdivision

During the post–Civil War era, the realities of Florida politics denied African Americans all but a few of the state's highest offices. Josiah T. Walls sat in the United States House of Representatives for all or part of three terms, while Jonathan C. Gibbs acted as the state's only black cabinet officer. Below that level, however, blacks occupied, at one time or another during the period beginning in 1867 and ending in 1924, almost every non-judicial public office of significance in state and local government.

The following list of officeholders reflects only a portion of the individuals who served in Florida. As explained in the introduction, this survey encompassed only the most significant elective and appointive offices for which appropriate records are available. Constables, while elected officers, generally are omitted, for example, due to lack of election returns, although individual constables are included when their service came to light during research for this book. Port wardens, health board members, school board members, and similar officers are not listed due to a comparable lack of records. In the case of county-level officials, comprehensive review of all available appointment and commissioning records extended only to appointments made from 1868 to 1876, the Reconstruction era. African Americans who received appointment thereafter are included only when their appointment otherwise came to light.

As to municipal officials, reference also should be made to the introduction. Readers should note, though, that in most cases all or portions of the lists of officers for some years are missing. In such cases, after the name of the municipality appear in brackets the words *missing* or *partially missing* followed by notation of the appropriate electoral cycles in years. If the calendar year served as the electoral cycle, only that year will appear. Most often calendar years overlapped, resulting in multiyear references.

Municipalities may be found under the listing for the county in which they lay during the Reconstruction period.

Unless otherwise specified in the endnotes, sources for state and county office appointments, elections, removals, and resignations may be found in Records of the Department of State, record group 156, Florida State Archives, as follows: Election Returns, 1824–1970, series 21 and 1258; Commissions, 1827–1978, series 259; Appointments, series 1284; Oaths and Bonds, series 622; Removals from Office, 1869–1885, series 261; Resignations from Office, 1868–1975, series 260. Also see Gubernatorial Appointment Nominations for County Offices, 1824–1873, series 74, record group 914, Florida State Archives; Florida *House Journals*, 1868–1889; Florida *Senate Journals*, 1868–1887; *Journal of the Proceedings of the Constitutional Convention of the State of Florida, Begun and Held at the Capitol, at Tallahassee, on Monday, January 20th, 1868;* and *Journal of the Proceedings of the Constitutional Convention of the State of Florida which convened at the Capitol, at Tallahassee, Tuesday, June 9, 1885*. For 1867–1868 voter registrars, see Correspondence of Ossian Bingley Hart, Superintendent of Registration, 1867, series 626, record group 156, Florida State Archives, and U.S. Department of War, Incoming Correspondence, Third Military District, 1867–68, Bureau of Civil Affairs, record group 393, National Archives. Sources for municipal officeholders are contained in the endnotes.

UNITED STATES HOUSE OF REPRESENTATIVES

Josiah Thomas Walls (1871–1873, 1873–1876)[1]

FLORIDA SECRETARY OF STATE

Jonathan C. Gibbs (1868–1873)[2]

FLORIDA SUPERINTENDENT OF PUBLIC INSTRUCTION

Jonathan C. Gibbs (1873–1874)[3]

CONSTITUTIONAL CONVENTION OF 1868

Owen B. Armstrong (Leon and Wakulla Counties)

William Bradwell (Duval, Nassau, and St. Johns Counties)

Homer Bryan (Washington, Calhoun, and Jackson Counties)
Alexander [Alonzo] Chandler (Putnam, Marion, and Levy Counties)
Green Davidson (Leon and Wakulla Counties)
Auburn H. Erwin (Columbia and Baker Counties)
Emanuel Fortune (Washington, Calhoun, and Jackson Counties)
Jonathan C. Gibbs (Duval, Nassau, and St. Johns Counties)
Frederick Hill (Gadsden County)
Major Johnson (Madison County)
Robert Meacham (Jefferson County)
Anthony Mills (Jefferson County)
Joseph E. Oates (Leon and Wakulla Counties)
Charles H. Pearce (Leon and Wakulla Counties)
William U. Saunders (Gadsden County)
Andrew Shuler (Hamilton and Suwannee Counties)
Josiah Thomas Walls (Alachua County)
Richard H. Wells (Leon and Wakulla Counties)
John W. Wyatt (Leon and Wakulla Counties)

CONSTITUTIONAL CONVENTION OF 1885

Wallace B. Carr (Leon County)
Henry Wilkins Chandler (Marion County)
Thomas Van Renssalaer Gibbs (Duval County)
Amos Hargret[t] (Wakulla County)
John W. Mitchell (Leon County)
Samuel Petty (Nassau County)
William F. Thompson (Leon County)

FLORIDA LEGISLATURE, 1868–1889

Edward I. Alexander, Sr. (House, Madison County, 1877, 1879, 1885)
John H. Anderson (House, Duval County, 1887)
Samuel Anderson (House, Duval County, 1887)
Josiah H. Armstrong (House, Columbia County, 1871, 1872, 1875)
William A. Bird [Byrd] (House, Jefferson County, 1883, 1885)
Richard Horatio Black (House, Alachua County, 1869, 1870)
Killis B. Bonner (House, Marion County, 1877)
Samuel Boyd (House, Nassau County, 1871, 1872)
William Bradwell (Senate, Duval County, 1868, 1869, 1870)

Richard Lewis Brown, Sr. (House, Duval County, 1881, 1883)
Wallace B. Carr (House, Leon County, 1881, 1887)
Phillip Carroll (House, Leon County, 1881)
Henry Wilkins Chandler (Senate, Marion County, 1881, 1883, 1885, 1887)
Joseph Newman Clinton (House, Alachua County, 1885)
George C. Coleman (House, Nassau County, 1881)
Oliver J. Coleman (House, Madison County, 1871, 1872, 1875; Senate, Madison County, 1874)
Singleton Coleman (House, Marion County, 1873, 1874)
Robert Cox (House, Leon County, 1868, 1869, 1870)
Harry Cruse (Senate, Gadsden County, 1869, 1870; House, Gadsden County, 1871, 1872, 1873, 1874, 1877)
Peter H. Davidson, Sr. (House, Escambia County, 1877)
Peter H. Davidson, Jr. (House, Escambia County, 1887)
Henry Mack Davis (House, Leon County, 1883)
Thomas S. Delaney (House, Nassau County, 1868, 1869, 1870)
Robert H. Dennis, Sr. (House, Jackson County, 1875)
Zebulon Elijah (House, Escambia County, 1871, 1872, 1873)
Auburn H. Erwin (House, Columbia County, 1868, 1869, 1870)
Lucien Fisher (House, Leon County, 1875)
William Henry Ford (House, Leon County, 1877, 1879)
Emanuel Fortune (House, Jackson County, 1868, 1869, 1870; House Sergeant at Arms, 1872)
Samuel W. Frazier (House, Leon County, 1879, 1885, 1887)
Robert Gabriel (House, Monroe County, 1879)
Theodore C. Gass (House, Alachua County, 1871, 1872, 1873, 1874, 1875)
Burton C. Gibbs (House, Jefferson County, 1881, 1885)
Thomas Van Renssalaer Gibbs (House, Duval County, 1885, 1887)
Birch Gibson (House, Marion County, 1872)
Noah Graham (House, Leon County, 1868, 1869, 1870, 1871, 1872)
Alfred Grant (House, Duval County, 1875, 1877)
Henry S. Harmon (House, Alachua County, 1868, 1869, 1870; House Chief Clerk, 1873, 1874, 1875)
Charles Harris (House, Jefferson County, 1875)
Frederick Hill (House, Gadsden County, 1868, 1869, 1870; Senate, Gadsden County, 1871, 1872, 1873, 1874, 1875, 1877)
David E. Jacobs (House, Marion County, 1877)
William James (House, Duval County, 1885)
T. Scipio Jasper (House, Marion County, 1871, 1872)

Isaac Jenkins (House, Leon County, 1881, 1883)
Everett C. Jones (Senate, Leon County, 1879—unseated)
Andrew Jackson Junius (House, Jefferson County, 1879)
Joseph E. Lee (House, Duval County, 1875, 1877, 1879; Senate, Duval County, 1881)
Matthew M. Lewey (House, Alachua County, 1883)
George A. Lewis (House, Duval County, 1889)
Benjamin F. Livingston (House, Jackson County, 1871, 1872, 1873, 1874, 1875)
Robert Livingston (House, Leon County, 1868)
Ephraim Logan (House, Jefferson County, 1871, 1872)
Thomas Warren Long (Senate, Marion County, 1873, 1874, 1875, 1877, 1879)
William Ryal Long (House, Jefferson County, 1873, 1874, 1877)
Moses W. C. McCardy (House, Jefferson County, 1883)
James McCaslin (House, Alachua County, 1885)
Lafayette N. B. McCray (House, Jefferson County, 1881)
Daniel M. McInnis (House, Duval County, 1871, 1872, 1873, 1874)
Daniel C. Martin (Senate, Alachua County, 1885, 1887)
Robert Meacham (Senate, Jefferson County, 1868, 1869, 1870, 1871, 1872, 1873, 1874, 1875, 1877, 1879)
John Willis Menard (House, Duval County, 1874)
Anthony Mills (House, Jefferson County, 1868, 1869, 1870)
John W. Mitchell (House, Leon County, 1887)
Claiborne Monroe (House, Gadsden County, 1879, 1883)
David Montgomery (House, Madison County, 1873, 1874, 1875; Senate Sergeant at Arms, 1871)
Zack H. Morehead (House, Leon County, 1875)
George Nixon (House, Gadsden County, 1875)
Alfred Brown Osgood (House, Madison County, 1868, 1869, 1870, 1871, 1872, 1873, 1874, 1879, 1883, 1885; Senate, Madison County, 1875, 1877)
Charles H. Pearce (Senate, Leon County, 1868, 1869, 1870, 1871, 1872, 1873, 1874)
Samuel Petty (House, Nassau County, 1873, 1874, 1875)
Salvador T. Pons (House, Escambia County, 1868, 1869, 1870, 1875)
Washington Pope (Senate, Jackson County, 1873, 1874, 1875)
George Willis Proctor (House, Jefferson County, 1883)
John Elias Proctor (House, Leon County, 1873, 1874, 1875, 1879; Senate, Leon County, 1883, 1885)
Dernard E. Quarterman (House, Leon County, 1877)

C. T. Redmon (House, Nassau County, 1879)
Jesse Robinson (House, Jackson County, 1868, 1869, 1870, 1873, 1874)
Riley Edward Robinson (House, Nassau County, 1883, 1885)
William K. Robinson (House, Jackson County, 1872)
Charles H. Rollins (House, Leon County, 1883)
Charles Rouse (House, Escambia County, 1874)
Egbert C. Sammis (Senate, Duval County, 1885)
John Robert Scott, Sr. (House, Duval County, 1868, 1869, 1870, 1871, 1872, 1873, 1879)
John Robert Scott, Jr. (House, Duval County, 1889)
Charles A. Shavers (House, Monroe County, 1887)
John Simpson (House, Marion County, 1868, 1869, 1870)
Samuel Small (House, Marion County, 1873, 1874, 1875)
Clinton Snead (House, Leon County, 1885, 1887)
Samuel Spearing (Senate, Duval County, 1874)
William G. Stewart (House, Leon County, 1873)
John N. Stokes (House, Leon County, 1874)
John Sunday, Jr. (House, Escambia County, 1874)
Benjamin W. Thompson (House, Jefferson County, 1868, 1869, 1870)
Charles H. Thompson (House, Columbia County, 1873, 1874, 1875)
Lemuel W. Thompson (House, Duval County, 1883)
Washington Thompson (House, Jefferson County, 1871, 1872, 1873, 1874)
William F. Thompson (House, Leon County, 1877)
Augustus Tilghman [Tillman] (House, Jefferson County, 1875)
Green B. Tillman (House, Jefferson County, 1877)
William Trapp (House, Alachua County, 1879, 1883)
John Wallace (House, Leon County, 1871, 1872, 1873, 1874; Senate, Leon County, 1875, 1877, 1879, 1881)
Josiah Thomas Walls (House, Alachua County, 1868; Senate, Alachua County, 1869, 1870, 1877, 1879)
George Washington (House, Alachua County, 1873, 1874, 1875)
Randolph W. Washington (House, Jefferson County, 1885)
Richard H. Wells (House, Leon County, 1868, 1869, 1870, 1871, 1872)
George Walter Wetmore (House, Duval County, 1883, 1885)
Mark S. White (House, Escambia County, 1883)
Wesley Asbury Wilkerson (House, Marion County, 1881, 1883, 1885)
John Wilkinson (House, Nassau County, 1883, 1885)
George Washington Witherspoon (House, Jefferson County, 1875, 1877, 1879, 1883)
John W. Wyatt (House, Leon County, 1871, 1872)

ALACHUA COUNTY[4]

Voter Registrar
Theodore C. Gass (1868)
Henry S. Harmon (1867)

Treasurer
Andrew D. Mayo (1873–1875)

Clerk
Henry S. Harmon (1871–1873)

County Commissioner
Mitchell H. Beattie (1872–1873?)
Theodore C. Gass (1868–1870, 1872–1873?)
Henry James (1873–1877)
William Trapp (1873–1874)
Joseph Valentine (1870–1871)
Josiah Thomas Walls (1876–1877)
George Washington (1868–1871, 1872)

Justice of the Peace
Richard Horatio Black (1868–1869)
Matthew M. Lewey (1875–1876)
Richard E. Shivery (1873–1875)
Joseph Valentine (1874–1875)

Constable
Joseph Adams (1874)

Gainesville, 1869–1891[5]
[Missing: 1871–1872; partially missing: 1874–1876, 1879–1881, 1885–1886]

Mayor
Josiah Thomas Walls (1873)

Clerk and Treasurer
Daniel C. Martin (1880–1885, 1888–1890)

Tax Assessor
Jennings Feltner (1882–1885, 1886–1887, 1888–1890)

Tax Collector
Jennings Feltner (1881–1882)

Councilman
Johnson Chestnut (1869–1870)
Joseph Newman Clinton (1883–1885)
Edward Dryer (1873–1874)
Theodore C. Gass (1878–1879, 1881–1885)
Henry S. Harmon (1869–1870)
Matthew M. Lewey (1886–1890, 1891)
Jeff McQueen (1879–1880)
Edward Martin (1889–1891)
Andrew D. Mayo (1873–1874, 1876–1880, 1882–1883)
Julius A. Parker (1886–1888)
William Porter (1878–1879)
Richard E. Shivery (1875–1876, 1882–1884)
Arthur Simmons (1877–1878, 1881–1886)
Milton Stewart (1877–1878)

BAKER COUNTY[6]

Voter Registrar
Warren Roundtree (1867–1868)

County Commissioner
Alfred Roberts (1870)

BRADFORD COUNTY[7]

Voter Registrar
Henry Brown (1867–1868)

County Commissioner
Henry Brown (1868–1870, 1873–1875)

Justice of the Peace
Samuel B. Williams (1874–1878)

BREVARD COUNTY[8]

Voter Registrar
Wright Brothers (1867–1868)

CALHOUN COUNTY[9]

Voter Registrar
Alexander B. Hawkins (1867–1868)

Superintendent of Schools
Alexander B. Hawkins (1873–1875)

County Commissioner
Alexander B. Hawkins (1874–1875)

Justice of the Peace
Oliver Byrd (1875–1879)

CLAY COUNTY[10]

Voter Registrar
Henry [Harry] Tillman (1867–1868)

County Commissioner
James Andrews [Andreu] (1871–1877)
Henry Bram (1876–1877)
Bird Miller (1871–1873)

Green Cove Springs, 1874–1906[11]

[Missing: 1876–1877, 1889–1890, 1900–1906; partially missing: 1874–1876, 1877–1882, 1884–1886, 1890–1894, 1895–1896]

Tax Assessor
Andrew Wiles (1886–1887)

Councilman
July Bram (1874–1876, 1878–1879, 1881–1882)
Edward Fells (1874–1876)
Lewis F. Forrester (1896–1900)
Samuel M. Patterson (1887–1891)
Richard W. Redmond (1890–1892)
Howard Taylor (1875–1876)
Andrew Wiles (1891–1893)

COLUMBIA COUNTY[12]

Voter Registrar
Romulus Spencer (1867–1868)

Tax Assessor
Francis B. Carolina (1873–1874)
Charles H. Thompson (1874–1875)

County Commissioner
Cato B. Carter (1871–1873, 1876–1877)
Edward Hall (1874–1877)
Primus Harrison (1869–1870)
Reuben Hart (1870–1871)
Lewis Johnson (1873–1875)
Archibald Niblack (1868–1870)
William Rafe (1873–1875)
Charles H. Thompson (1875–1877)
Edward Williams (1870)

Justice of the Peace
Romulus Spencer (1876)

Lake City, 1871–1892[13]

[Partially missing: 1872–1873, 1874–1876, 1887–1888, 1889–1890]

Tax Assessor
Edward Hall (1873–1874, 1876–1877)
Romulus Spencer (1877–1879)

Marshal
Harry Drake (1873–1874)

Councilman
Francis B. Carolina (1874–1875)
John Edwards (1872–1873)
Elbert T. Holmes (1890–1892)
Thomas McCoy (1876–1877)
York Mizell (1878–1879)
Asa Richard (1873–1874)
Benjamin Simpson (1873–1874, 1876–1877, 1878–1879)
Romulus Spencer (1876–1877)
Hugh Watson (1876–1877)

DADE COUNTY[14]

Voter Registrar
Nelson Francis deSales English (1867–1868)

County Commissioner
Andrew Price (1869–1873, 1874–1876)

DUVAL COUNTY[15]

Voter Registrar
George K. Sammis (1867)
Cataline B. Simmons (1868)

Clerk of the Circuit Court
Joseph E. Lee (1889?)

Tax Assessor
William T. Garvin (1871–1874)

Tax Collector
John J. Month (1871–1873)
Samuel Spearing (1875–1877)

County Commissioner
Emanuel Fortune (1873–1877)
William T. Garvin (1871)
Abram [Abraham] Grant (1876–1877)
Richard L. Jones (1873, 1874–1876)
Cataline B. Simmons (1868–1870, 1872–1874)

Justice of the Peace
John H. Ballou (1889–1891)
W. Samuel Burgess (1873–1874)
Mitchell P. Chappell[e] (1874–1877)
Auburn H. Erwin (1873–1874)
John Willis Menard (1874, 1877)
Edmund G. Sammis (1877–1881?)
William W. Sampson (1871–1875?)
Samuel Spearing (1868–1870?)
Norman Bascom Sterrett (1875–1876)
Henry C. Tison (1869–1871, 1873–1877)

Constable
John H. Brown (1871, 1874–1875)
Auburn H. Erwin (1872, 1877–1878)
James J. Forbes (1873–1875)
James D. Garvin (1872)
Moses Hicks (1868–1870)
James Lane (1873–1875)
Henry McIntyre (1868–1870)
George H. Mays (1873–1875, 1878–1880?)
Jesse H. Oxendine (1877–1878)
James K. Robinson (1879–1880)
Joseph Smith (1873–1874)
Sanders Wilson (1873–1874)

Jacksonville, 1869–1907[16]

Municipal Judge
Joseph E. Lee (1888)

Clerk
James D. Garvin (1871–1873)

Tax Assessor
Thomas Lancaster (1874–1876, 1880–1881, 1882–1883)
Cataline B. Simmons (1872–1874)

Marshal
Emanuel Fortune (1873–1875)
George H. Mays (1878–1882)

Councilman
Samuel Maxwell Dennis (1888–1889)
Emanuel Fortune (1888–1889)
Frank Franklin (1871–1872)
William T. Garvin (1869–1871, 1873–1874)
Richard L. Jones (1873–1874, 1879–1880)
Thomas Lancaster (1871–1874)
Cato Lee (1872–1873)
Charles C. Manigault (1899–1901)
David Petty (1875–1876)
George Eugene Ross (1901–1907)
William W. Sampson (1872–1873, 1879–1880)
John Robert Scott, Jr. (1897–1899)
Cataline B. Simmons (1869–1871)
John E. Spearing (1888–1889)
J. G. Thompson (1871–1872)
Capers Michael Vaught, Sr. (1888–1889)
Benjamin Wright (1888–1889)

LaVilla, 1869–1887[17]

[Missing: 1869–1870, 1872–1873, 1880–1881; partially missing: 1870–1871]

Mayor
Mitchell P. Chappell[e] (1874–1876)
Alfred Grant (1876–1877)

Clerk
George W. Andrews (1882–1884)
James F. Elliott (1881–1882)
Charles B. Gallaway (1877–1878)
Sylvanus H. Hart (1884–1887)
Mack Hollingsworth (1878–1879)
James Johnson (1876–1877)

Tax Assessor
William P. Braddock (1871–1872)
Alfred Grant (1878–1879)

Tax Collector
Mitchell P. Chappell[e] (1873–1874, 1876–1877)
Thomas C. Claiborne (1881–1887)
Samuel Spearing (1871–1872)

Treasurer
Samuel Spearing (1882–1887)

Marshal
Frank Andrews (1870–1872)
Handy [Hiram] N. Huggins (1876–1879, 1881–1887)
Benjamin Redding (1874–1876)
Smart Tillman (1873–1874)

Councilman
Moody Baker (1870–1871, 1875–1876)
Simon Booth (1886–1887)
Benjamin Brooks (1873–1874)
John H. Brown (1871–1872)
Alexander E. Campbell (1884–1886)
Lewis [Louis] H. Chappell[e] (1875–1877)
Mitchell P. Chappell[e] (1877–1878)
William Frank Epps (1884–1886)
Reddish Evans (1874–1875)

Alfred Grant (1871–1872, 1874–1875)
Robert Green (1873–1876, 1881–1887)
Henry Griffin (1876–1877)
Robert Hall (1870–1871)
Bristow Henderson (1886–1887)
Noah Henderson (1870–1871, 1873–1874)
Joseph Holder (1871–1872)
John Hughes (1887)
Lee Jackson (1873–1876)
James Johnson (1871–1872)
Wiley Jones (1887)
Thomas LeGrand [LeGrant] (1870–1872, 1876–1877)
Peter W. Morrison (1870–1872, 1873–1875, 1876–1878)
March Ponder (1874–1875)
James A. Scott (1874–1875)
James E. Scott (1878–1879, 1883–1885)
John Robert Scott, Sr. (1877–1879)
Henry Smith (1878–1879)
John E. Spearing (1881–1887)
Samuel Spearing (1873–1875)
November Squire (1876–1877)
Smart Tillman (1878–1879, 1881–1884)
John Tucker (1885–1887)
George Turner (1877–1878)
George Washington (1877–1878)
Hilliard Wheaton (1886–1887)
James C. Williamson (1879–1880, 1882–1884)

ESCAMBIA COUNTY[18]

Voter Registrar
John W. Baptiste (1867–1868)

Tax Assessor
Richard Gagnet (1873–1874)
John Pons (1874–1875)

Superintendent of Schools
George W. Lindsley (1873–1875)

County Commissioner
John [Jack] Butterfield (1873–1875)
Augustus Dupont (1876–1877)
Zebulon Elijah (1872–1873)
Richard Gagnet (1874–1876)
Thomas Harrod (1871–1873)
Heraldo Hernandez (1873–1874)
John Pons (1868–1870)
Charles Rouse (1874–1875)
Joseph Wyer (1869–1871)

Justice of the Peace
John W. Baptiste (1868–1874?)
W. H. Turner (1874–1875)

Pensacola, 1869–1889[19]
[Partially missing: 1869–1870, 1871–1877, 1878–1882]

Mayor
Salvador T. Pons (1874)

Clerk
Salvador T. Pons (1877–1880, 1882–1884)

Tax Assessor
Zebulon Elijah (1881–1882)
George A. Parsons (1883–1884)
Warren Calway Vester [Vesta] (1885)

Tax Collector
Joseph Wyer (1869)

Marshal
John [Jack] Butterfield (1881)
Richard Gagnet (1878–1880, 1883–1884)
Duncan H. [Dank] Mallett (1885)
William Warren (1874)

Councilman
John [Jack] Butterfield (1877)
Augustus Dupont (1870–1872, 1874, 1877, 1885)
Richard Gagnet (1872, 1882)
John A. Gibson (1879, 1882–1883, 1885)
Anthony Headsby [Headcopy or Headspey] (1874)
Heraldo Hernandez (1869, 1871, 1884–1885)
Elias Johnson (1883)
Ed McGovern (1883)
John Pons (1879)
Salvador T. Pons (1869–1870, 1874)
Richard Ramsey (1874)
Jasper Shanks (1877)
John Sunday, Jr. (1878?–1885)
Jerry Washington (1874)
George Washington Witherspoon (1885–1889)

FRANKLIN COUNTY[20]

Voter Registrar
Emanuel Smith (1867–1868)

Sheriff
Henry Hutchinson (1874–1877)

County Commissioner
John B. Collins (1873–1875)
Calvin Herndon (1872–1877)
Anthony Porter (1875–1881)
Emanuel Smith (1869–1872)

Justice of the Peace
Samuel Hutchinson (1873–1876?)
Emanuel Smith (1872–1881?)

Apalachicola, 1871–1890[21]
[Missing: 1869–1870; partially missing: 1870–1873, 1874–1882, 1883–1887]

Councilman
Thomas Clark (1871–1874)
Henry Hutchinson (1886–1890)
Thomas Kilby (1887–1889)
Louis Robinson (1885–1886)
George W. Smith (1882–1883)

GADSDEN COUNTY[22]

Voter Registrar
George W. Morris (1867–1868)

County Commissioner
William H. Eckles [Eckels] (1873–1877)
Frederick Hill (1870)
Allen Jones, Sr. (1870–1874)
Alexander C. Lightbourn[e], Sr. (1871–1873)
George Nixon (1869–1872)
William G. Stewart (1870–1872)

Justice of the Peace
Sir Sidney Gilchrist (1868–1871)
Jesse F. King (1872–1873)
Alexander C. Lightbourn[e], Sr. (1871–1874)
Austin [Mack] McGriff (1873–1874)

Quincy, 1869–1881[23]

[Missing: 1876–1877, 1881–1882; partially missing: 1870–1871, 1874–1875, 1878–1882]

Councilman
John Moss (1877?–1878?)[24]

HAMILTON COUNTY[25]

Voter Registrar
James Livingston (1868)
Andrew Shuler (1867)

Sheriff
Benjamin F. Collier (1872–1874)

Tax Assessor
Benjamin F. Collier (1872–1873)

County Commissioner
Daniel F. Lee (1873–1877)
Charles Lumpkin (1872)
Robert Peaden (1875–1877)
James Peterson (1872–1875)

Justice of the Peace
James Peterson (1870–1872)

Jasper, 1878–1890[26]
No known black officials

HERNANDO COUNTY[27]

Voter Registrar
Arthur W. St. Clair (1867–1868)

County Commissioner
Henry Harper (1871–1875?)
Sampson Jourdan (1873–1875)
Joseph Mills (1876–1877)
Arthur W. St. Clair (1875–1877)

Justice of the Peace
George W. Geiger (1876–1877)

Brooksville, 1880–1890[28]
No known black officials

HILLSBOROUGH COUNTY[29]

Voter Registrar
Frederick D. Newberry (1867–1868)

County Commissioner
Cyrus Charles (1868–1871)
Adam Holloman (1873–1877)
Mills Holloman (1868–1870, 1870–1871)
Robert Johnson (1871–1873)
John Thomas (1871–1873)

Justice of the Peace
Peter W. Bryant (1877–1881)
Frederick D. Newberry (1868–1869?)

Tampa, 1869–1888[30]

Councilman
Henry Brumick (1876–1877)
Cyrus Charles (1869)
Joseph A. Walker (1887–1888)

HOLMES COUNTY[31]

Voter Registrar
George W. Barkley (1867–1868)

JACKSON COUNTY[32]

Voter Registrar
Emanuel Fortune (1867)
Oscar Granberry (1868)

Tax Collector
Homer Bryan (1868–1871)

Treasurer
Homer Bryan (1871–1872)

County Commissioner
Benjamin F. Livingston (1868–1870, 1874–1877)
Washington Pope (1870–1872)

Jesse Waller (1871–1872, 1873–1875)
Fuller M. White (1872, 1873–1875)
Isham White, Sr. (1875–1877)
Elijah L. Williams (1868–1872)
Anderson Wynans [Anson Wynns] (1870–1871)

Justice of the Peace
Edward Barkley (1872–1875)
Alfred Barnes (1874–1877)
David Campbell (1874–1877)
George B. Robinson (1872–1875)
Jesse Robinson (1876–1880)
Benjamin Williams (1868–1873?)
Elijah L. Williams (1868–1870?)

Constable
Richard Pousser (1870)
Calvin Rogers (1869–1870)

Marianna, 1876–1886[33]
[Missing: 1878–1881, 1884–1886]

Councilman
William Everett (1877–1878)
Benjamin F. Livingston (1882–1884?)
John Livingston (1876–1877)
Jesse Waller (1876–1877)
Fuller M. White (1877–1878)

JEFFERSON COUNTY[34]

Voter Registrar
Robert Meacham (1867–1868)
Daniel M. Pembroke (1868)

Clerk
Robert Meacham (1868)

Sheriff
Lafayette N. B. McCray (1876)
George W. Monroe (1876–1877)

Tax Assessor
William Ryal Long (1869–1870)

Treasurer
John A. Potter (1874–1876)

Superintendent of Schools
Robert Meacham (1868–1872, 1873–1877)

County Commissioner
Anthony Bellamy (1877–1878)
Benjamin Franklin Dilworth, Sr. (1870–1872, 1873–1877)
William Ryal Long (1870–1874)
John Mays (1870–1872, 1873–1877)
Anthony Mills (1872–1873?)
Charles Parrish, Sr. (1868–1869)
Daniel M. Pembroke (1869–1870)
Joseph Taylor (1876–1877)
Hampton [Hamilton] Williams (1872–1873?)

Justice of the Peace
George Hadley (1871–1877)
Moses W. C. McCardy (1874–1876)
Daniel M. Pembroke (1868–1869?, 1876–1877)

Monticello, 1869–1886[35]
[Missing: 1869, 1871–1872, 1874–1875, 1879–1881, 1884–1885]
No known black officials

LAFAYETTE COUNTY[36]

Voter Registrar
Morris M. Sampson (1867–1868)

LEON COUNTY[37]

Voter Registrar
James Page (1867–1868)

Sheriff
Philip L. DeCourcey [DeCoursey] (1875)

Tax Assessor
Charles H. Pearce (1876–1877)

Superintendent of Schools
Charles H. Pearce (1868–1872)

County Commissioner
Owen B. Armstrong (1869–1870)
Lloyd Crampton (1872–1873?)
Noah Graham (1868)
Alexander B. Hawkins (1868–1870)
James W. Jefferson (1875–1877)
Benjamin Jones (1873)
Robert Kent (1871–1874?)
Richard Mickens (1873–1874)
James Page (1868–1870?)
Charles H. Pearce (1868)
Lewis Plater (1873)
Charles H. Rollins (1874–1877)
Benjamin Ross (1872)
Jonas W. Toer (1870–1872)
Samuel Crawford Watkins (1873–1874)
Robert Williams (1868–1871)
John W. Wyatt (1872)

Justice of the Peace
Joseph Broadenax (1873)
Alfred Cobb (1868–1872, 1873–1877)
Charles F. Daly (1872–1873)
Herbert B. DeVaughn (1873–1874)
Samuel W. Frazier (1872–1873)
John D. Haynes (1872–1873)

Clement Manley (1875–1877)
John W. Mitchell (1877–1879)
Zack H. Morehead (1874)
James Page (1872–1877)
John H. Peterson (1872)
Samuel Snowden (1873–1874)
James D. Thompson (1872–1874)
William F. Thompson (1872–1873, 1874)
Jonas W. Toer (1868–1870)
Milton A. Trapp (1876)
John Wallace (1877)
Noah Williams (1873–1876)
John W. Wyatt (1872–1874)

Constable
William Henry Ford (1870, 1873–1874)
Dernard E. Quarterman (1873–1874)
Bradley Robinson (1875–1877)

Tallahassee, 1869–1891[38]
[Missing: none]

Clerk and Treasurer
W. T. Chester (1880)
Everett C. Jones (1876–1877)
William G. Stewart (1872)

Tax Assessor
Philip L. Decourcey [DeCoursey] (1874–1875)
Esau W. Hall (1889)
James W. Jefferson (1877, 1879, 1881–1883, 1886, 1888)
William Matthews (1880)
John Sheppard (1878)
William F. Thompson (1884, 1887)
Edward W. Yellowhair (1885)

Marshal and Tax Collector
Archer D. Crowell (1880)
Henry Douglass (1881–1882, 1884)
Henry N. Douglas[s] (1883)

Henry Fitzgiles (1876, 1878)
Henry Sutton (1877)

Marshal
Henry Douglass (1885–1886)
Henry Sutton (1872–1875)

Councilman
Alfred Cobb (1882–1883, 1886–1890)
Lloyd Crampton (1873)
Wesley Davis (1880)
Andrew DeCourcey [DeCoursey] (1874)
Benjamin DeCourcey [DeCoursey] (1875, 1878, 1880–1881)
Henry N. Douglas[s] (1884, 1888–1889)
George S. Fitzgiles (1875, 1878, 1880–1882, 1885–1886)
William [Frank] Franklin (1876)
Henry Garnett (1876)
Jonathan C. Gibbs (1872)
Stanford Harrison (1879–1880)
Henry Hicks (1875)
James W. Jefferson (1873)
Isaac Jenkins (1876)
Everett C. Jones (1872–1873)
Henry Jones (1879, 1881)
Henry Matthews (1875, 1877)
Charles H. Pearce (1876)
Andrew Ramsey (1874)
John Sheppard (1877)
William G. Stewart (1873)
John N. Stokes (1878, 1881–1882)
Jonas W. Toer (1872)
Daniel Vaughn (1875)
Samuel Crawford Watkins (1876, 1880)
Henry Williams (1876)
Edward W. Yellowhair (1883–1884)

LEVY COUNTY[39]

Voter Registrar
Tillman Valentine (1867–1868)

County Commissioner
William Canty (1876–1877)
Fred E. Miller (1876–1877)
Jackson Parrish (1873–1875)
Edward B. Stidum (1870–1872)

Justice of the Peace
Peter Hart (1874)
Edward B. Stidum (1871–1872)
John G. Williams (1871–1874, 1876–1877)

Bronson, 1885–1888[40]
[Partially missing: 1886–1887]

Councilman
George Washington (1885–1886)

Cedar Key(s), 1869–1909[41]
[Missing: 1869–1873]

Mayor
John G. Williams (1874)

Clerk
John V. Cornell, Sr. (1874–1875)

Marshal
Fred E. Miller (1874–1876)

Councilman
Crummie Alston (1883–1885, 1898–1909)
Charles H. Benson (1878–1879, 1882–1884, 1888–1898)
William Canty (1874–1875, 1876–1877, 1888–1894, 1898–1902)
Samuel Forrester (1876–1877)
Peter Hart (1874–1876)
James Hearn (1875–1876)
Morris Jordan (1875–1876)
Jeff McQueen (1874–1875, 1885–1889)

Boston P. Martin (1893–1895, 1909)
Arthur Simmons (1873–1874)
Bulley William Wiley (1878–1879)
John G. Williams (1873–1874, 1876–1877)
William Young (1889–1891)

LIBERTY COUNTY[42]

Voter Registrar
Israel Shuler (1867–1868)

County Commissioner
Walter Sanders (1876–1877)
Ephraim Summers (1871–1876)

Justice of the Peace
Ephraim Summers (1876–1877)

MADISON COUNTY[43]

Voter Registrar
Peter Wright (1867–1868)

Clerk
John C. Gambia (1871–1874)

Sheriff
David Montgomery (1868–1873)

Tax Assessor
John C. Gambia (1870–1872)

Tax Collector
David Montgomery (1868–1869, 1872–1877)

Superintendent of Schools
Thomas Warren Long (1868–1869)

County Commissioner
Oliver J. Coleman (1874–1877)
Robert Cray (1868–1873, 1875–1877)
David King (1868–1873)
David Montgomery (1873–1874)
Edmund Murray (1873–1875)

Justice of the Peace
William Brown (1874–1877)
Oliver J. Coleman (1873)
Jefferson J. Evans (1872–1873?)
Anthony Hall (1870–1872, 1874–1878)
John B. Mays (1870–1879?)
Morris M. Sampson (1874–1877)
Edwin Smith (1874)
Samuel E. Tillman (1874–1877)
Charles Woodward [Woodard] (1872–1873)

Constable
Bristow Foxworth (1872)

Madison, 1869–1896[44]
[Missing: 1869–1875, 1879–1882; partially missing: 1875–1876, 1877–1878]

Marshal
Thomas McLeary (1876–1877)

Councilman
Edward I. Alexander, Sr. (1882)
Edmund Burroughs (1884)
Oliver J. Coleman (1883–1884, 1887–1896)
Anthony Johnson (1876–1877)
James Mosely (1878, 1885–1886)
Ulysses Grant Nixon (1890–1891)
Robert Richardson (1876–1878)

MANATEE COUNTY[45]

Voter Registrar
John Lomans (1868)
Robert Taylor (1867)

MARION COUNTY[46]

Voter Registrar
Samuel Small (1867–1868)

Superintendent of Schools
Isaac Black (1868–1869)

County Commissioner
Primus Gowens (1868–1870?)
David E. Jacobs (1875–1876)
Gilbert Little (1873–1877)
Samuel Small (1868–1872?)
Alfred Tooley (1872–1875)
John Williams (1873)
Charles M. Woodward (1869–1873?)

Justice of the Peace
Peter R. Anderson (1872)
Birch Gibson (1873–1875)
Charles M. Scott (1875–1879)
Edward B. Stidum (1872–1876)
Frank Ward (1871–1875?)
Wesley Asbury Wilkerson (1873–1877)

Ocala, 1869–1893[47]

[Missing: 1870–1871, 1872–1873; partially missing: 1871–1872, 1873–1874, 1878–1880]

Clerk, Tax Assessor, and Tax Collector
Reuben S. Mitchell (1877–1878)

Clerk
Henry Wilkins Chandler (1883–1884)

Treasurer and Tax Collector
Frank P. Gadson (1890–1892)

Treasurer
Frank P. Gadson (1884–1886)

Tax Collector
Frank P. Gadson (1888–1890)

Marshal
Burrell Dawkins (1873–1876, 1880–1881)
Watson Murphy (1876–1877)

Councilman
Henry Wilkins Chandler (1886–1893)
Robert Coleman (1880–1881)
Alfred Davis (1874–1877, 1879–1883)
Wallace D. Dawkins (1882–1883)
Richard Dinkins (1869–1870)
Frank P. Gadson (1886–1888)
Birch Gibson (1877–1878, 1881–1883)
Watson Murphy (1875–1876, 1877–1880, 1883–1885)
Elias Glasco Smith (1875–1880, 1882–1883, 1885–1887, 1888–1890)

MONROE COUNTY[48]

Voter Registrar
Washington Clarke (1867–1868)

County Judge
James Dean (1889)

Sheriff
Charles F. Dupont (1889–1893)
James A. Roberts (1874–1877)

County Commissioner
Robert W. Butler (1876–1877)
James D. English (1868–1875)
Benjamin W. Roberts (1875–1876)

Constable
Charles Brown (1872)
James A. Roberts (1872–1874)

Key West, 1869–1907[49]
[Missing: 1870–1871, 1872–1875, 1885–1886, 1887–1888, 1899–1900;
partially missing: 1871–1872, 1876–1877, 1878–1881, 1882–1885, 1888–1889]

Clerk
John V. Cornell, Sr. (1875–1876)

Tax Assessor
Frank Adams (1886–1887, 1888–1889)

Councilman
Charles R. Adams (1880–1882, 1887–1888)
Frank Adams (1882–1884)
William Middleton Artrell (1875–1876)
Washington A. Cornell (1884–1885, 1887–1888)
Jose Juan Figueroa (1875–1876)
Robert Gabriel (1876–1880, 1897–1898, 1901–1907)
Benjamin W. Roberts (1875–1876, 1877–1878)
James A. Roberts (1875–1876)
Charles A. Shavers (1898–1901)
Roman M. Stevens (1887–1888)

NASSAU COUNTY[50]

Voter Registrar
Thomas S. Delaney (1867)
Farley W. Redmon (1868)

Tax Assessor
Cornelius Bell (1876–1877)

County Commissioner
Caesar Baker (1868–1872)
John Gordon (1875–1877)
Charles Knabb (1872–1874)
C. T. Redmon (1874)
George Washington (1874–1875)

Justice of the Peace
Samuel Boyd (1870?–1871)
Furney B. Bryant (1875–1876)
Turner Duling (1871–1877)
James Goodbread (1876–1877)
Farley W. Redmon (1873–1875, 1876–1877)
John H. Stays (1889–1901)

Constable
John Wilkinson (1874)

Fernandina, 1869–1902[51]
[Partially missing: 1870–1871, 1873–1877, 1881–1882, 1887–1888]

Clerk and Treasurer
Peter Bonaud (1873–1874)
Samuel Boyd (1869–1871)
Port W. King (1875–1876)
George Washington (1874–1875)

Tax Assessor
Jacob R. Ballard (1877–1878)
Richard E. Eddin (1880–1881)
Richard Jones (1883–1884)
Port W. King (1878–1879)
John H. Stays (1884–1887)
Floyd Wright (1879–1880)

Marshal and Tax Collector
Turner Duling (1871–1881)
Henry Hannahan (1870–1871)

Marshal
Richard L. Denefield [Delafield] (1881–1883, 1884–1886)
Stephen Morris (1886–1887)
Robert Friday Smith (1883–1884)

Councilman
R. W. Atkinson (1887–1888)
Daniel R. Baxter (1877–1882)
Samuel Brown (1879–1880)
James Bush (1884–1885)
Romain Cribb (1880–1881)
Ray S. Delaney (1870–1871, 1880–1881)
Richard L. Denefield [Delafield] (1894–1902)
Romeo Denegal (1873–1875)
Willoughby Dorsey (1873–1875, 1876–1877, 1884–1887)
Richard E. Eddin (1890–1892)
Paul Francis (1870–1871, 1878–1880, 1881–1882)
Henry Franklin (1898)
Harry Johnson (1871–1873)
Simon A. Johnson (1899–1900)
William Joseph (1881–1882)
Port W. King (1883–1885)
Charles Knabb (1869–1870)
Edward Francis Langley (1870–1871, 1875–1876)
Obit McDonald (1872–1874)
Robert McDonald (1882–1884, 1885–1887, 1900–1902)
John A. McDyer (1896–1898)
Peter B. Middleton (1879–1881)
Edward Mordecai (1873–1874)
Samuel Petty (1870–1871, 1875–1879, 1881–1882, 1888–1889)
Albert S. Reynolds (1892–1896)
Riley Edward Robinson (1875–1876, 1877–1879, 1883–1890, 1892–1894)
Julius Triay [Traeye] (1872–1874)
Reuben Walker (1885–1887)
John Wilkinson (1871–1872)

Richard Wilkinson (1872–1873, 1874–1875, 1885–1887)
Peter Williams (1875–1876, 1881–1884)

ORANGE COUNTY[52]

Voter Registrar
James Chaires (1867–1868)

Eatonville, 1887–1924[53]

[Missing: 1888–1889, 1890–1900; partially missing: 1900–1924]

Mayor
Columbus H. Boger, Sr. (1887–1888)
Matthew B. Brazell (1916–1920)
Joseph E. Clark (1889–1890, 1900–1912)
John Hurston (1912–1916)
Hyrum N. Lester (1922–1924)
Samuel M. Moseley (1920–1922)

Clerk
J. R. Johnson (1887–1888)

Tax Assessor
J. B. Brazell (1887–1888)

Tax Collector
John N. Watson (1887–1888)

Treasurer
L. D. Brazell (1887–1888)

Marshal
Walter T. Thomas (1887–1888)

Councilman
Matthew B. Brazell (1887–1888)
Joseph E. Clark (1887–1888)
E. L. Horn (1887–1888)
E. J. Shines (1887–1888)
David Yelder (1887–1888)

Goldsboro, 1891–1911[54]
[Missing: 1892–1910; partially missing: 1911]

Mayor
Morris B. Bellamy, Sr. (1911)
George W. Benton, Sr. (1911)
Walter Williams (1891–1892)

Clerk
T. T. Green (1911)

Clerk and Tax Assessor
John Wesley Small (1891–1892)

Treasurer
Joseph White (1891–1892)

Marshal and Tax Collector
William M. Clark (1891–1892)

Councilman
George W. Benton, Sr. (1911)
Evans Charlton Carolina (1891–1892)
Hubbard [Herbert] Jewett (1891–1892)
Aren T. Shepard (1891–1892)
Joseph A. Williams (1891–1892)
David Wilson (1891–1892)

Maitland, 1885–1889[55]
[Missing: 1887–1888]

Councilman
Tony Taylor (1885–1886)

Mellonville, 1876–1877[56]
No known black officials

Sanford, 1877–1881[57]
[Missing: 1878–1879]
No known black officials

POLK COUNTY[58]

Voter Registrar
Stepney Blount Dixon (1867–1868)

PUTNAM COUNTY[59]

Voter Registrar
George Brash Rivers (1867–1868)

County Commissioner
Albert N. Doyle (1868–1877)

Justice of the Peace
Alfred [Alford] Davis (1868–1873?, 1875–1877)
Edward S. Francis (1873–1875)
Dennis Wood (1868–1873?)

Palatka, 1869–1924[60]

[Missing: 1869–1870, 1874–1875; partially missing: 1870–1871; 1875–1876, 1879–1880, 1881–1883]

Clerk and Tax Assessor
Joseph J. Sawyer (1882–1884)

Clerk
Joseph W. Purcell (1888–1890)

Marshal and Tax Collector
Albert N. Doyle (1870–1874)

Marshal
Albert N. Doyle (1876, 1880–1881, 1882–1884)

Councilman
Joseph A. Adams (1900–1902, 1908–1912)
William Bell (1871–1873, 1876, 1879–1881)
John Brown (1881–1882)
Albert Lewis Browning (1903–1909, 1912–1914, 1920–1924)
Francis B. Carolina (1875–1876)

Milton Cooper (1882–1883)
Albert N. Doyle (1889–1890)
Edward S. Francis (1870?–1873)
Elbert T. Holmes (1904–1908)
John McMillan (1902–1904)
Joseph A. Nottage (1917–1920, 1922–1924)
Isaac L. Purcell (1885–1887, 1891–1893)
Lee N. Robinson (1896–1898, 1909–1917)
Littleton Louis Trapp (1916–1920)
A. J. Williams (1883)
Daniel Williams (1883–1885)
Samuel Wilson (1882–1883)
Thomas N. Wilson (1887–1889)
Dennis Wood (1870–1871, 1873–1874, 1877–1878)

SANTA ROSA COUNTY[61]

Voter Registrar
John Kelker (1867–1868)

Milton, 1869–1887[62]

[Partially missing: 1869]

Tax Assessor
Alexander M. Collins (1885)

Councilman
Alexander M. Collins (1882)
Anthony Hawthorne (1882)

ST. JOHNS COUNTY[63]

Voter Registrar
Joseph C. Crews [Cruse or LaCruse] (1867)
John Robinson (1868)

Tax Assessor
Domingo M. Papy (1876–1877)

County Commissioner
Stacio Benjamin (1871–1873)
Henry M. Emmerly (1875–1877)
James H. Lang (1868–1871)
Antonio Papy (1868–1871)
Domingo M. Papy (1873–1875)
William Vandyke (1872–1874)

Justice of the Peace
Stacio Benjamin (1870–1871)
Henry M. Emmerly (1873–1875)
Samuel Sevilly (1868–1877?)
Francis E. Witsell (1875–1877?)

St. Augustine, 1869–1904[64]
[Missing: none]

Tax Assessor
William B. Hicks (1873–1874)
Alfonso A. Papy (1885–1886)
Domingo M. Papy (1880–1881)
Frank A. Papy (1881–1882)

Tax Collector
Edward J. Houston (1882–1883, 1884–1885)
Jacob Clarence Jordan (1882)
Alfonso A. Papy (1888–1889)
Francis E. Witsell (1881–1882)

Marshal and Tax Collector
William Vandyke (1873–1874)

Marshal
George Adams (1880–1883)
John Blake (1888–1889)
John Papino (1884–1886)
William Vandyke (1877–1878)

Councilman
Charles Benedee (1881–1882)
Joseph Blanchard (1901–1904)

William B. Hicks (1878)
Jacob Clarence Jordan (1885–1886)
Jesse McLain (1897–1902)
John Papino (1891–1897, 1899–1901, 1902–1903)
Domingo M. Papy (1877–1878, 1884–1886, 1888–1890)
James Benjamin Thomas (1882–1884)
William A. Watts (1888–1889)
Francis E. Witsell (1873–1874, 1877–1878, 1880–1881, 1889–1891)

SUMTER COUNTY[65]

Voter Registrar
Edward McMullen [McMillen] (1867–1868)

County Commissioner
Henry Brooks (1873–1877)
Tanner Henderson (1868–1870)

SUWANNEE COUNTY[66]

Voter Registrar
George Manker (1867–1868)

County Commissioner
Tully C. Denham (1875–1876)
Lewis Fields (1870–1873)
Berry M. Gardner (1873–1877)
Nathaniel Goodman (1870)
Nelson M. Kerby (1868–1869)
Samuel McIver (1873–1875)
George Manker (1869–1870)
Caleb Simpkins (1876–1877)
Frank Stockton (1870–1873)

Justice of the Peace
Robert Allen (1876–1877)

Live Oak, 1878–1890[67]

Councilman
Thomas T. Thompson (1878–1879)

TAYLOR COUNTY[68]

Voter Registrar
Jesse Colson (1867–1868)

VOLUSIA COUNTY[69]

Voter Registrar
Richard Horatio Black (1867–1868)

Justice of the Peace
Anthony E. Freeman (1876–1880)

DeLand, 1882–1890[70]

[Missing: none]
No known black officials

WAKULLA COUNTY[71]

Voter Registrar
Turner Duling (1867–1868)

County Commissioner
Anthony Bradham (1870–1872)
Robert Braswell (1876–1877)
Isaac Gavin (1870–1871, 1873–1875)
Amos Hargret[t] (1868–1870)
Richard H. Hargrett (1873–1875)
Joseph Poole (1873–1877)
Edward Wise (1868–1872)

Justice of the Peace
Anthony Bradham (1873–1877)
Amos Hargret[t] (1876–1877)

WALTON COUNTY[72]

Voter Registrar
Henry Call (1868)
Willis Johnson (1867–1868)

County Commissioner
Henry Call (1875–1877)

Justice of the Peace
Henry Call (1873–1875)
Joseph T. Daniels (1872–1873?)
Anderson A. Pittman (1875–1879)

WASHINGTON COUNTY[73]

Voter Registrar
Henry Call (1868)
Jesse Robinson (1867–1868)

Abbreviations

Census	Manuscript returns, United States Decennial Census or Florida State Census, as appropriate
CR	Philadelphia *Christian Recorder*
DCI	Combined Index of Deaths, Marriages, and Divorces [Death Certificate Index], Florida Office of Vital Statistics
DFU	Jacksonville *Daily Florida Union*
DN&H	Savannah *Daily News and Herald*
DS&P	Jacksonville *Daily Sun and Press*
FDT	Jacksonville *Florida Daily Times*
FM	Fernandina *Florida Mirror*
FP	Tampa *Florida Peninsular*
FSA	Florida State Archives, Tallahassee
FT-U	Jacksonville *Florida Times-Union*
FT-U&C	Jacksonville *Florida Times-Union and Citizen*
FU	Jacksonville *Florida Union*
LC	Library of Congress, Washington, D.C.
MPR	Military pension records, Veterans' Administration, RG 15, NA.
MSR	Military service records, Union soldiers in the Civil War, RG 94, NA.
NA	National Archives, Washington, D.C.
N-H	Jacksonville *News-Herald*
NYA	*New York Age*
NYF	*New York Freeman*
NYG	*New York Globe*

PKY	P. K. Yonge Library of Florida History, University of Florida, Gainesville
SAE	St. Augustine *Examiner*
SAHSRL	St. Augustine Historical Society Research Library
SDA	*Savannah Daily Advertiser*
SDR	*Savannah Daily Republican*
SMN	*Savannah Morning News*
TS	*Tallahassee Sentinel*
VR corr.	Incoming correspondence, Third Military District, 1867–68, Bureau of Civil Affairs
WF	Tallahassee *Weekly Floridian*
WFU	Jacksonville *Weekly Florida Union*
WS&P	Jacksonville *Weekly Sun and Press*

NOTES

INTRODUCTION: BLACK LEADERSHIP IN THE POST–CIVIL WAR ERA

1. Richardson, *Negro in the Reconstruction of Florida;* Davis, *Civil War and Reconstruction;* Shofner, *Nor Is It Over Yet.*
2. Akin, "When a Minority Becomes the Majority"; Richardson, "History of Blacks in Jacksonville"; Kenney, "LaVilla."
3. Foner, *Freedom's Lawmakers*, vii.
4. Ibid., xiii.
5. Ibid.
6. Klingman, *Josiah Walls;* Warner, *Free Men in an Age of Servitude;* Dodd, "'Bishop' Pearce"; Richardson, "Jonathan C. Gibbs"; Brown, "Robert Meacham"; Clark, "John Wallace"; Beatty, "John Willis Menard"; Rivers, "James Page"; Wallace, *Carpetbag Rule in Florida.*
7. See Brown, *Ossian Bingley Hart.*
8. Brown, "Carpetbagger Intrigues."

CHAPTER 1: THE FOUNDERS

1. Coles, " 'Terrible and Sad Result,' " 158–59.
2. Foster and Foster, "Aid Societies," 316–17.
3. Trefousse, *Andrew Johnson*, 216–17; Shofner, *Nor Is It Over Yet*, 34–55.
4. Wallace, *Carpetbag Rule*, 38–39; "Public meeting at Fernandina, Feb. 25, 1866," undated clipping from Jacksonville *Florida Times*, box 19, Yulee papers, PKY; *Savannah Daily Herald*, March 17, 1866.
5. *DN&H*, June 28, 1866; Davis, *Civil War and Reconstruction*, 426.

6. Shofner, *Nor Is It Over Yet*, 169; *New York Times*, July 23, 1866.
7. Jacksonville *Florida Times*, quoted in Washington (D.C.) *Daily Morning Chronicle*, October 24, 1865.
8. *FU*, June 1, 1867; Brown, *Ossian Bingley Hart*, 159–60.
9. Wallace, *Carpetbag Rule*, 42–44; Richardson, *Negro in the Reconstruction of Florida*, 141.
10. Wallace, *Carpetbag Rule*, 42; Shuften, *Colored Man's Exposition*, 20.
11. Rivers, "James Page."
12. Anderson, *A. Philip Randolph*, 30.
13. Ibid., 29.
14. McKinney and McKinney, *History of Black Baptists*, 37–40.
15. Dodd, " 'Bishop' Pearce," 6.
16. Long, *History of the A.M.E. Church*, 52–60; *CR*, June 9, 1866.
17. See Schafer, "Freedom Was as Close as the River," and Coles " 'They Fought Like Devils.' "
18. Clark, "John Wallace"; Owen B. Armstrong MPR 783295; William Henry Ford MPR 487862.
19. Klingman, *Josiah Walls*, 6–11; Richard H. Black MPR C2534208; Henry S. Harmon MSR, M-589, roll 37.
20. Foner, *Freedom's Lawmakers*, 261–91.
21. *DN&H*, April 22, 1867.
22. Tallahassee *Semi-Weekly Floridian*, March 26, 1867; *New York Herald*, April 8, 17, 1867; *SAE*, May 11, 1867.
23. *DN&H*, May 8, 1867; *SDR*, May 4, 1867; *SAE*, May 11, 1867.
24. Klingman, *Neither Dies Nor Surrenders*, 17–19; Brown, *Ossian Bingley Hart*, 187–89; *FU*, August 6, 1868; *SDR*, May 4, 1867; *DN&H*, May 8, 1867; *CR*, August 10, 1867.
25. *FU*, June 1, 1867.
26. Brown, *Ossian Bingley Hart*, 190–95; Davis, *Civil War and Reconstruction*, 470–74.
27. *FU*, July 20, 1867; *New York Daily Tribune*, July 27, 1867.
28. *FU*, July 20, 1867; Pensacola *Daily News*, November 18, 1906.
29. *New York Daily Tribune*, February 5, 1868; *WF*, February 11, 1868.
30. Brown, *Ossian Bingley Hart*, 200–201; John T. Sprague to J. F. Meline, June 4, 5, 1867, VR corr., RG 393, entry 5782, box 2, NA.
31. O. B. Hart to James F. Meline, September 5, 1867, VR corr., RG 393, entry 5782, box 2, NA; Brown, "Robert Meacham," 6; *TS*, April 9, 1868.
32. *CR*, September 28, 1867.
33. Shofner, *Nor Is It Over Yet*, 174–76; *DN&H*, October 2, 1867; *FU*, November 23, 1867.

34. Wallace, *Carpetbag Rule*, 49–57; Shofner, *Nor Is It Over Yet*, 177–82; Long, *History of the A.M.E. Church*, 68–69; *New York Daily Tribune*, February 5, 1868.
35. O. B. Hart to John T. Sprague, February 4, 1868, Telegrams Sent and Received, Hd. Qtrs., Dist. of Fla., Sept. 23, 1867–October 1, 1868, RG 393, entry 1692, vol. 1, NA.
36. Shofner, *Nor Is It Over Yet*, 182–84; Brown, *Ossian Bingley Hart*, 209–11; *FU*, February 15, 1868; *DN&H*, February 12, 13, 27, 1868.
37. Shofner, *Nor Is It Over Yet*, 184–87.
38. *TS*, February 13, 1868; Shofner, *Nor Is It Over Yet*, 180.
39. *DN&H*, February 27, 1868; Brown, *Ossian Bingley Hart*, 213–16; Jacksonville *East Floridian*, quoted in *TS*, April 9, 1868.
40. *DN&H*, April 17, 1868.
41. Daniel Richards to Elihu P. Washburn, May 7, 1868, vol. 59, Washburn papers, LC.
42. *CR*, April 4, 1868; Daniel Richards to Thaddeus Stevens, March 18, 1868, box 4, Stevens papers, LC.
43. Davis, *Civil War and Reconstruction*, 524; *TS*, April 9, 1868; *WF*, April 14, 1868.
44. *TS*, June 18, 1868; *DN&H*, June 23, 1868.
45. Brown, *Ossian Bingley Hart*, 217–19; Newark (N.J.) *Sentinel of Freedom*, July 7, 1868.

CHAPTER 2: THE STRUGGLE FOR POWER

1. *DN&H*, June 24, 1868.
2. *SMN*, July 23, 1873.
3. Shofner, *Nor Is It Over Yet*, 196–97; Wallace, *Carpetbag Rule*, 81; *SMN*, November 11, 1868. On local black appointments, generally, see the biographical directory and appendix in this volume.
4. *New York Times*, August 18, 1868.
5. *FP*, August 22, 1868.
6. Ibid.
7. Wallace, *Carpetbag Rule*, 83–84; Davis, *Civil War and Reconstruction*, 542–46.
8. *Norfolk* (Va.) *Journal and Guide*, October 15, 1927.
9. Wallace, *Carpetbag Rule*, 54; *New York Tribune*, February 5, 1868; Osborn, "Letters," 267; *Norfolk* (Va.) *Journal and Guide*, October 15, 1927.
10. Shofner, *Nor Is It Over Yet*, 203; Wallace, *Carpetbag Rule*, 88.

11. *WF*, November 3, 1868; Brown, "Robert Meacham," 11. For local appointments, generally, see the appendix to this volume.
12. *TS*, January 29, 1870; Shofner, *Nor Is It Over Yet*, 204.
13. Shofner, *Nor Is It Over Yet*, 204–05.
14. Ibid.; Brown, *Ossian Bingley Hart*, 232–33.
15. Wallace, *Carpetbag Rule*, 91, 98–100.
16. *SMN*, January 4, 1869.
17. *FU*, February 11, 1869.
18. Shofner, *Nor Is It Over Yet*, 150–51.
19. *FU*, February 18, 1869; *SDA*, March 6, 1869; Davis, *Civil War and Reconstruction*, 569; Shofner, *Jackson County*, 279–93.
20. Shofner, *Nor Is It Over Yet*, 209–11. For more on the Swepson-Littlefield fraud, see Fenlon, "Notorious Swepson-Littlefield Fraud."
21. Brown, "Carpetbagger Intrigues," 278–81; *TS*, February 12, 1870; Ambrose B. Hart to "My dear Bro. Ed," September 2, 1870, Hart letters, PKY.
22. Menard, "Negro in Politics," 594.
23. Jacksonville *Evening Telegram*, August 15, 1893; *FT-U*, May 10, 1894.
24. Klingman, *Josiah Walls*, 33–34.
25. *SDR*, August 25, 1870; *WF*, August 23, 1870; *TS*, August 20, 1870; Klingman, *Josiah Walls*, 33–35; Brown, "Robert Meacham," 15–16; Richardson, *Negro in the Reconstruction of Florida*, 178.
26. Shofner, *Nor Is It Over Yet*, 214–16; Brown, "Robert Meacham," 17; *SMN*, November 14, 1870.
27. *TS*, January 7, 1871; Dodd, " 'Bishop' Pearce," 8; Rivers, "James Page."
28. *CR*, October 21, 1871.
29. Ibid., July 29, 1871.
30. Dodd, " 'Bishop' Pearce, 9–10.
31. *TS*, July 8, 1871; Brown, "Carpetbagger Intrigues," 283.
32. Brown, "Carpetbagger Intrigues," 283–85; Jonathan C. Gibbs to O. O. Howard, February 14, 1872, Howard papers, Bowdoin College Library.
33. *SMN*, January 19, 1872.
34. Wallace, *Carpetbag Rule*, 154, 159.
35. Brown, "Carpetbagger Intrigues," 286–87.
36. Ibid., 288–90.
37. *WF*, July 30, August 6, 1872; Brown, "Carpetbagger Intrigues," 291–93.
38. *WF*, August 13, 1872.
39. Ibid., March 24, 1874.
40. Brown, "Carpetbagger Intrigues," 296–98; *WF*, September 17, 1872; New Orleans *Daily Picayune*, November 3, 1872; Carson, "William Dunnington Bloxham," 76.

41. "The Florida Election [1872]—Official State Canvass" in Election Returns (1862–87), vol. 1, 70, RG 156, series 1258, FSA; *CR*, December 28, 1872.
42. Brown, *Ossian Bingley Hart*, 274. See also the biographical directory and appendix in this volume.
43. Ibid., 274–81.
44. Ibid., 272–74. For local appointments, see the appendix to this volume.
45. Ossian B. Hart to Ozias Buddington, March 1, 1873, Governors' Letterbooks, RG 101, series 32, vol. 8, folder 1 (Jan.–Apr. 1873), FSA.
46. Brown, *Ossian Bingley Hart*, 283–84.
47. Newark (N.J.) *Sentinel of Freedom*, March 25, 1873.
48. Florida *Senate Journal* (1874), 12.
49. Savannah *Advertiser-Republican*, February 22, 1874.
50. *WF*, May 27, 1873; Brown, *Ossian Bingley Hart*, 293–96.

CHAPTER 3: THE COLLAPSE OF DREAMS

1. Wallace, *Carpetbag Rule*, 295.
2. Savannah *Advertiser-Republican*, April 29, 1874.
3. *SMN*, July 29, 1874.
4. Jacksonville *Tri-Weekly Florida Union*, June 18, 1874; Wallace, *Carpetbag Rule*, 293.
5. Brown, "Robert Meacham," 23; Wallace, *Carpetbag Rule*, 299; Jacksonville *Tri-Weekly Florida Union*, August 18, 1874.
6. *TS*, August 29, 1874.
7. Brown, "Robert Meacham," 23–29; *TS*, August 29, 1874.
8. *TS*, quoted in Jacksonville *Tri-Weekly Florida Union*, August 18, 1874.
9. Jacksonville *Tri-Weekly Florida Union*, August 18, 1874.
10. *WF*, December 15, 1874; Shofner, *Nor Is It Over Yet*, 295–96; Wallace, *Carpetbag Rule*, 307–08.
11. *Jacksonville Press*, quoted in *WF*, August 3, 1875.
12. Dodd, " 'Bishop' Pearce," 12; *DFU*, June 13, 1876; Klingman, *Josiah Walls*, 111–14.
13. *CR*, February 18, 1875.
14. *TS*, April 9, 1868; *CR*, January 30, 1873; Jacksonville *Evening Telegram*, January 6, 1892.
15. *CR*, June 12, 1873; *Key West Democrat*, November 1, 1880; *WF*, September 29, October 6, 1874, August 17, 1875; Davis, *Civil War and Reconstruction*, 644; Shofner, *Jefferson County*, 330.
16. *CR*, April 13, 1876.
17. *DFU*, December 6, 1881.

18. Washington (D.C.) *People's Advocate*, July 19, 1879.
19. *FT-U*, April 26, 1889.
20. *SMN*, May 30, 1870; *TS*, November 5, 1870; Brown, "Robert Meacham," 30; *Norfolk* (Va.) *Journal and Guide*, October 1, 1927.
21. *Norfolk* (Va.) *Journal and Guide*, October 1, 1927.
22. Stanaback, *History of Hernando County*, 162.
23. J. M. Hawks to Secretary of State, March 18, 1871, Resignations and Removals, RG 150, series 24, box 6, FSA; Executive Order, dated January 17, 1873, included with S. C. Cobb to J. M. Tarble, July 21, 1882, Customhouse Nominations, Pensacola, RG 56, entry 246, box 074, NA.
24. William G. Stewart to Ossian B. Hart, May 15, 1873, James D. English to Hart, March 2, 1873, and James D. English to Marcellus Stearns, October 23, 1875, Resignations and Removals, RG 150, series 24, box 6, FSA; *WF*, March 4, 1873; *SDA*, March 11, 1873; Savannah *Advertiser-Republican*, November 6, 1873; John V. Cornell to B. H. Bristow, October 30, 1874, Customhouse Nominations, Cedar Keys, box 063, and Charles V. Hillyer to John Sherman, August 18, 1879, Customhouse Nominations, Fernandina, RG 56, entry 246, box 066, NA.
25. Foner, *Freedom's Lawmakers*, 564–601; Shofner, *Nor Is It Over Yet*, 303.
26. Shofner, *Nor Is It Over Yet*, 301–03; Klingman, *Josiah Walls*, 110–14.
27. Shofner, *Nor Is It Over Yet*, 306; *Gainesville Times*, October 5, 1876.
28. *Quitman* (Ga.) *Reporter*, September 14, 1876; Thomasville (Ga.) *Southern Enterprise*, November 1, 1876.
29. *SMN*, October 25, 1876.
30. *WF*, June 5, 1877.
31. Shofner, *Nor Is It Over Yet*, 310–11.
32. Klingman, *Josiah Walls*, 115; Davis, *Civil War and Reconstruction*, 731.
33. Shofner, *Nor Is It Over Yet*, 314–27; *WF*, December 19, 1876.
34. See the biographical directory and the appendix in this volume.
35. *Laws of Florida* (1877), 64–73; *DS&P*, July 20, 1877; DeLand *Volusia County Herald*, July 12, 1877; *FT-U*, February 7, 1884.
36. *WFU*, July 14, 1877; *WF*, June 19, 1877.
37. *DS&P*, July 8, 1877; Shuften, *Colored Man's Exposition*, 40.
38. Dodd, " 'Bishop' Pearce," 12; Brown, "Robert Meacham," 31–32; WF, March 11, 1879; *New York Tribune*, April 26, 1878.
39. Drake, *Florida Legislature*, 55; *NYG*, June 30, 1883.
40. *FM*, April 17, 1880.

41. For biographical information on Thomas V. Gibbs, John R. Scott, Jr., and Peter H. Davidson, Jr., see the biographical directory in this volume.
42. *WF*, December 10, 1878, December 12, 1886; *FM*, December 11, 1880; Florida *Senate Journal* (1885); Florida *House Journal* (1885).
43. *WF*, May 14, 1878; Brown, "Robert Meacham," 31–32; *CR*, June 13, October 3, 10, 1878; *FT-U*, January 25, 1885; Birmingham (England) *Good Templars' Watchword*, April 4, 1877, January 8, 1879; Washington (D.C.) *People's Advocate*, March 27, 1880. On the Good Templars in Florida, see Fahey, *Temperance and Racism*, 119–25.
44. *WF*, May 11, 1880.
45. Tallahassee *Semi-Weekly Floridian*, August 13, October 22, 1880; *New York Tribune*, October 19, 1880.
46. *DFU*, June 2, December 15, 1882; Williamson, *Florida Politics*, 85–89; *WF*, August 29, September 12, October 17, 1882; *FDT*, September 10, 1882; Shofner, *Jefferson County*, 342.

CHAPTER 4: A REFUGE IN THE TOWNS

1. *New York Herald*, April 17, 1867; Gainesville *New Era*, March 30, April 6, 1867.
2. Nassau County Deed Records, Book L, a; Pensacola *West Florida Commercial*, January 26, 1869; Pensacola *Tri-Weekly Observer*, February 3, 1869; *FU*, March 18, July 1, 1869; Grismer, *Tampa*, 155; record of incorporation, city clerk's office, Gainesville.
3. Walker, *Ninth Census—Volume 1*, 97–99; Davis, *History of Jacksonville*, 500.
4. U.S. Department of the Interior, Census Office, *Statistics of the Population of the United States at the Tenth Census (June 1, 1880)*, 117–19.
5. Morris, *Florida Handbook*, 565; Department of the Interior, Census Office, *Report on the Population of the United States at the Eleventh Census 1890, Part 1*, 83–87.
6. *NYF*, February 28, 1885, May 8, 1886; *NYG*, August 18, 1883, April 26, 1884; Brown, "Bishop Payne," 26–27.
7. *NYA*, May 25, 1889.
8. See Smith, *Slavery and Plantation Growth in Antebellum Florida.*
9. *FDT*, March 17, 1882.
10. Census Office, *Eleventh Census 1890*, 13; *WF*, December 19, 1891; *FT-U*, September 20, 1885. For black officials at Marianna, Quincy, Tallahassee, and Madison, see the appendix to this volume.

11. Walker, *Ninth Census—Volume 1*, 97–99; *CR*, August 26, 1880.
12. *CR*, October 27, 1887.
13. See the appendix to this volume.
14. Gainesville *Florida Sentinel*, 1895 special edition.
15. Walker, *Ninth Census—Volume 1*, 98. See also the appendix to this volume.
16. Tebeau, *History of Florida*, 272–92; Brown, *Florida's Peace River Frontier*, 255–91.
17. Live Oak Minute Book (April 24, 1878–April 13, 1903), 3–31, city clerk's office; *FT-U*, March 31, 1885; roster of city officials, office of DeLand city clerk and auditor; Sanford incorporation minutes, Sanford Museum; Sanford town council minute books, city clerk's office.
18. Department of Commerce, Bureau of the Census, *Negro Population*, 778; *FT-U*, July 30, 1885; Otey, *Eatonville*, 1–3; *Orange County Black Communities Survey*, 81.
19. *SMN*, March 9, 1881. See also the appendix to this volume.
20. *Palatka Daily News*, April 8, 1887.
21. See the appendix to this volume.
22. Ibid.; *FT-U&C*, November 2, 1902.
23. See the appendix to this volume.
24. *DFU*, April 4, 17, 1876; *Gainesville Times*, April 14, 1877; *TS*, January 1, August 5, 1876; *SMN*, August 16, 1877; *WF*, April 10, 1877; St. Augustine City Council Minute Book (August 7, 1871–August 12, 1878), 381, 476–77; *FM*, April 19, 1879.
25. *WF*, February 24, 1880; St. Augustine City Council Minute Book (August 7, 1871–August 12, 1878), 160, 216; *FDT*, April 14, 1882; *FT-U*, April 17, 1886.
26. *SMN*, March 21, 1877; *WF*, December 26, 1876; *TS*, December 23, 1876; *DFU*, March 25, 1882; *DS&P*, July 14, 1877; *WFU*, July 21, 1877.
27. *FT-U*, January 28, 1885.
28. Ibid., November 28, 1993.
29. Madison *New Enterprise*, December 22, 1904.
30. Jacksonville *Metropolis*, December 26, 1918.
31. Ocala *Evening Star*, January 23, 1901.
32. Madison *Enterprise-Recorder*, June 4, 1926.
33. Rivers and Brown, "African Americans in South Florida." See also the biographical directory and appendix in this volume.
34. *FT-U*, April 7, 1885.
35. Ibid., April 5, 1887.
36. *NYA*, May 25, 1889; Mobile (Ala.) *Daily Register*, January 10, 1873.
37. Wallace, *Carpetbag Rule;* Davis, *Civil War and Reconstruction.*

38. *FP*, November 16, 1870; *WF*, November 25, 1873; *DFU*, October 16, 1876.
39. *WF*, November 26, 1878.
40. *Laws of Florida* (1881), 110–16; *SMN*, April 19, 1881; *FM*, July 9, 1881.
41. Williamson, *Florida Politics*, 107, 125–26, 130–32; Boyd and Reder, "History of the Supreme Court of Florida," 1040; *Laws of Florida* (1885), 46–49; *CR*, May 28, 1885.

CHAPTER 5: THE ROAD TO DISFRANCHISEMENT

1. *DFU*, May 16, 1882.
2. Williamson, *Florida Politics*, 83–91.
3. *DFU*, January 5, 26, 27, 1883; Williamson, *Florida Politics*, 93.
4. *NYG*, April 21, 1883.
5. Ibid., May 26, 1883.
6. Hall, *Magic Mirror*, 145–46; Woodward, *Strange Career*, 70–71.
7. *FT-U*, December 15, 1883.
8. *NYG*, February 9, 1884.
9. Eustis *New Yorker*, quoted in *FT-U*, May 24, 1884.
10. Williamson, *Florida Politics*, 114.
11. Ibid., 104–08; Klingman, *Neither Dies Nor Surrenders*, 89; *FT-U*, June 29, 1884.
12. *FT-U*, November 18, 1884.
13. Williamson, *Florida Politics*, 125.
14. *WF*, December 2, 1884.
15. *Laws of Florida* (1885), 46–49; *CR*, May 28, 1885; *FT-U*, February 12, 1885.
16. *FT-U*, February 10, 18, 1885; *WF*, February 19, 1885.
17. *CR*, May 7, 1885.
18. *FT-U*, February 22, August 22, 1889, January 7, 1892.
19. *NYA*, July 14, 1888.
20. Williamson, *Florida Politics*, 133.
21. Ibid., 129–41. See also the appendix to this volume.
22. *NYF*, September 12, 1885.
23. McLauren, *Knights of Labor*, 47, 131–48; Brown, "Prelude to the Poll Tax."
24. J. A. Bodenhamer to T. V. Powderly, April 15, 1889, reel 30, Powderly papers, Catholic University.
25. Brown, "Prelude to the Poll Tax."
26. See the appendix to this volume. As to blacks voting for Democrats, see, for example, *NYF*, June 4, 1887.

27. Williamson, *Florida Politics*, 142–43; *FT-U*, November 2, 1886; Brown, "Prelude to the Poll Tax"; *SMN*, April 12, 1887.
28. Brown, "Prelude to the Poll Tax."
29. Ibid.; Hawes, "Diary leads to rediscovery"; Philadelphia *Journal of United Labor*, August 13, 1887.
30. *NYF*, June 25, 1887.
31. Brown, "Prelude to the Poll Tax"; Akin, "When a Minority Becomes the Majority," 134.
32. Philadelphia *Journal of United Labor*, December 3, 1887.
33. *FT-U*, January 29, 1888.
34. Jacksonville *Southern Leader*, ca. January 1887, quoted in *NYF*, February 5, 1887.
35. *NYA*, July 28, 1888.
36. Brown, "Prelude to the Poll Tax."
37. Ibid.; *WF*, January 1, 1889. See also the appendix to this volume.
38. *Laws of Florida* (1889, 2d sess.), 13–14; *FT-U*, June 13, July 11, 1889; Akin, "When a Minority Becomes the Majority," 137–39; Jackson, "Negro and the Law," 94; Brown, "Prelude to the Poll Tax."
39. Ayers, *Promise of the New South*, 146–49; Proctor, *Napoleon Bonaparte Broward*, 154–55, 173–75.
40. McLauren, *Knights of Labor*, 158–59, 174–79; *FT-U*, May 4, 1890.
41. *FT-U*, August 20, 1890.
42. Ibid., May 19, 1890.
43. Indianapolis *Freeman*, November 11, 1893.
44. *FT-U*, June 20, 1890.
45. Ayers, *Promise of the New South*, 214–37; Williamson, *Florida Politics*, 183; *NYA*, November 2, 1889; *WF*, April 16, 1890.
46. Ayers, *Promise of the New South*, 237–48; Gainesville *Florida Sentinel*, July 17, 1891; *FT-U*, June 4, 1890.
47. Williamson, *Florida Politics*, 183–87.
48. Klingman, *Neither Dies Nor Surrenders*, 109; Casdorph, *Republicans, Negroes, and Progressives*, 10, 49, 97–98, 162; Menard, "Negro in Politics," 600.
49. Lee papers, box 1, folder: "Collector of Internal Revenue, Schedules for Stamps, etc. 1913," FSA; *FT-U*, April 12, 1913; *NYA*, March 26, 1914; *FT-U&C*, November 9, 1898; Hawes, "One official's untold story."
50. See the appendix to this volume.
51. See, for example, *Madison Recorder*, September 18, 1896, April 10, 1903; *FT-U*, April 9, 1896, April 7, 1898; St. Augustine City Council Minute Book I (March 2, 1898–June 25, 1904), 658–59.

52. *FT-U*, June 19, 21, 22, 1921; *Tampa Tribune*, June 22, 1921.
53. Report of the acting secretary, November 1920, and report of the secretary, December 1920, part 1, reel 4, National Association for the Advancement of Colored People papers, LC; Jones and McCarthy, *African Americans in Florida*, 81–82; McCluskey, "Ringing Up a School," 213–14.
54. Flynt, *Duncan Upshaw Fletcher*, 134–35.
55. Dodd, " 'Bishop' Pearce," 6.

BIOGRAPHICAL DIRECTORY

1. Monroe County census, 1885, 1900; Key West burial records, Monroe County May Hill Russell Library.
2. F. N. Wicker to Sec. of Treas., March 22, 1880, Customhouse Nominations, Key West, RG 56, entry 246, box 68, NA; 1870, 1910 Monroe County censuses; Key West burial records.
3. St. Johns County census, 1885; DCI (card) 01504.
4. Putnam County census, 1910, 1920; Hoffman, "Westview Cemetery."
5. Madison County census, 1885; Duval County probate file 3745-D.
6. Suwannee County census, 1880, 1885.
7. Levy County census, 1900; Cedar Key cemetery records.
8. Duval County census, 1900; *FT-U*, October 29, 1916.
9. Marion County census, 1870, 1885.
10. MPR 1,039,614; 1900 Duval County census.
11. Duval County census, 1870; Jacksonville *Tri-Weekly Florida Union*, January 18, 1873.
12. Duval County census, 1870, 1885; 1893 Jacksonville city directory.
13. Clay County census, 1870.
14. Wright, *Centennial Encyclopaedia*, 25; MPR 559523; 1870 Columbia County census; Kealing, *History of African Methodism in Texas*, 207–09, quote on p. 209.
15. Leon County census, 1870, 1885; 1910 DeSoto County census; MPR 783295; *A.M.E. Church Review* 25 (July 1908), 81–82; Vernon Peeples interview.
16. Birmingham (England) *Good Templars' Watchword*, December 27, 1876, March 12, 1879; 1885 Monroe County census; FT-U, April 3, 1903.
17. Nassau County census, 1870, 1895; November 1864 Fernandina census, Amelia Island Museum of History; Nassau County probate file 39.
18. Duval County census, 1870; Duval County probate file 180-D.

19. Jacob Reed Ballard to Sec. of Treas., February 12, 1876, records relating to Customhouse Nominations, Fernandina, RG 56, entry 246, box 66, NA; 1880 Nassau County census; *FT-U*, February 11, 1892; MPR Navy SC 13678/XNS C0012944.
20. *NYA*, April 13, 1889, August 22, 1891; Shofner, "Florida," 102; DCI v. 303, #12657 (1926).
21. Thomes, *Early Vital Records*, 1:249; 1870 Escambia County census; Pensacola *Daily News*, March 12, 1893.
22. Jackson County census, 1870, 1880.
23. Ibid.
24. Ibid., 1870, 1880, 1885.
25. Nassau County census, 1870, 1900, 1910.
26. Alachua County census, 1870.
27. Nassau County census, 1870, 1900; Nassau County probate file 61.
28. Putnam County census, 1870, 1885, 1900, 1910, 1920; DCI v. 112, #12281 (1920).
29. Jefferson County census, 1870, 1900; *CR*, October 13, 1887; Jefferson County Deed Book BB, 494.
30. Orange County census, 1900; 1920 Seminole County census; DCI v. 966, #20449 (1941).
31. St. Johns County census, 1885.
32. Ibid., 1870; 1875 list of registered voters, St. Johns County, in Election Returns, RG 156, series 21, box 21, FSA.
33. Levy County census, 1885; 1900 Alachua County census; DCI v. 221, #8995 (1924).
34. Orange County census, 1900; DCI v. 393, #14740 (1928).
35. Drake, *Florida Legislature*, 38–39; 1880 Jefferson County census; DCI v. 134, #8650 (1921).
36. Marion County census, 1870.
37. Alachua County census, 1870; MPR #C2534208; Davis, *Civil War and Reconstruction*, 731.
38. St. Johns County census, 1880, 1900, 1910.
39. Ibid., 1885, 1900.
40. Orange County census, 1885; 1910 Duval County census; *NYF*, May 22, 1886; Otey, *Eatonville*, 7; DCI v. 39, #5805 (1918).
41. Nassau County census, 1870; MPR #798832.
42. Marion County census, 1880, 1885; Ocala *East Florida Banner*, May 13, 1876.
43. Duval census, 1885, 1900; 1905 Jacksonville city directory.
44. Nassau County census, 1870; Bosque Bello cemetery records, Amelia Island Museum of History.

45. Wakulla County census, 1870, 1885, 1900, 1920; DCI v. 148, #2141 (1922).
46. Freedmen's Bank register of signatures, Tallahassee, M816, roll 5, NA; 1870 Jefferson County census; Long, *History of the A.M.E. Church*, 196; *CR*, August 18, 1887; Butler, *Butler's History*, 64; *FU*, July 20, 1867; *WF*, November 26, 1867.
47. Clay County census, 1870; Clay County Probate Records (July Bram), Order Book 2 (1889–1902), 137.
48. Clay County Census, 1880; Clay County Probate Records, Order Book 2 (1889–1902), 137.
49. Wakulla County census, 1885.
50. Orange County census, 1900, 1910; DCI v. 650, #21158 (1934).
51. Jacksonville *Tri-Weekly Florida Union*, January 9, 1873.
52. DCI v. 113, #12845 (1920).
53. Sumter County census, 1870, 1880, 1885, 1900.
54. Monroe County census, 1870.
55. MPR #427340; Long, *History of the A.M.E. Church*, 197.
56. Putnam County census, 1885, 1900, 1910, 1920; DCI v. 374, #5030 (1928).
57. Duval County census, 1880, 1885; 1896 Jacksonville city directory.
58. Drake, *Florida Legislature*, 54; 1880 Duval County census; Duval County probate file 18743-D; *FT-U*, February 19, 1995.
59. Nassau County census, 1870, 1880, 1900.
60. Madison County census, 1870; Madison County probate file A-147.
61. Putnam County census, 1900, 1920; DCI v. 1189, #4641 (1946).
62. Gordon, *Afro-Americans*, 126; Tampa *Sunland Tribune*, April 7, 1877; Hillsborough County probate packets, file #388.
63. Jackson County census, 1870.
64. MPR #587872.
65. Julius J. Gordon, Tampa, Fla., to author, January 22, 1992, collection of the author; Peter W. Bryant to John F. Horr, August 26, 1889, records relating to Customhouse Nominations, Key West, RG 56, entry 246, box 69, NA; *NYA*, August 1, 1912; Rivers and Brown, "African Americans in South Florida," 12–13.
66. Duval County census, 1870; DCI v. 16, #7984 (1917).
67. Madison County census, 1870, 1880, 1885; 1910 Duval County census.
68. MPR #520610.
69. Monroe County census, 1880, 1885; 1895 Nassau County census; 1900, 1910 Duval County censuses; Jacksonville *Evening Telegram*, March 3, 1892.
70. Escambia County census, 1870; Thomes, *Early Vital Records*, 3:45.
71. Calhoun County census, 1885; 1900 Duval County census; 1908 Jacksonville city directory.

72. Hiram Potter, Jr., to Sec. of Treas., May 16, 1874, records relating to Customhouse Nominations, Pensacola, RG 56, entry 246, box 73, NA; 1880 Escambia County census; 1910 Walton County census; Long, *History of the A.M.E. Church*, 54–56.
73. Duval County census, 1885; 1899 Jacksonville city directory.
74. Jackson County census, 1880, 1885; Jackson County Deed Book CC, 241.
75. Levy County census, 1885, 1900.
76. Polk County census, 1900; 1885 Orange County census; DCI v. 135, #9325 (1921).
77. Talbert, *Sons of Allen*, 68–69.
78. Whitfield, *Florida State Government*, 50; 1885, 1900, 1920 Leon County censuses; DCI v. 512, #12767 (1931); *WF*, November 16, 1880.
79. Leon County census, 1880, 1885, 1900, 1920; *WF*, November 16, 1880.
80. Columbia County census, 1870, 1880, 1900.
81. Orange County census, 1870.
82. Marion County census, 1870.
83. Drake, *Florida Legislature*, 55; 1885 Marion County census; Lakeland *Evening Ledger and Star-Telegram*, March 27, 30, 31, 1938; Work, "Some Negro Members," 70. As to Chandler in Lakeland, see Hubener, "Lakeland Jubilee"; Rivers and Brown, "African Americans in South Florida," 14–15.
84. Duval County census, 1870, 1880, 1900; 1905 Jacksonville city directory.
85. *NYG*, September 27, 1884; *FT-U*, September 17, 1884; 1880 Duval County census.
86. Hillsborough County census, 1870; Hillsborough County probate packet 534; Welch, *Tampa's Elected Officials*, 15.
87. Leon County census, 1885; Leon County probate file 2024.
88. Alachua County census, 1870, 1880; Alachua County probate administration file 67.
89. Duval County census, 1880; *FDT*, April 21, 1882; 1889 Jacksonville city directory.
90. Orange County census, 1885, 1900, 1910; Otey, *Eatonville*, 16; DCI v. 062, #6586 (1916).
91. Franklin County census, 1870.
92. Orange County census, 1910, 1920; *Orange County Black Communities Survey*, 81; DCI v. 377, #6678 (1928).
93. Joseph N. Clinton death certificate, Florida Office of Vital Statistics; 1880 Alachua County census; *FT-U*, February 11, 1892; Richardson, *National Cyclopedia of the Colored Race*, 1:381; Hawes, "One official's untold story"; *Tampa Tribune*, September 8, 1927; *Tampa Daily Times*,

September 8, 1927; Rivers and Brown, "African Americans in South Florida," 13–14.

94. Leon County census, 1870, 1885, 1900.
95. Nassau County census, 1880; 1900, 1920 Duval County censuses; DCI v. 278, #165 (1926).
96. Madison County census, 1880, 1900; *Madison Recorder*, October 4, 1889; Madison County probate file A-223; Madison *Enterprise-Recorder*, June 4, 1926.
97. Marion County census, 1885.
98. Ocala *East Florida Banner*, October 24, 1874.
99. Hamilton County census, 1870.
100. Santa Rosa County census, 1885.
101. Franklin County census, 1870.
102. Taylor County census, 1870.
103. Putnam County census, 1885; Janice S. Mahaffey, Office of the Putnam County Clerk of the Circuit Court, to author, April 5, 1994, collection of the author.
104. Monroe County census, 1870, 1885, 1900.
105. Ibid., 1870, 1885; Key West burial records.
106. Freedmen's Bank register of signatures, Tallahassee; 1870, 1880, 1885, 1900 Leon County censuses.
107. Leon County census, 1870; 1880 Duval County census.
108. Madison County census, 1885.
109. Jefferson County census, 1870; Long, *History of the A.M.E. Church*, 199; Wright, *Centennial Encyclopaedia*, 309.
110. Nassau County census, 1880, 1895, 1900, 1910; DCI v. 033, #4105 (1914).
111. Leon County census, 1870.
112. Gadsden County census, 1870, 1885; Womack, *Gadsden*, 136.
113. Walton County census, 1880.
114. Freedmen's Bank register of signatures, Tallahassee.
115. Thomes, *Early Vital Records*, 3:74; 1885 Escambia County census.
116. Peter H. Davidson, Jr., to J. M. Tarble, July 17, 1882, records relating to Customhouse Nominations, Pensacola, RG 56, entry 246, box 74, NA; 1885 Escambia census; DCI v. 085, #12405 (1919); *NYF*, February 12, 1887.
117. Marion County census, 1880, 1885, 1900.
118. Putnam County census, 1885.
119. Drake, *Florida Legislature*, 35–36.
120. Leon County census, 1870, 1885, 1900; DCI; *WF*, April 8, 1879.

121. Marion County census, 1870; *SMN*, March 9, 1881; Marion County probate file, cabinet 1, box 13.
122. Marion County census, 1885; Gainesville *Daily Sun*, November 2, 1890; Marion County probate file, cabinet 1, box 14.
123. Key West *Daily Equator and Democrat* (trade edition), March 1889; 1870 Suwannee County census; *CR*, August 23, 1888, May 1, 1902; *NYA*, January 14, 1915; *FT-U*, December 23, 1914; *NYG*, February 16, 1884.
124. Leon County census, 1870; *WF*, February 23, 1875.
125. Leon County census, 1870; 1885 Duval County census; Duval County probate file 587 (Margaret N. DeCoursey).
126. Leon County census, 1870; *WF*, November 16, 1875; *TS*, November 13, 1875.
127. Bosque Bello cemetery records; 1870, 1880, 1895 Nassau County censuses.
128. Bosque Bello cemetery records; 1870 Nassau County census; *FT-U*, February 21, 1891.
129. Nassau County census, 1895, 1900; Nassau County probate file 194.
130. Nassau County census, 1870, 1880, 1895; Bosque Bello cemetery records.
131. Jefferson County census, 1870; 1880 Columbia County census; *CR*, May 9, 1889; *DFU*, March 7, 1876; Smith, *The African Methodist Episcopal Church*, 261.
132. Escambia census, 1885; Thomes, *Early Vital Records*, 3:81.
133. *History and Souvenir of Bethel Baptist Institutional Church;* 1900 Duval County census; Duval County probate file 3257-D.
134. Leon County census, 1870; 1880 Liberty County census; *Minutes of the Seventeenth Session of the Florida Annual Conference of the African Methodist Episcopal Church.*
135. Jefferson County census, 1870; Jacksonville *Evening Telegram*, January 30, 1894; *FT-U*, January 26, 1886; *FT-U&C*, December 2, 1900; Duval County probate file 588-D.
136. Marion County census, 1870, 1885.
137. Polk County census, 1870; 1880 Hillsborough County census; Brown, *Florida's Peace River Frontier*, 97, 177–78, 188, 206–07.
138. Nassau County census, 1870, 1880, 1895, 1900; DCI v. 034, #3016 (1918).
139. Freedmen's Bank register of signatures, Tallahassee; 1870, 1885 Leon County censuses; Leon County probate file 1419.
140. Leon County census, 1885, 1900, 1910, 1920.
141. MPR #478229; 1870 Putnam County census; Hoffman, "Westview Cemetery."

142. Columbia County census, 1870.
143. Alachua County census, 1870 and 1880 (mortality schedule); Long, *History of the A.M.E. Church*, 198.
144. Nassau County census, 1870, 1880, 1895, 1900; MPR #665733 (Edward F. Langley).
145. Escambia County census, 1870, 1885; DCI v. 001, #322 (1888); Hunter, *History of Pensacola's Black Community*.
146. Monroe County census, 1870, 1885, 1900, 1920; Key West burial records; *Key West Citizen*, October 3, 1938.
147. Gadsden County census, 1885, 1900, 1910; Gadsden County Deed Book CC, 180.
148. Nassau County census, 1880.
149. Columbia County census, 1870.
150. Zebulon Elijah to John M. Tarble, July 24, 1882, records relating to Customhouse Nominations, Pensacola, RG 56, entry 246, box 74, NA; 1870 Escambia County census; Zebulon Elijah biographical materials, Pensacola Historical Society; *Pensacola Journal*, December 3, 1910.
151. Duval County census, 1885, 1900, 1920; DCI v. 123, #3488 (1921).
152. St. Johns County census, 1880, 1885, 1900; DCI (card) 08622.
153. English, *James D. English;* 1870 Monroe County census.
154. N. F. English to George W. Allen, March 30, 1898, records relating to Customhouse Nominations, Key West, RG 56, entry 246, box 070, NA; 1870 Monroe County census; English, *Nelson Francis deSales English*.
155. *FT-U*, October 4, 1914; 1885 Duval County census.
156. Hillsborough County census, 1885; 1900 Manatee County census; *CR*, April 11, 1878.
157. Madison County census, 1870, 1885, 1910.
158. Jackson County General Index to Marriage Records (Males), 2:53; Genealogy Department, *Jackson County Tombstone Inscriptions*, 213.
159. Clay County census, 1880, 1900, 1920.
160. Alachua County census, 1880, 1900, 1910; Alachua County probate administration file 57.
161. Suwannee County census, 1870.
162. Monroe County census, 1880.
163. Leon County census, 1870, 1880.
164. Ibid., 1885.
165. Ibid., 1870, 1900.
166. Duval County census, 1870, 1880; 1887 Jacksonville city directory.
167. MPR #487862; 1885 Leon County census; Varick and Smith, *Tallahassee and Leon County Cemeteries*, 49.

168. Clay County census, 1900, 1920; DCI v. 728, #16686 (1936).
169. Hillsborough County census, 1870; 1900, 1920 Duval County censuses; DCI v. 477, #15198 (1930).
170. *FT-U*, January 28, 1897; 1870, 1880 Duval County censuses; Cleveland (Ohio) *Gazette*, February 6, 1897.
171. Madison County census, 1870; 1880 Duval County census.
172. *NYG*, August 18, 1883; 1870 Putnam County census; *FT-U*, July 28, 1883.
173. Nassau County census, 1870, 1900, 1910.
174. MPR #328117; 1870 Duval County census; *FT-U*, June 24, 1886.
175. Nassau County census, 1895; Fernandina Council Proceedings, Book B, 198.
176. Varick and Smith, *Tallahassee and Leon County Cemeteries*, 45; 1885 Leon County census; MPR #623587.
177. Leon County census, 1885, 1900.
178. Volusia County census, 1885, 1900, 1910; DCI v. 7, #3415 (1917).
179. Robert Gabriel to John F. Horr, August 1, 1889, records relating to Customhouse Nominations, Key West, RG 56, entry 246, box 069, NA; 1870, 1900 Monroe County censuses; Tom Hambright, Monroe County May Hill Russell Library, to author, July 13, 1993, collection of the author; *FT-U*, December 1897.
180. Payne, *Recollections*, 316; 1885 Marion County census; *NYA*, July 10, 1913; Marion County probate file, cabinet 1, box 143; Tallahassee *Florida Bureau of Immigration Monthly Bulletin*, February 1891.
181. Richard Gagnet to Hiram Potter, December 16, 1874, records relating to Customhouse Nominations, Pensacola, RG 56, entry 246, box 073, NA; 1870 Escambia County census; Thomes, *Early Vital Records*, 1:294; Pensacola *Daily News*, August 20, 1893.
182. Duval County census, 1870; 1876–1877 Jacksonville city directory.
183. Madison County census, 1870; 1885 Putnam County census.
184. Suwannee County census, 1870, 1880; 1900, 1910 Orange County censuses; 1920 Seminole County census; DCI v. 372, #4273 (1928).
185. Leon County census, 1870, 1885, 1900.
186. Duval County census, 1870, 1885; 1887 Jacksonville city directory.
187. Duval County census, 1870; Edwards, *Grave Markers*, 113.
188. Alachua County census, 1870, 1880.
189. Wakulla County census, 1870, 1885, 1900, 1910; DCI v. 123, #3431 (1921).
190. Jefferson County census, 1880, 1885; *CR*, June 19, 1902; *FT-U&C*, October 10, 1902.
191. Richardson, "Jonathan C. Gibbs"; Neyland, *Twelve Black Floridians*, 1–5; Jones and McCarthy, *African Americans in Florida*, 44–45; *New York Daily Tribune*, February 5, 1868.

192. *NYF,* April 11, 1885; Neyland and Riley, *History of Florida Agricultural and Mechanical University;* 14, 40; Johnson, *Along This Way*, 58.
193. Marion County census, 1870; *FT-U*, September 12, 1895.
194. Escambia County census, 1900; Thomes, *Early Vital Records*, 3:108, *Pensacola Journal*, October 7, 1906.
195. Gadsden County census, 1885; Gadsden County Deed Book L, 613.
196. Nassau County census, 1880, 1895, 1900.
197. Suwannee County census, 1885, 1900, 1910.
198. Nassau County census, 1870; *FU*, November 2, 1867; MPR #798832 (Peter Bonaud).
199. Marion County census, 1900, 1910; *TS*, December 23, 1871; Marion County probate files, cabinet 1, box 66.
200. Freedmen's Bank register of signatures, Tallahassee; Long, *History of the A.M.E. Church*, 171; 1870 Leon County census; 1885 Jefferson County census (mortality schedule).
201. Shofner, *Jackson County*, 284.
202. Kealing, *History of African Methodism in Texas*, 199–203; *A.M.E. Church Review* 5 (April 1889): 325–26; *NYA*, January 26, 1911.
203. Duval County census, 1870, 1880; *FT-U*, March 28, 1883.
204. Duval County census, 1870; Duval County probate file 822-D.
205. Seminole County census, 1920.
206. Duval County census, 1880, 1885; 1899 Jacksonville city directory.
207. Jefferson County census, 1880, 1885; Hardy, *Brown and Martin Family Reunion History*.
208. Madison County census, 1870, 1880, 1900, 1920; DCI v. 107, #9899 (1920).
209. Columbia County census, 1870, 1880.
210. Leon County census, 1885, 1900.
211. Duval County census, 1870, 1880, 1900; DCI v. 027, #1456 (1914).
212. MPR #721857; 1870, 1895 Nassau County censuses.
213. Whitfield, *Florida State Government*, 61; 1880, 1885 Wakulla County censuses; records of appointments of postmasters, M841, roll 21, NA; Tallahassee *True Democrat*, December 8, 1905.
214. Wakulla County census, 1870, 1880, 1885, 1900; Wakulla County probate records, Letters of Administration, Book 1, 118.
215. Leon County census, 1880, 1885; Jacksonville *Tri-Weekly Florida Union*, June 30, 1874; *WF,* November 12, 1878, August 26, 1886, December 31, 1889; *Norfolk* (Va.) *Journal and Guide*, October 22, 1927.
216. Hernando County census, 1870, 1880, 1885; 1900 Hillsborough County census; *NYG*, November 10, 1883.
217. Columbia County census, 1870; 1880 Duval County census.
218. Leon County census, 1870, 1885, 1900, 1910, 1920; DCI v. 199, #13931 (1923).

219. Escambia County census, 1870; Hiram Potter, Jr., to Sec. of Treas., December 2, 1873, records relating to Customhouse Nominations, Pensacola, RG 56, entry 246, box 073, NA.
220. Levy County census, 1870.
221. Columbia County census, 1870; *FP,* October 28, 1871; Columbia County Will Book A, 56–57.
222. Duval County census, 1885, 1900, 1910; 1935 Jacksonville city directory.
223. Calhoun County census, 1870; records of commissions, 1827–1978, series 259, RG 156, FSA.
224. Santa Rosa County census, 1880; 1910 Escambia County census; DCI v. 441, #17417.
225. Jacksonville *Tri-Weekly Florida Union*, January 9, 1873; *DFU*, March 7, 1876.
226. Escambia County census, 1870, 1885; Thomes, *Early Vital Records*, 1:308.
227. Levy County census, 1870.
228. Duval County census, 1880; 1900 Brevard County census.
229. Duval County census, 1870, 1885; 1892 Jacksonville city directory.
230. Sumter County census, 1885.
231. DCI lists Hernandez as white. Escambia County census, 1870; 1885–1886 Pensacola city directory; DCI v. 06, #3056 (1888).
232. Franklin County census, 1885.
233. Leon County census, 1870; *WF,* January 11, 1876; *TS*, January 8, 1876.
234. Duval County census, 1870, 1885; 1887 Jacksonville city directory.
235. St. Johns County census, 1870, 1885; *FT-U&C*, January 24, 1901.
236. Gadsden County census, 1870; *New York Daily Tribune*, February 5, 1868; Womack, *Gadsden*, 136; *WF,* August 17, 1875, April 2, 1878; Jacksonville *Evening Telegram*, May 18, 1893.
237. MPR #XC–2527134; *FT-U*, January 25, 1917.
238. Gordon, *Afro-Americans*, 61–62; 1870, 1900 Hillsborough County censuses.
239. Gordon, *Afro-Americans*, 63; 1860 Hillsborough County census.
240. Putnam County census, 1900; Janice S. Mahaffey, Office of the Putnam County Clerk of the Circuit Court, to the author, April 4, 1994, collection of the author.
241. St. Johns County census, 1880, 1885, 1910; 1918–19 St. Augustine city directory.
242. Duval County census, 1870, 1885; *FT-U*, January 23, 1889.
243. Duval County census, 1885, 1900; 1907 Jacksonville city directory.
244. Orange County census, 1900, 1910; *Sanford Herald*, November 25, 1910; Bordelon, "Zora Neale Hurston."

245. Gadsden County census, 1870; 1880, 1900 Franklin County censuses; Willie Speed interview.
246. Walton County census, 1870.
247. Duval County census, 1870.
248. Marion County census, 1885; *FT-U*, January 28, 1893; Jacksonville *Evening Telegram*, January 30, 1894; Ocala *East Florida Banner*, May 13, 1876.
249. Alachua County census, 1870, 1880; Alachua County will file 100.
250. Marion County census, 1885; *Struggle for Survival*, 7.
251. Leon County census, 1885; Leon County probate file 1109.
252. Drake, *Florida Legislature*, 36; 1870 Leon County census; Leon County probate file 1408.
253. Orange County census, 1900.
254. Madison County census, 1870.
255. Escambia County census, 1885, 1900, 1910; 1916 Pensacola city directory.
256. Nassau County census, 1870, 1880, 1895.
257. Johnson, *Along This Way*, 4, 16–17, 276; 1870 Duval County census.
258. Columbia County census, 1870; 1900 Suwannee County census; Lake City *Florida Index*, March 25, 1904.
259. Marion County census, 1880; Long, *History of the A.M.E. Church*, 65, 172.
260. Hillsborough County census, 1870; Gordon, *Afro-Americans*, 73.
261. Bosque Bello cemetery records; 1870, 1910 Nassau County censuses.
262. Walton County census, 1870.
263. Gadsden County census, 1870; Long, *History of the A.M.E. Church*, 197; *FT-U*, March 8, 1888; Jacksonville *Evening Telegram*, February 12, 1894.
264. Leon County census, 1870, 1885.
265. Ibid., 1880; 1885, 1900 Orange County censuses; *WF*, July 9, 1889; *Miami Metropolis*, September 29, 1899.
266. *WF*, April 8, 1879; Jacksonville *Florida Weekly Times*, April 26, 1883; Leon County probate file 893.
267. Nassau County census, 1870.
268. Duval County census, 1870; *NYF*, June 27, 1885; Duval County probate file 1160-D.
269. Duval County census, 1885, 1900, 1910; 1910 Jacksonville city directory.
270. Duval County census, 1910; DCI v. 152, #4235; St. Augustine biographical files, SAHSRL.
271. Nassau County census, 1880, 1895, 1900.

272. Hernando County census, 1870.
273. Santa Rosa County census, 1860, 1870, 1880; Jupiter, "Agustina," 274–75.
274. Leon County census, 1870.
275. Columbia County census, 1870, 1900.
276. Franklin County census, 1880, 1900, 1910; Willie Speed interview.
277. Madison County census, 1870, 1885.
278. Gadsden County census, 1870; Gadsden County Deed Book D, 359.
279. Nassau County census, 1870, 1895; DCI (card) 07273 (1903).
280. November 1864 Fernandina census; MPR #291883; 1870 Nassau County census; Bosque Bello cemetery records.
281. Duval County census, 1870; *DFU,* March 25, 1882; Akin, "When a Minority Becomes the Majority," 130; 1902 Jacksonville city directory.
282. Duval County census, 1870; Duval County probate file 1301-D.
283. MPR #1166518.
284. Nassau County census, 1870, 1880; MPR #665733; Bosque Bello cemetery records.
285. Duval County census, 1880; *FT-U,* September 21, 1891.
286. Hamilton County census, 1870, 1885.
287. Jacksonville *Daily News-Herald,* April 16, 1888; 1880 Duval County census; *CR,* November 24, 1881; *FT-U,* March 26, 1920; Jacksonville *Evening Telegram,* February 8, 1892; J. D. Wetmore to W. E. B. DuBois, April 19, 1926, xerographic copy in collection of David Nolan, St. Augustine.
288. Orange County census, 1920; DCI v. 268, #14410.
289. Drake, *Florida Legislature,* 45; 1900 Escambia County census; Neyland, *Twelve Black Floridians,* 7–14; DCI; Shofner, "Florida," 97–100.
290. *FT-U,* February 6, 1889; 1910 Duval County census; Jacksonville *Metropolis,* July 2, 1910; Duval County probate file 3475-D.
291. Gadsden County census, 1870; 1900 Dade County census; Womack, *Gadsden,* 137; Kleinberg, "Discovering black participation"; idem, "Miami pioneer Lightburn"; Rivers and Brown, "African Americans in South Florida," 11–12.
292. Marion County census, 1880, 1900.
293. Jackson County census, 1870, 1880, 1900; Jackson County Deed Book QQ, 684; *CR,* December 23, 1880.
294. Jackson County census, 1880, 1900, 1910, 1920; DCI v. 305, #13751.
295. Florida *House Journal* (1869), 138–39; *WF,* December 15, 1868.
296. Manatee County census, 1880, 1885; Punta Gorda *Sun-Herald,* December 6, 1992; Brown, *Florida's Peace River Frontier,* 181, 188, 205, 244–45; Manatee County circuit court records, folder: Trials (Grand Jury) 1870–1875.

297. Long, *History of the A.M.E. Church*, 75–79; 1870 Duval County census; MPR #GZ [CZ] 491417; Schafer, "Freedom," 113.
298. Jefferson County census, 1870; Jefferson County Deed Book W, 450; *WF*, October 6, 1874, March 14, 1896.
299. Hamilton County census, 1870, 1885, 1910; 1900 Columbia County census.
300. Drake, *Florida Legislature*, 38; 1870 Jefferson County census; 1900 Duval County census.
301. Alachua County census, 1875, 1880, 1900, 1910; DCI v. 108, #10326.
302. Columbia County census, 1870, 1880, 1900, 1920; DCI v. 341, #9050.
303. *CR*, June 4, 1885.
304. November 1864 Fernandina census; 1880 Nassau County census; Nassau County probate dockets, Book 1 (1873–1930), 162.
305. November 1864 Fernandina census; 1880, 1895, 1900 Nassau County censuses; DCI (card) 05417.
306. November 1864 Fernandina census; 1895 Nassau County census; Bosque Bello cemetery records.
307. Escambia County census, 1885; 1885, 1893–1894 Pensacola city directories; DCI v. 08, #668 (1905).
308. Jacksonville *Tri-Weekly Florida Union*, January 9, 1873.
309. Duval County census, 1885; Duval County probate file 1538-D; Wallace, *Carpetbag Rule*, 129.
310. MPR #538136; 1885 Marion County census.
311. Suwannee County census, 1885.
312. St. Johns County census, 1900; 1910 Putnam County census.
313. Madison County census, 1870, 1900; Madison *New Enterprise*, December 22, 1904.
314. Putnam County census, 1900, 1920; DCI v. 292, #7458 (1926).
315. Sumter County census, 1870, 1885, 1900.
316. Alachua County census, 1880; 1885 Levy County census.
317. Escambia census, 1900, 1910.
318. Alachua County census, 1870; 1885, 1920 Duval County censuses; DCI v. 917, #20157.
319. Levy County census, 1885; 1910, 1920 Duval County censuses; 1930 Jacksonville city directory.
320. Duval County census, 1880; Gainesville *Daily Sun*, July 2, 1890; *Palatka Daily News*, quoted in *NYF*, June 4, 1887.
321. Alachua County census, 1880, 1900, 1910; DCI v. 330, #3661.
322. Leon County census, 1870.
323. Ibid., 1885; Jacksonville *Evening Telegram*, October 4, 1892.
324. Alachua County census, 1870, 1880.

325. Jacksonville *Metropolis*, December 26, 1918; *FT-U*, December 28, 1918.
326. Jefferson County census, 1870.
327. Madison County census, 1870, 1885.
328. Brown, "Robert Meacham"; *CR*, August 10, 1867; *Punta Gorda Herald*, March 7, 1902; Rivers and Brown, "African Americans in South Florida," 15–16.
329. *NYG*, June 2, 1883; Gibbs, "John Willis Menard"; Beatty, "John Willis Menard"; Menard, "John Willis Menard"; Shofner, "Florida," 92–96; Johnson, *Along This Way*, 58; *Gainesville Times*, October 5, 1876; Rivers and Brown, "African Americans in South Florida," 12.
330. Leon County census, 1870, 1880; Leon County probate file 869.
331. Nassau County census, 1880.
332. Clay County census, 1870; Duval County probate file 1421.
333. *WF*, November 26, 1878.
334. Jefferson County census, 1870; *A.M.E. Church Review* 25 (April 1909): 458; *SMN*, July 29, 1874.
335. Hernando County census, 1870, 1880, 1900.
336. Whitfield, *Florida State Government*, 38; *FT-U&C*, March 29, 1901.
337. Marion County census, 1870, 1910; Marion County probate file, cabinet 1, box 97.
338. Columbia County census, 1870, 1880, 1900.
339. Drake, *Florida Legislature*, 33; 1885, 1900 Gadsden County censuses.
340. Jefferson County census, 1880, 1900; Jefferson County Deed Book II, 194.
341. "Testimony Taken by the Joint Select Committee," 125–36; *New York Tribune*, April 26, 1878; *Quitman* (Ga.) *Reporter*, June 22, 1876; *TS*, November 5, 1870.
342. Duval County census, 1870.
343. Nassau County census, 1870, 1880; Bosque Bello cemetery records.
344. Leon County census, 1870, 1885.
345. Nassau County census, 1870.
346. Duval County census, 1870, 1880.
347. Orange County census, 1900; Jacksonville *Evening Telegram*, November 20, 1891, November 7, 1892; DCI v. 603, #18279 (1933).
348. Madison County census, 1870; Madison County Letters of Administration, Book H, 265, 66.
349. Gadsden County census, 1880, 1900; Gadsden County Deed Book R, 259.
350. Marion County census, 1885.
351. Madison County census, 1880, 1900; Madison County Deed Book 28, 536.
352. Columbia County census, 1870, 1880.
353. Gadsden County census, 1870; *WF*, October 5, 1875; *Quincy Journal*, quoted in Palatka *Eastern Herald*, October 9, 1875.

354. Madison County census, 1900, 1920; *Madison Recorder*, October 4, 1889, August 1, 1890; DCI v. 406, #19 (1929).
355. Marion County census, 1900; 1920 Putnam County census; DCI v. 254, #7245 (1925).
356. Freedmen's Bank register of signatures, Tallahassee; Wallace, *Carpetbag Rule*, 38–39; Davis, *Civil War and Reconstruction*, 495.
357. Drake, *Florida Legislature*, 39–40; *Madison Recorder*, October 4, 1889; Madison *New Enterprise*, November 30, 1905; Madison *Enterprise-Recorder*, December 15, 1911; *Norfolk* (Va.) *Journal and Guide*, October 29, 1927.
358. Duval County census, 1885, 1900.
359. McKinney and McKinney, *History of Black Baptists*, 23; 1870 Leon County census; *WF*, March 20, 1883.
360. St. Johns County census, 1900; John Papino biographical information, SAHSRL; 1914 St. Augustine city directory.
361. St. Johns County census, 1885, 1900; A. A. Papy biographical materials, SAHSRL.
362. MPR #363496 (William Pappy).
363. St. Johns County census, 1880, 1885, 1900; DCI v. 724, #14636.
364. MPR #363496 (William Pappy).
365. *FT-U*, November 8, 1898.
366. Jefferson County census, 1870; Charles Parrish, Sr., probate file, Keystone Genealogical Library, Monticello.
367. Levy County census, 1870; *WF*, May 4, 1875; Jacksonville *New South*, May 5, 1875.
368. Thomes, *Early Vital Records*, 3:249; 1870 Escambia County census.
369. Clay County census, 1900, 1910, 1920.
370. Hamilton County census, 1885, 1900.
371. Freedmen's Bank register of signatures, Tallahassee; 1885 Putnam County census; Dodd, " 'Bishop' Pearce"; *CR*, November 17, 1887; Charles H. Pearce to George G. Meade, VR corr., RG 393, entry 5738, box 8, part 1, NA; *New York Daily Tribune*, February 5, 1868.
372. Jefferson County census, 1885; Shofner, *Jefferson County*, 309; *FT-U*, February 1, 1887.
373. Hamilton County census, 1870, 1885.
374. *CR*, February 10, 1872.
375. Duval County census, 1880; Duval County probate file 1700.
376. Whitfield, *Florida State Government*, 50; 1880, 1895 Nassau County censuses; *Fernandina Observer*, quoted in Ocala *East Florida Banner*, August 8, 1874; *WF*, March 14, 1896.
377. Marion County census, 1885.

378. *FT-U*, May 6, 1915; 1870 Duval County census.
379. Escambia County census, 1870; Bruington, *St. Michael's Cemetery*, 148; Escambia County probate file, "John Pons."
380. Bruington, *St. Michael's Cemetery*, 28; Pensacola *Daily News*, March 22, 1890; 1870 Escambia County census; Pensacola *Tri-Weekly Observer*, August 13, 1868; *Norfolk* (Va.) *Journal and Guide*, October 22, 1927.
381. Wakulla County census, 1870, 1880, 1900; DCI v. 44, #8135 (1918).
382. Jackson County census, 1870; Shofner, *Jackson County*, 324; Washington (D.C.) *People's Advocate*, May 8, 1880.
383. Apalachicola census, 1884–1885; 1870 Franklin County census.
384. Marion County census, 1880, 1900.
385. Jefferson County census, 1870, 1885; *WF*, July 9, 1889; McKinney and McKinney, *History of Black Baptists*, 114.
386. "Testimony Taken by the Joint Select Committee," 272; 1870 Jackson County census.
387. Dade County census, 1870, 1885, 1900.
388. Drake, *Florida Legislature*, 38; 1870 Leon County census; Warner, *Free Men*, 95.
389. Warner, *Free Men*, 49, 95, 136–37, 139; *TS*, October 21, 1871; Drake, *Florida Legislature*, 34–35; 1885 Leon County census.
390. Putnam County census, 1885; Tallahassee *Florida Bureau of Immigration Monthly Bulletin*, February 1891; Janice S. Mahaffey, Office of the Putnam County Clerk of the Circuit Court, to the author, April 5, 1994, collection of the author.
391. Putnam County census, 1885, 1900; DCI v. 047, #5736 (1915).
392. Columbia County census, 1870, 1900.
393. Leon County census, 1870.
394. Escambia County census, 1870; Escambia County probate files, "Richard Ramsey."
395. MPR #XC2666058; 1870 Duval County census.
396. Nassau County census, 1880, 1895.
397. Ibid., 1870, 1900; Nassau County probate file 998.
398. Clay County census, 1900, 1910, 1920; DCI v. 394, #15044 (1928).
399. Nassau County census, 1895, 1900, 1920.
400. Columbia County census, 1870, 1900; DCI v. 96, #4201 (1920).
401. Madison County census, 1870, 1885.
402. Putnam County census, 1870, 1885.
403. Baker County census, 1870, 1885, 1900, 1910.

404. Talbert, *Sons of Allen*, 126–27; 1880 Franklin County census; *CR*, April 29, 1880; F. N. Wicker to Sec. of Treas., March 31, 1879, records relating to Customhouse Nominations, Key West, RG 56, entry 246, box 067, NA.
405. MPR #681174; James A. Roberts to John F. Horr, August 22, 1890, records relating to Customhouse Nominations, Key West, RG 56, entry 246, box 069, NA; *DFU*, February 28, 1876.
406. Leon County census, 1870.
407. Jackson County census, 1885.
408. Duval County census, 1880; Duval County probate file 1848-D.
409. Jackson County census, 1870, 188; *WF*, June 30, 1874.
410. St. Johns County census, 1870, 1880; MPR #468527.
411. Putnam County census, 1900; DCI v. 69, #4470 (1919).
412. Franklin County census, 1885; Franklin County probate records, Book 3, 294.
413. Drake, *Florida Legislature*, 51; 1880 Nassau County census; Jacksonville *Evening Telegram*, January 30, 1894; *FM*, August 19, 1882; Bosque Bello cemetery records.
414. Jackson County census, 1870, 1880; *FT-U*, December 11, 1893.
415. Jackson County census, 1870 (mortality schedule); FP, February 16, 1870; Shofner, *Jackson County*, 282–87.
416. Drake, *Florida Legislature*, 36–37; Varick and Smith, *Tallahassee and Leon County Cemeteries*, 50; 1870 Leon County census; Tallahassee *Daily True Democrat*, August 30, 1919.
417. Leon County census, 1870, 1885, 1900, 1910; DCI v. 80, #9808 (1919).
418. Duval County census, 1900; 1918, 1966 Jacksonville city directories; Akin, "When a Minority Becomes the Majority," 140; DCI v. 2780, #2419 (1966).
419. Baker County census, 1870, 1885, 1900.
420. DCI indicates that Charles Rouse was white, but census records differ. Escambia County census, 1870, 1880; DCI v. 02, #968 (1891); Pensacola *Daily News*, November 11, 1906.
421. Duval County census, 1885; Duval County probate file 2024-D.
422. Ibid.; *FT-U*, July 11, 1889.
423. Madison County census, 1870, 1880; Madison County Deed Book M, 127.
424. Duval County census, 1885; Long, *History of the A.M.E. Church*, 196; *CR*, December 28, 1872, November 22, 1888; *FT-U*, October 2, 1888.
425. Liberty County census, 1870, 1885.

426. MPR #577402; *New York Daily Tribune*, February 5, 1868; Klingman, *Josiah Walls*, 66; Jacksonville *Tri-Weekly Florida Union*, June 30, 1874; *FU*, November 9, 1867; Davis, *Civil War and Reconstruction*, 496.
427. Duval County census, 1900; Gainesville *Florida Sentinel*, January 26, 1900; 1900, 1907 Jacksonville city directories.
428. Marion County census, 1880, 1900, 1910.
429. Jacksonville city directory, 1886.
430. *WF*, March 11, 1879; 1870 Duval County census; Long, *History of the A.M.E. Church*, 197; *SMN*, March 11, 1879; *CR*, December 28, 1872, March 1, 1877.
431. Talbert, *Sons of Allen*, 154; 1870 Duval County census; John R. Scott, Jr., death certificate, Florida Office of Vital Statistics; *CR*, October 30, 1884; *FT-U*, February 6, 1889.
432. St. Johns County census, 1885, 1900.
433. Escambia County census, 1885; DCI v. 03, #1322 (1892).
434. Monroe County census, 1885, 1900; Key West burial records; *Fort Myers News-Press*, October 21, 1943.
435. Orange County census, 1885, 1900, 1910.
436. Leon County census, 1870, 1900, 1910.
437. Volusia County census, 1910.
438. Alachua County census, 1870, 1875, 1880; *NYF*, May 23, 1885; Gainesville *Florida Sentinel*, July 17, 1891; Alachua County probate administration file 63.
439. Suwannee County census, 1870, 1885; *FU*, January 25, 1868.
440. Alachua County census, 1870, 1880, 1900, 1910.
441. *FT-U*, July 14, 1883; *NYG*, August 18, 1883; 1870 Duval County census.
442. Suwannee County census, 1885, 1900.
443. Columbia County census, 1870, 1880.
444. Marion County census, 1870; *Struggle for Survival*, 7.
445. *Struggle for Survival*, 8; 1870 Marion County census; Ocala *East Florida Banner*, quoted in *NYG*, November 10, 1883.
446. Duval County census, 1880.
447. Marion County census, 1870, 1880; Marion County probate file, cabinet 1, box 48; Ocala *Evening Star*, January 23, 1901.
448. Apalachicola census, 1884–85; 1885 Franklin County census; *CR*, April 1, 1886; Willie Speed interview.
449. Franklin County census, 1885; *FT-U*, July 28, 1888.
450. Duval County census, 1880.
451. Ibid., 1870.
452. Bosque Bello cemetery records; MPR #769402; 1880 Nassau County census.

453. Leon County census, 1885, 1900; DCI v. 034, #4982 (1914).
454. Leon County census, 1870.
455. Duval County census, 1870, 1885; 1932–1933 Jacksonville city directory.
456. Duval County census, 1870, 1880; Jacksonville *New South*, December 5, 1874; *DFU*, February 9, 1882; 1887 Jacksonville city directory.
457. Columbia County census, 1880; *CR*, July 20, 1882; *FT-U&C*, February 22, 1898; *Journal of Proceedings and Year Book*, 18.
458. Duval County census, 1870, 1885; 1889 Jacksonville city directory.
459. Hernando County census, 1870; *WFU*, July 14, 1877; *WF*, July 17, 1877.
460. Bosque Bello cemetery records; 1880, 1895 Nassau County censuses; Nassau County probate file 1031.
461. Caldwell, *History of the American Negro*, 570–72; *CR*, January 27, 1876, December 29, 1881.
462. Monroe County census, 1880, 1885, 1900.
463. Alachua County census, 1875, 1880, 1900; DCI v. 191, #9692.
464. *NYF*, March 27, 1886; Tallahassee *Weekly True Democrat*, June 16, 1911; 1870 Gadsden County census; *CR*, December 28, 1872.
465. Levy County census, 1870; Long, *History of the A.M.E. Church*, 109.
466. Suwannee County census, 1870, 1885.
467. Freedmen's Bank register of signatures, Tallahassee; 1870, 1880 Leon County censuses; Wallace, *Carpetbag Rule*, 227; 1900 Suwannee County census; Suwannee County Deed Records, Book DD, 480; *WF*, February 24, 1880.
468. Liberty County census, 1870, 1880.
469. Escambia County census, 1885; MPR #962790; Bruington, *St. Michael's Cemetery*, 134–35; *Pensacola Journal*, January 8, 1925; *Bliss' Quarterly* 3 (January 1897): 139–40.
470. Clay County census, 1880.
471. Jefferson County census, 1870, 1885.
472. Orange County census, 1885; Otey, *Eatonville*, 4.
473. St. Johns County census, 1870, 1885; DCI v. 163, #9734 (1922).
474. Volusia County census, 1885; *TS*, November 15, 1870; Jacksonville *Evening Telegram*, March 3, 1892; *Journal of Proceedings and Year Book*, 18.
475. Orange County census, 1900, 1910; DCI v. 195, #11823 (1923).
476. Jefferson County census, 1870; Shofner, *Jefferson County*, 316; Jefferson County Deed Book P, 473; Monticello *Advertiser*, quoted in *WF*, June 11, 1872.
477. Columbia County census, 1880, 1900; Jacksonville *Evening Telegram*, July 21, 1893.
478. Jacksonville city directory, 1871.

479. Leon County census, 1870, 1900; 1885 Escambia County census; *TS*, October 21, 1871; Wallace, *Carpetbag Rule*, 295–96; *CR*, May 28, 1885.
480. Drake, *Florida Legislature*, 54.
481. Wayman, *Cyclopaedia*, 163; 1870 Suwannee County census; 1880 Columbia County census; Long, *History of the A.M.E. Church*, 198; *Journal of Proceedings and Year Book*, 18.
482. Jefferson County census, 1870.
483. Whitfield, *Florida State Government*, 40; 1885 Leon County census; *FT-U*, February 21, 1891.
484. Jefferson County census, 1870, 1885, 1900.
485. Jefferson County census, 1885, 1900.
486. MPR #904104; 1880 Duval County census.
487. Madison County census, 1870, 1880, 1885; 1900 Gadsden County census; DCI v. 21, #10134 (1917).
488. MSR; 1885 Duval County census; Duval County probate file 2131-D.
489. Edwards, *Grave Markers*, 57; 1880 Duval County census; Duval County probate file 2145.
490. *TS*, May 25, 1872; Jacksonville *Tri-Weekly Florida Union*, May 28, 1872; 1870 Leon County census.
491. Marion County census, 1880, 1900.
492. Alachua County census, 1870, 1900; DCI v. 555, #14350 (1932).
493. Leon County census, 1880; 1885 Jackson County census; Wright, *Centennial Encyclopaedia*, 311.
494. Drake, *Florida Legislature*, 46; 1870, 1880, 1900 Alachua County censuses; Alachua County probate administration file 64.
495. November 1864 Fernandina census; 1875–1876 Nassau County voter registration list, RG 156, series 21, FSA.
496. Jacksonville city directory, 1892.
497. Duval County census, 1870, 1885; 1907 Jacksonville city directory.
498. Alachua County census, 1870; *SMN*, June 3, 1876.
499. MPR #433791; 1880 Duval County census; *FT-U*, January 20, 1884, March 13, 1895.
500. St. Johns County census, 1870, 1885, 1900, 1910; biographical information files, SAHSRL.
501. Leon County census, 1870; Varick and Smith, *Tallahassee and Leon County Cemeteries*, 51.
502. Thompson and Thompson, *Capers Michael Vaught;* 1885 Duval County census.
503. Escambia County census, 1885; 1900, 1920 Hillsborough County censuses; *FT-U*, February 11, 1892; DCI v. 185, #6653 (1923).

504. Hillsborough County census, 1900, 1910; Hawes, "Diary leads to rediscovery"; Joseph A. Walker death certificate, Florida Office of Vital Statistics.
505. Nassau County census, 1880, 1900, 1910.
506. Clark, "John Wallace," 409, 427; 1870 Leon County census; Philadelphia *Times*, quoted in *FT-U*, December 12, 1883; *FM*, December 20, 1879.
507. Jackson County probate file 1055.
508. Klingman, *Josiah Walls*, 6, 141, 143; 1870 Alachua County census; *CR*, May 25, 1872; *NYG*, February 9, 1884.
509. Marion County census, 1870, 1885.
510. Escambia County census, 1870; Escambia County probate files, "William Warren."
511. *WF*, May 18, 1880.
512. Jacksonville city directory, 1876–1877.
513. Levy County census, 1885; *CR*, January 23, 1890.
514. Escambia County census, 1870; DCI v. 05, #2322 (1895).
515. Jefferson County census, 1885; Samuel Pasco to Joseph E. Lee, October 14, 1886, Lee papers.
516. Leon County census, 1870, 1880.
517. Columbia County census, 1870.
518. Orange County census, 1900, 1910, 1920.
519. Duval County census, 1900; DCI v. 107, #9580 (1920).
520. Freedmen's Bank register of signatures, Tallahassee; 1870 Leon County census; Leon County probate file 1131.
521. Drake, *Florida Legislature*, 53; 1870 Leon County census; *NYG*, April 14, June 9, 1883; *FT-U*, January 7, 1920.
522. Duval County census, 1880.
523. Jackson County census, 1880, 1885; *TS*, January 15, 1870; Long, *History of the A.M.E. Church*, 172; *WF*, August 15, 1876.
524. Jackson County census, 1870; Jackson County probate files, "Isham White, Sr."
525. Drake, *Florida Legislature*, 24; 1885, 1910 Escambia County censuses; *Tampa Tribune*, May 19, 1912; Mark S. White to F. C. Humphreys, May 6, 1878, records relating to Customhouse Nominations, Pensacola, RG 56, entry 246, box 073, NA; *FT-U*, September 21, 1891.
526. Clay County census, 1880, 1900.
527. Volusia County census, 1885; 1900 Hillsborough County census; 1903 Tampa city directory; *Journal of Proceedings and Year Book*, 18.
528. Drake, *Florida Legislature*, 55; 1900 Marion County census; *Struggle for Survival*, 8; *FT-U*, May 19, 1890.

529. Drake, *Florida Legislature*, 50–51; Gainesville *Florida Sentinel*, July 17, 1891.
530. Nassau County census, 1870, 1880, 1895.
531. Jackson County census, 1870, 1885.
532. Columbia County census, 1870.
533. Jackson County census, 1870, 1880; Shofner, *Jackson County*, 259.
534. Jefferson County census, 1870; DCI v. 35, #3946 (1918).
535. Leon County census, 1870.
536. John G. Williams to Sec. of Treas., September 26, 1874, records relating to Customhouse Nominations, Cedar Keys, RG 56, entry 246, box 063, NA; 1880 Chatham County, Georgia, census.
537. Leon County census, 1870.
538. Nassau County census, 1870, 1880, 1895; Nassau County probate dockets, Book 1, 257.
539. Leon County probate file 706.
540. DCI v. 51, #11994 (1918).
541. Duval County census, 1885; *FT-U*, August 22, 1888.
542. Orange County census, 1885.
543. Putnam County census, 1885.
544. Ibid., 1900; 1910 Duval County census.
545. Putnam County census, 1900, 1910; Janice S. Mahaffey, Office of the Putnam County Clerk of the Circuit Court, to the author, April 4, 1994, collection of the author.
546. Wakulla County census, 1870.
547. Drake, *Florida Legislature*, 37–38; 1880 Jefferson County census; *FT-U*, January 7, 1892; Davis, *Civil War and Reconstruction*, 644; *CR*, May 28, 1885; Jacksonville *Evening Telegram*, January 6, 1892; Rivers and Brown, "African Americans in South Florida," 15–17.
548. St. Johns County census, 1870, 1885; Francis E. Witsell biographical materials, SAHSRL.
549. Putnam County census, 1870, 1885; Jacksonville *Evening Telegram*, April 19, 20, 1893; *CR*, June 9, 1866.
550. Madison County census, 1870, 1880.
551. Marion County census, 1880.
552. Indianapolis *Freeman*, June 3, 1892; Akin, "When a Minority Becomes the Majority," 134; 1904 Jacksonville city directory.
553. Nassau County census, 1880; DCI v. 45, #4847 (1915).
554. Madison County census, 1870.
555. Freedmen's Bank register of signatures, Tallahassee; *CR*, September 26, 1878; Philadelphia *Times*, November 30, 1883.

556. Columbia County census, 1870; Escambia County probate files, "Joseph Wyer."
557. Jackson County census, 1870; 1885 Jefferson County census.
558. Orange County census, 1885; Otey, *Eatonville*, 9.
559. Leon County census, 1885, 1900, 1920; *CR*, May 28, 1885; DCI v. 309, #15720.
560. Levy County census, 1885.

APPENDIX: OFFICIALS BY POLITICAL SUBDIVISION

1. See Klingman, *Josiah Walls.*
2. See Richardson, "Jonathan C. Gibbs."
3. Ibid.
4. Unidentified in Alachua County: County Clerk J. E. Webster; Sheriff John W. Howell; County Commissioners D. Warren L. Barton and Paul Brown; Justices of the Peace W. H. Denmark, J. Keen, Reuben W. Roberts, W. A. Geiger, George N. Moody; Allen M. Jones, W. C. Andrews, A. J. Weeks, Green R. Moore, William H. Belton; and Constable J. M. McCullum.
5. Unidentified at Gainesville: Councilman W. A. "Gus" Walters. Record of incorporation and Gainesville officials materials, city clerk's office, Gainesville; *TS*, April 23, 1870, April 20, 1872; *SMN*, April 23, 1872, April 23, 29, 1873, April 21, 1874; Gainesville *Florida Independent*, May 10, 1873; Gainesville *New Era*, August 30, 1873; *WF*, November 4, 1873, April 28, 1874, April 24, 1877; Gainesville *Alachua Citizen and New Era*, January 28, 1876; Ocala *East Florida Banner*, October 2, 1875; *DFU*, April 17, July 14, 1876; *Gainesville Times*, April 14, July 7, 1877, April 17, 1878; *WS&P*, April 25, 1878; *Gainesville Sun*, April 19, 1879; *FM*, November 8, 1879, April 24, 1880, April 23, 1881; Gainesville *Sun and Bee*, March 19, April 14, July 7, 1881; Gainesville *Weekly Bee*, April 14, 21, 1882, April 19, 1884; *FDT*, April 14, 1882; *FT-U*, April 17, 1883, April 16, 1884, April 11, 1895, April 15, September 3, 1896; Davis, *History of Gainesville*, 39–40; *Gainesville News*, April 4, 1885; Gainesville *Daily Sun*, August 23, 1891, September 14, 1892; Gainesville *Florida Sentinel*, July 17, 1891; *FT-U&C*, April 14, 1898.
6. Unidentified in Baker County: none.
7. Unidentified in Bradford County: Assessor J. S. Howell; Treasurer T. N. B. Oliver; County Commissioners John B. Roundtree and N. E. Roberts; Justices of the Peace Charles P. Perry, L. G. Stringfellow, and Morris Moore.

8. Unidentified in Brevard County: none.
9. Unidentified in Calhoun County: County Clerk Henry Clark; Assessor Henry Clark; County Commissioners Henry Clark and James S. Fannin; Justice of the Peace David S. Kerwin.
10. Unidentified in Clay County: Justices of the Peace W. S. Harris, W. C. Clark, N. L. Cannon, and Samuel Jackson.
11. Unidentified at Green Cove Springs: Treasurer W. J. Nelson; Councilmen —— Johnson (1874), L. W. Rim, J. S. Lens. Case file, *Theodore T. Edgerton* vs. *The Mayor and Aldermen of Green Cove Springs*, supreme court case files, file #0587 (Jan. term 1882), series 49, RG 970, FSA; *DFU*, April 4, 1882; *FDT*, April 4, 1882; *FT-U*, April 13, 1883, April 1, 15, 24, 1884, April 14, 1885, April 15, 1886, April 12, 1887, April 3, May 22, 1888, April 4, 1894, April 9, 1896, April 8, 1897; *FT-U&C*, April 7, 1898; Green Cove Springs *The Spring*, April 26, 1884; Blakey, *Parade of Memories*, 260; records of municipal officials and Minute Book, June 2, 1891–April 25, 1900, Green Cove Springs city clerk's office.
12. Unidentified in Columbia County: Assessor Gabriel J. Jones; Treasurer B. F. Ridgell; Superintendent of Schools William W. Keep; County Commissioner G. J. Jones; Justices of the Peace Simeon H. Hampton, S. P. Shuman, John T. Wofford, and L. A. Keegan.
13. Unidentified at Lake City: Councilmen Charley Smith and W. J. Edwards. *TS*, February 18, November 11, 1871; *SMN*, February 3, April 16, 1872, April 22, 1873, April 17, 1877, April 17, 1878, April 9, 1879, April 14, 1880, April 19, 1881; Jacksonville *Tri-Weekly Florida Union*, April 15, 1873; *WF*, April 21, 1874, April 21, 1887; Savannah *Advertiser-Republican*, April 22, 1874; *FT-U*, April 14, 1883, April 11, 1884, April 9, 16, 1885, April 15, 1886, April 19, 1889, April 11, 1890, April 13, 1891, April 15, 1892, April 2, 1893; *SDA*, April 18, 1875; *Thomasville* (Ga.) *Times*, April 8, 1876; Talbert, *Sons of Allen*, 68; *DFU*, April 17, 1876, April 16, 1882; *DS&P*, April 10, 1878; *N-H*, April 14, 1888; Minute Book (November 14, 1892–February 16, 1904), Lake City clerk's office.
14. Unidentified in Dade County: none.
15. Unidentified in Duval County: Superintendent of Schools A. J. Pickard; County Commissioners M. Bowes, Emmett Densmore, and Miles Price; Justices of the Peace Charles F. Daly, William Allright, William M. Robinson, Howell A. Baisden, and Amos H. Norris.
16. Unidentified at Jacksonville: none. *FU*, October 28, 1868, March 18, December 30, 1869; *WF*, October 26, 1869, March 14, April 11, 1871, April 13, 1875, April 10, 1877, April 8, 1886; *TS*, April 9, 1870, April

8, 1871; *SMN*, April 9, 1872, April 30, July 22, 1879, March 30, April 7, 1880; Jacksonville *Tri-Weekly Florida Union*, April 5, 1873, April 7, 1874; Jacksonville *New South*, April 7, 1875; *DFU*, April 4, 1876, April 4, 1882; Jacksonville *Daily Evening Chronicle*, November 1, 1877; *FM*, July 19, 1879, April 7, 1880, April 9, 1881; *DS&P*, September 17, 1880; *FT-U*, April 3, 1883, April 8, 1884, April 7, 1885, April 3, 7, 1886, April 5, December 14, 1887; Akin, "When a Minority Becomes the Majority," 134–40.

17. LaVilla became a part of Jacksonville in 1887. Unidentified at LaVilla: Clerk George W. Adams; Assessor H. P. Walker; Collector Simon Rouse; Councilmen Eli Fretwell, Henry Ross, Harrington Kyler, Raymond Davis, William Wadham, John Hewlett, and J. E. Holt. Jacksonville city directory, 1870, 5; Jacksonville city directory, 1871; Kenney, "LaVilla," 25; Jacksonville *Tri-Weekly Florida Union*, February 8, 1873, February 10, 1874; Jacksonville *New South*, February 19, 1875; *DFU*, January 19, July 28, 1876, February 8, 1882; *SMN*, February 13, 1877; *DS&P*, February 20, 1878; *FM*, January 24, 1880; *Webb's Jacksonville Directory*, 1882, 234; *FT-U*, February 8, 1883, February 8, 1884, February 8, 1885, February 8, 1886, February 8, 1887.
18. Unidentified in Escambia County: County Commissioners Edward Hughes, John J. Lindsey, A. C. Fisher, and Eugene St. Guiron; Justices of the Peace John J. Lindsey, S. M. Williamson, M. G. Hardy, and G. E. McCord.
19. Unidentified at Pensacola: Councilmen —— Hutchinson (1869–1870), A. C. Fisher, —— Stinson (1874–1875), —— Stevens (1878–1879), —— Hoffman (1879–1880), R. H. Matthews, and George B. Loud. Pensacola *West Florida Commercial*, January 26, 1869; Pensacola *Tri-Weekly Observer*, February 3, 1869; Pensacola *Semi-Weekly Commercial*, June 15, July 13, 1869, December 29, 1882; *FU*, June 24, July 22, December 30, 1869; *Pensacola Journal*, December 17, 1905, February 6, 1912; *History of Local Government in Pensacola and Escambia County*, 90–91; Pensacola *Florida Weekly Express*, September 9, 1871; *SMN*, January 9, 1872, January 3, March 7, 1877; *Pensacola Mail*, January 30, February 16, 1872; Jacksonville *Tri-Weekly Florida Union*, January 11, 1873; Savannah *Advertiser-Republican*, January 6, 1874; Pensacola *Republican*, July 4, 1874; Jacksonville *New South*, September 5, 1874; *SDA*, August 10, 1875; *TS*, January 1, 1876 *Pensacola Weekly Gazette*, January 17, 1876; Pensacola *Echo*, February 15, 1878; *WS&P*, May 30, 1878; Hunter, *History of Pensacola's Black Community; Pensacola Gazette*, March 30, 1880; Ellsworth and Ellsworth, *Pensacola*, 74; *DFU*, January 28, 1882; *Pensacola Weekly*

Commercial, February 14, 1882; *Pensacola Commercial*, December 22, 1883, January 2, 1884; *FT-U*, January 5, December 24, 30, 1884, March 2, 1889; Pensacola *Advance-Gazette*, January 1, 1884; *WF*, February 19, 1885.

20. Unidentified in Franklin County: County Commissioners Daniel Rowlett and M. H. Scott; Justice of the Peace A. M. Harris.
21. Unidentified at Apalachicola: Councilman M. W. Keating. Mayor's Court Record (1855–1882), Ordinance Book (1871–1921), and City Council Minute Book (July 3, 1884–May 3, 1889), Apalachicola city clerk's office; *TS*, December 21, 1868; *WF*, June 4, 1872, February 11, 1873; *DFU*, December 29, 1881, February 18, 1882; *FT-U*, November 16, 1887, February 18, 1888, February 6, 13, 1890.
22. Unidentified in Gadsden County: County Clerk S. E. Stewart; Sheriff Charles Williams; Assessors M. D. Overacker and Lafayette Mitchell; Treasurer Samuel Hamblen; Superintendent of Schools Samuel Hamblen; County Commissioners John Dickson, Michael H. Murray, and M. J. Johnson; Justices of the Peace C. C. Hilton and Lafayette Mitchell.
23. Unidentified at Quincy: none. *FU*, February 11, 1869; *WF*, February 28, 1871, March 3, 1872, February 23, 1875, March 4, 1879, February 21, 1882; *TS*, February 25, 1871; *Quincy Journal*, January 9, 1874; *SMN*, January 30, 1877; *WS&P*, February 21, 1878; *FM*, March 6, 1880; *DFU*, February 17, 1882.
24. Moss offered himself on the Quincy municipal ticket favored for election, but his election is not confirmed. *SMN*, January 30, 1877.
25. Unidentified in Hamilton County: County Clerk and Tax Collector William J. Lee; County Commissioners William J. Lee, Smart Stokes, and William G. Knowles; and Justices of the Peace William J. Lee, Levi F. Dasher, E. M. Lee, and Londy Tracy.
26. Hamilton County Bicentennial Committee, Early History, 62–63.
27. Unidentified in Hernando County: County Commissioner A. T. Sykes [Howell T. Lykes?].
28. Stanaback, *History of Hernando County*, 56.
29. Unidentified in Hillsborough County: none.
30. Hawes, "Diary leads to rediscovery"; Grismer, *Tampa*, 155; Tampa *Sunland Tribune*, April 7, 1877.
31. Unidentified in Holmes County: Clerk James J. Newton.
32. Unidentified in Jackson County: County Commissioners Henry A. Henneman, Stewart Hardin, and W. R. Swain; Justices of the Peace James A. Price, William W. Boykin, Smith Dawson, George B. Roberson,

and W. L. Robinson. Jackson County Commission Order Book C and Record Book (January 2, 1871–November 5, 1883).

33. Unidentified at Marianna: none. *DFU*, March 21, 1876, December 15, 1881, January 17, 1883; *SMN*, March 21, 1877; *WS&P*, April 25, 1878.
34. Unidentified in Jefferson County: Assessor L. A. Reed; County Commissioners Augustine Ward, Henry E. Bryan, R. C. Parkhill, Emery Brooks, Joseph Mitchell, and John T. Edwards; Justices of the Peace C. G. Edwards and C. J. Hunter. Shofner, *Jefferson County*, 309.
35. Unidentified at Monticello: none. *TS*, January 22, 1870; *SMN*, January 23, 1872, January 16, 21, 1873, January 17, 1877; *WF*, January 23, 1873, January 19, 1875, January 11, 1876, January 22, 1884; Jacksonville *Tri-Weekly Florida Union*, May 12, 1874; *DFU*, January 17, 1876, January 13, 1882, January 16, 1883; *DS&P*, January 20, 1878; *FT-U*, January 20, 1886.
36. Unidentified in Lafayette County: none.
37. Unidentified in Leon County: Superintendent of Schools Josephus Anderson; County Commissioners H. C. Rippy and James Monroe; Justices of the Peace Weld Hamlin, Thomas H. West, John H. Rhodes, D. Cameron, A. F. Berry, J. M. Earnest, A. J. Miller, Alonzo Napier, William K. Harley, H. C. Wyche, B. C. Chaires, and Washington Ransom.
38. Unidentified at Tallahassee: Assessor J. B. Hall; Councilmen William R. Pettes and J. A. Pearce. Tallahassee Council Minute Book II; *FU*, January 14, December 30, 1869; *TS*, December 24, 1870, December 23, 1871, December 23, 1876; *WF*, December 27, 1870, November 28, 1871, December 24, 1872, December 23, 1873, December 22, 1874, December 28, 1875, December 26, 1876, December 22, 1877, February 25, 1879, February 24, 1880, February 22, December 13, 1881, February 28, 1882, February 27, 1883, February 26, 1884; *FDT*, February 24, 1882; *FT-U*, February 20, 1885, February 21, 1886, February 22, 1888, February 18, 1891.
39. Unidentified in Levy County: County Commissioner John E. McFedder; Justices of the Peace Thomas A. Britt and Joseph W. Shelton.
40. Unidentified in Bronson: none. *FT-U*, March 31, 1885, April 14, 1886, April 12, 1887; Bronson *Levy County Times*, April 1, 1886.
41. Unidentified at Cedar Key(s): Collector Joseph Boothby; Councilmen H. O. Richard, George W. McCumber, E. H. McLeod, and T. W. Brewer; and Marshals G. C. Kersey and R. R. Richard. Fishburne, *Cedar Keys in the 19th Century*, 86–172; Charles Carroll Fishburne, Jr., personal notes; Cedar Key Council Record II (1899–1915); *WS&P*, March 14, 1878; Bronson *Levy County Enterprise*, February 23, 1883;

FT-U, March 12, 1884, March 11, 1885, March 4, 1886; Cedar Key *Gulf View,* April 14, 1888.

42. Unidentified in Liberty County: Superintendents of Schools M. J. Solomon and T. J. Gregory.

43. Unidentified in Madison County: County Commissioner R. H. Williams; Justices of the Peace A. A. Taylor, Frank V. Ferrill, and W. M. Elliott.

44. Unidentified in Madison: none. *SMN,* April 16, 1875, June 7, 1876, January 15, 1878; TS, June 17, September 23, 1876; *Quitman* (Ga.) *Reporter,* July 5, 1877; *DFU,* January 5, 1882, January 5, 1883; *FT-U,* January 11, 1884, January 13, 1885, January 8, 1886, January 9, 1887, January 5, 10, 1888, May 17, 1891, January 9, 1892, January 6, 1893; Madison *New Era,* August 7, 1884; *Madison Recorder,* August 25, 1885, December 14, 21, 1888, January 11, 1889, August 1, 1890; Madison Council Minute Book 2 (July 9, 1894–July 4, 1911).

45. Unidentified in Manatee County: none.

46. Unidentified in Marion County: Clerk W. H. LeCain; Assessor Philip S. Cosgrove; Treasurer John A. Ferguson; County Commissioners Lewis McGee and J. Monroe Smith; Justices of the Peace B. G. Mills, John F. McDonell, S. L. Williams, William Knoblock, James H. Johnson, Edward W. Perry, C. F. Waterman, Edwin Smith, and Edwin Spencer.

47. Unidentified in Ocala: Assessor C. D. Royale; Marshal J. H. Whitfield; Councilmen J. Black, S. Herman, J. A. Ferguson, J. A. Reynolds, W. G. Jones, W. R. Hillyer, Charles A. Rapp, —— Reddick (1878), C. F. Robinson, H. P. Robinson, H. E. Thomas, and W. G. Marshal. *FU,* July 1, 1869; *WF,* August 8, 1871, July 21, 1877; *SMN,* March 20, 1873; Jacksonville *Tri-Weekly Florida Union,* March 20, 1873; Ocala *East Florida Banner,* June 27, August 8, 1874, May 22, June 5, 12, 26, July 10, 1875, June 13, 1876, July 20, 1878; *DS&P,* July 14, 1877; *WFU,* July 21, 1877; *WS&P,* April 11, 1878; lists of Ocala officers, Ocala city clerk's office; Ocala Council Record Book (December 15, 1879–January 2, 1894).

48. Unidentified in Monroe County: Assessor William Sutton; Justice of the Peace Robert Wilkinson.

49. Unidentified in Key West: Marshal Phillip Griffin; Councilmen L. Torregross and Samuel Roberts. *FP,* January 9, 1869; *WF,* October 17, 1871, October 31, 1876, October 25, 1881, October 24, 1882; Maloney, *Key West,* 76; *SMN,* October 20, 1877, October 13, 1886; Tom Hambright, Monroe County May Hill Russell Library, to author, December 27, 1993, collection of the author; Tallahassee *Semi-Weekly Floridian,* October 19, 1880; Key West *Key of the Gulf,* October 14, 1882, August 6, 1887; *FT-U,* October 26, 1883, February 5, 1896,

September 9, 1897, September 10, 1898, September 8, 1900, April 28, September 7, 1901, September 6, 1902, July 12, 1904, October 16, 1905, November 18, 1907, November 13, 1909, November 16, 1911; *Elliott's Florida Encyclopedia*, 172; Appointments, vol. 8, 355–56, RG 156, series 1284, FSA.

50. Unidentified in Nassau County: County Commissioner Lewis Wade; Justices of the Peace A. A. Gifford, Fred Saprutoire, C. W. Bullard, J. E. E. Jones, and Frank S. Chester. *Negro History in Florida*, 35; Drake, *Florida Legislature*, 50–51.

51. Unidentified in Fernandina: Collector C. Hallen; Councilmen N. S. Easton and John L. Clay. Case file, *Joseph Finegan* vs. *The Mayor and Aldermen of the City of Fernandina*, #0831, Florida supreme court case files; Nassau County Deed Records, Book L, a, Book Q, 85–86; *FU*, June 3, 1869; *TS*, January 15, 1870, January 20, 1872; *FM*, April 12, 1879, March 27, 31, April 7, 1880, April 2, 1881, August 5, 1882, April 7, 1883, April 12, 1884, April 4, 18, 1885, April 10, 1886, May 14, August 13, 1887, April 6, July 20, August 3, 1889, January 16, July 5, 15, 17, 1890, July 20, 25, 28, 1891; *SMN*, January 16, 1872, April 19, 1881; *Fernandina Observer*, January 18, 1873, August 25, 1874, January 22, 29, February 12, 1876; Turner Duling affidavit, May 29, 1896, Edward F. Langley MPR, NA; Savannah *Advertiser-Republican*, January 20, 1874; *Fernandina Observer*, February 28, March 24, 1874, in case file, *Joseph Finegan* vs. *City of Fernandina and George Washington, Clerk of said City*, #0764, Florida supreme court case files; *WF*, April 13, 1875, April 11, 1882; Fernandina *Nassau Citizen*, February 3, 1877; *DFU*, March 27, April 7, 1877; *WS&P*, January 3, April 4, 1878; *Fernandina Express*, April 9, July 18, 1881; *FDT*, April 4, 1882; *FT-U*, April 3, 1883, April 8, 10, 1884, April 7, 1886, April 5, 1887, July 19, 1888, March 9, 1890, July 24, 1892, July 19, 1895, August 22, 1896; Jacksonville *Weekly News-Herald*, July 21, 1887; *FT-U&C*, July 19, August 8, 1899; Fernandina Council Proceedings, Book A, 378–442, Book B, 1–601; Fernandina Council Minutes, Book 1, 58–582; Fernandina *News*, August 27, 1900; Fernandina *Nassau County Star*, June 30, 1904.

52. Unidentified in Orange County: Commissioner Thomas Walker; Justices of the Peace L. M. Moore, Samuel Bridges, and John H. Hemphill.

53. Unidentified at Eatonville: none. Otey, *Eatonville*, 4–28; *FT-U*, May 6, 1889.

54. Unidentified at Goldsboro: none. *Orange County Black Communities Survey*, 81–89.

55. Unidentified at Maitland: Clerk K. A. Faulkner; Treasurer L. B.

Courier. *FT-U*, July 30, 1885, March 18, 1886; Jacksonville *Weekly News-Herald*, March 15, 1888.

56. Unidentified at Mellonville: Councilmen T. P. McKey and S. M. Tucker. *DFU*, July 11, 1876.
57. Unidentified at Sanford: none. Sanford incorporation minutes, September 28, 1877, Sanford Museum, Sanford; Sanford Permanent Minute Book, March 3, 1879–April 11, 1881, 35–98.
58. Unidentified in Polk County: none.
59. Unidentified in Putnam County: Collector A. J. Curtis; Superintendent of Schools Edward McClure; Commissioner C. O. Hutchings; Justices of the Peace Robert N. Ellis, Charles B. Fenwick, W. P. Wright, A. S. Foster, and Charles E. Cook.
60. Unidentified at Palatka: Assessors Frederick J. Ballard and George W. Ransom; Treasurer W. O. Woltz; Marshals James Adams and J. F. Santina; Councilmen E. S. Jennings and D. Falk. Putnam County First Election Record Book; *FU*, July 15, 1869; *TS*, August 20, 1870, April 19, 1871, August 5, 1876; *WF*, August 15, October 10, 1871, August 13, 1872, August 19, 1873; Palatka *Eastern Herald*, April 5, 1873, January 5, September 12, 1878, February 5, 1881; Talbert, *Sons of Allen*, 68; *DFU*, January 14, 1876, April 9, 1882; *SMN*, March 24, August 16, 1877, April 11, 1878; Palatka Ordinance Book (September 25, 1878–March 6, 1916), 21–35; Palatka Town Council Minute Book (April 6, 1882–December 13, 1895); Palatka Council Minute Books (January 7, 1896–May 5, 1908) and (May 19, 1908–May 19, 1913); Palatka Lists of Town Officials, city clerk's office; Key West *Island City News*, April 20, 1882; *FT-U*, April 5, 1883.
61. Unidentified in Santa Rosa County: Justices of the Peace F. A. Alston and Tip Warren.
62. Unidentified at Milton: none. Minutes of the Town of Milton, vol. 1.
63. Unidentified in St. Johns County: none.
64. Unidentified at St. Augustine: Collector W. A. Kernan; Councilmen J. H. Kimball and H. A. Barling, Jr. St. Augustine Council Minutes (November 16, 1854–July 31, 1871) and (August 7, 1871–August 12, 1878); St. Augustine City Council Minute Books D (August 1878–July 1887), E (August 1887–June 1892), H (June 6, 1892–February 23, 1898), and I (March 2, 1898–June 25, 1904); St. Augustine Report of Elections (1890–1897), SAHSRL.
65. Unidentified in Sumter County: Commissioner R. H. Johnson.
66. Unidentified in Suwannee County: Justices of the Peace Zacheus Shepard, Edward J. Benton, and J. Padgett.

67. Unidentified in Live Oak: Marshals and Tax Collectors B. S. Hankins, W. M. Bacom, and E. S. Elliott; Councilmen William Flake, C. R. Jones, and James S. White. Live Oak Minute Book (April 24, 1878–April 13, 1903).
68. Unidentified in Taylor County: Justices of the Peace David G. Connel, A. Bird, and John W. Black.
69. Unidentified in Volusia County: Commissioners Benjamin W. Brown and William Allen; Justices of the Peace Silas Allen, LaFayette Allen, A. L. Anderson, and D. Thaddeus Goodwin.
70. Unidentified in DeLand: none. Roster of City Officials, DeLand city clerk's office.
71. Unidentified in Wakulla County: Justices of the Peace U. S. Hosford, Charles L. Rhame, and G. A. Lamb.
72. Unidentified in Walton County: none.
73. Unidentified in Washington County: none.

BIBLIOGRAPHY

MANUSCRIPTS

Apalachicola, Florida, census of 1884–1885. Apalachicola Public Library.

Bosque Bello cemetery records. Amelia Island Museum of History, Fernandina Beach, Fla.

Cedar Key, Florida, cemetery records. Collection of Mary Mizell, Cedar Key, Fla.

Elijah, Zebulon, biographical materials. Pensacola Historical Society, Pensacola, Fla.

Fernandina, Florida, census of November 1864. Photographic copy at Amelia Island Museum of History.

Fishburne, Charles Carroll, Jr. Personal notes and historical files. Collection of Charles Carroll Fishburne, Jr., Quincy, Fla.

Hart, Ambrose B. Letters. P. K. Yonge Library of Florida History, University of Florida, Gainesville.

Howard, O. O. Papers. Bowdoin College Library, Brunswick, Maine.

Key West burial records. Monroe County May Hill Russell Library, Key West, Fla.

Lee, Joseph E. Papers. M86-27, Florida State Archives, Tallahassee.

National Association for the Advancement of Colored People. Papers. Library of Congress, Washington, D.C.

Nolan, David. Historical notes and files. St. Augustine, Fla.

Powderly, Terrence V. Papers. Catholic University of America, Washington, D.C.

Stevens, Thaddeus. Papers. Library of Congress, Washington, D.C.

St. Augustine residents' biographical materials. St. Augustine Historical Society Research Library.

Washburn, Elihu P. Papers. Library of Congress, Washington, D.C.
Yulee, David Levy. Papers. P. K. Yonge Library of Florida History, University of Florida, Gainesville.

PUBLIC DOCUMENTS AND PUBLIC RECORDS

Alachua County. Probate administration files, will files, and docket books.
Apalachicola. Office of the City Clerk. Mayor's Court Record (1855–1882), Ordinance Book (1871–1921), and City Council Minute Book (July 3, 1884–May 3, 1889).
Cedar Key. Office of the City Clerk. Council Record Book II (1899–1915).
Clay County. Probate records.
Columbia County. Will books.
DeLand. Office of the City Clerk. Roster of City Officials.
Duval County. Probate files and docket books.
Escambia County. Probate files.
Fernandina Beach. Office of the City Clerk. Council Proceedings, Books A and B; Council Minutes, Book 1.
Florida. Combined Index of Deaths, Marriages, and Divorces [Death Certificate Index]. Office of Vital Statistics, Jacksonville.
———. Death certificates. Office of Vital Statistics, Jacksonville.
———. *House Journal*, 1868–1889.
———. House of Representatives. Office of the Clerk. *People of Lawmaking in Florida, 1922–1989.* Tallahassee: Florida House of Representatives, 1989.
———. *Journal of the Proceedings of the Constitutional Convention of the State of Florida, Begun and Held at the Capitol, at Tallahassee, on Monday, January 20th, 1868.* Tallahassee: Edward M. Cheney, 1868.
———. *Journal of the Proceedings of the Constitutional Convention of the State of Florida which convened at the Capitol, at Tallahassee, Tuesday, June 9, 1885.* Tallahassee: N. M. Bowen, 1885.
———. *Laws of Florida*, 1868–1889.
———. *Senate Journal*, 1868–1887.
———. State Census, 1875 (Alachua County), 1885 (all counties except Alachua, Clay, Columbia, and Nassau), 1895 (Nassau County). Available on microfilm at Florida State Archives, Tallahassee, and State Library of Florida, Tallahassee.
Florida State Archives. Elections, Division of. Appointments. RG 156, series 1284.
———. Commissions, 1827–1978. RG 156, series 259 and 259A.
———. Correspondence of Ossian Bingley Hart, Superintendent of Registration, 1867. RG 156, series 626.

———. Election Returns, 1824–1970. RG 156, series 21 and 1258.
———. Oaths and Bonds. RG 156, series 622.
———. Removals from Office, 1869–1885. RG 156, series 261.
———. Resignations from Office, 1868–1975. RG 156, series 260.
Florida State Archives. Governor's Office. Governors' Letterbooks. RG 101, series 32.
———. Gubernatorial Appointment Nominations for County Offices, 1824–1873. RG 914, series 74.
Florida State Archives. State Department. Resignations and Removals. RG 150, series 24.
Florida State Archives. Supreme Court. Case Files. RG 1100, series 49.
Franklin County. Probate records.
Freedmen's Bank, Tallahassee. Register of signatures. M816, roll 5, National Archives, Washington, D.C.
Gadsden County. Deed records.
Gainesville. Office of the City Clerk. Record of Incorporation and Gainesville officials materials.
Green Cove Springs. Office of the City Clerk. Records of municipal officials and Minute Book, June 2, 1891–April 25, 1900.
Hillsborough County. Probate packets.
Jackson County. County Commission Order Book C and County Commission Record Book, January 2, 1871–November 5, 1883.
———. Deed records.
———. General indexes to marriage records.
———. Probate files.
Jacksonville. City directories, 1870–1966. Hayden Burns Public Library.
Jefferson County. Deed records.
———. Probate records. At Keystone Genealogical Library, Monticello.
Lake City. Office of the City Clerk. Minute Book, November 14, 1892–February 16, 1904.
Leon County. Probate files and docket books.
Live Oak. Office of the City Clerk. Minute Book, April 24, 1878–April 13, 1903.
Madison. Office of the City Clerk. Council Minute Book 2, July 9, 1894–July 4, 1911.
Madison County. Deed records.
———. Probate files, docket books, and letters of administration books.
Manatee County. Circuit court records. At Manatee County Public Records Library, Bradenton.
Marion County. Probate files and docket books.
Milton. Office of the City Clerk. Town minutes.

Nassau County. Deed records.

———. Probate files and docket books.

Ocala. Office of the City Clerk. Lists of Ocala officers and Ocala Council Record Book, December 15, 1879–January 2, 1894.

Orange County. *Orange County Black Communities Survey, Phase 1—Seminole County: Project Report.* Orlando: Yeilding and Provost, 1990.

Palatka. Office of the City Clerk. Ordinance Book (September 25, 1878–March 6, 1916); Town Council Minute Book (April 6, 1882–December 13, 1895); Council Minutes (January 7, 1896–May 5, 1908, and May 19, 1908–May 28, 1913); and Lists of Palatka Officials.

Pensacola. City directories, 1880–1930.

Putnam County. First Election Record Book.

Sanford. Office of the City Clerk. Permanent Minute Book, March 3, 1879–April 11, 1881.

———. Incorporation minutes, September 28, 1877. Sanford Museum.

St. Augustine. City directories, 1914–1930.

———. City Council Minute Books and Reports of Elections. St. Augustine Historical Society Research Library.

Suwannee County. Deed records.

Tallahassee. Office of the City Clerk. Council Minute Book II.

United States Congress Serial Set. Washington, D.C. "Testimony Taken by the Joint Select Committee to Inquire Into the Condition of Affairs in the late Insurrectionary States." House Rpt. 22, pt. 13, 42d Congress, 2d sess.

U.S. Decennial Censuses, 1860–1920. Manuscript returns. Available on microfilm at Florida State Archives, Tallahassee, and State Library of Florida, Tallahassee.

U.S. Department of Commerce, Bureau of the Census. *Negro Population in the United States, 1790–1915.* Washington, D.C.: Government Printing Office, 1918.

U.S. Department of the Interior, Census Office. *Report on the Population of the United States at the Eleventh Census 1890.* Washington, D.C.: Government Printing Office, 1895.

———. *Statistics of the Population of the United States at the Tenth Census (June 1, 1880).* Washington, D.C.: Government Printing Office, 1883.

U.S. Department of the Treasury. Customhouse Nominations. RG 56, National Archives, Washington, D.C.

U.S. Department of War. Incoming Correspondence, Third Military

District, 1867–68, Bureau of Civil Affairs. RG 393, entry 5782, National Archives, Washington, D.C.

———. Military service records of Union soldiers in the Civil War. RG 94, National Archives, Washington, D.C.

U.S. Postal Service. Records of appointments of postmasters, 1832–September 30, 1971: Florida. M-841, National Archives, Washington, D.C.

Veteran's Administration. Military pension records. RG 15, National Archives, Washington, D.C.

Wakulla County. Probate records.

Walker, Francis A. *Ninth Census—Volume 1*. Washington, D.C.: Government Printing Office, 1872.

NEWSPAPERS AND PERIODICALS

A.M.E. Church Review, 1889–1909.

Birmingham (England) *Good Templars' Watchword*, 1876–1879.

Bliss' Quarterly, 1897.

Bronson *Levy County Enterprise*, 1883.

Bronson *Levy County Times*, 1886.

Cedar Key *Gulf View*, 1888.

Cleveland (Ohio) *Gazette*, 1897.

DeLand *Volusia County Herald*, 1877.

Eustis *New Yorker*, 1884.

Fernandina Express, 1881.

Fernandina *Florida Mirror*, 1879–1891.

Fernandina *Nassau Citizen*, 1877.

Fernandina *Nassau County Star*, 1904

Fernandina *News*, 1900.

Fernandina Observer, 1873–1876.

Florida Baptist, 1888.

Fort Myers News-Press, 1943.

Gainesville *Alachua Citizen and New Era*, 1876.

Gainesville *Daily Sun*, 1890–1892.

Gainesville *Florida Independent*, 1873.

Gainesville *Florida Sentinel*, 1891, 1895, 1900.

Gainesville *New Era*, 1867, 1873.

Gainesville News, 1885.

Gainesville Sun, 1879.

Gainesville *Sun and Bee*, 1881.
Gainesville Times, 1876–1878.
Gainesville *Weekly Bee*, 1882–1884.
Green Cove Springs *The Spring*, 1884.
Indianapolis *Freeman*, 1892–1893.
Jacksonville *Daily Evening Chronicle*, 1877.
Jacksonville *Daily Florida Union*, 1876–1883.
Jacksonville *Daily News-Herald*, 1888.
Jacksonville *Daily Sun and Press*, 1877–1880.
Jacksonville *Evening Telegram*, 1891–1894.
Jacksonville *Florida Daily Times*, 1882.
Jacksonville *Florida Times-Union*, 1883–1898, 1903–1921, 1993, 1995.
Jacksonville *Florida Times-Union and Citizen*, 1897–1902.
Jacksonville *Florida Union*, 1867–1869.
Jacksonville *Florida Weekly Times*, 1883.
Jacksonville *Metropolis*, 1910–1918.
Jacksonville *News-Herald*, 1888.
Jacksonville *New South*, 1874–1875.
Jacksonville *Tri-Weekly Florida Union*, 1872–1874.
Jacksonville *Weekly Florida Union*, 1877.
Jacksonville *Weekly News-Herald*, 1887–1888.
Jacksonville *Weekly Sun and Press*, 1878.
Key West Citizen, 1938.
Key West *Daily Equator and Democrat*, 1889.
Key West Democrat, 1880.
Key West *Island City News*, 1882.
Key West *Key of the Gulf*, 1882, 1887.
Lake City *Florida Index*, 1904.
Lakeland Evening Ledger and Star-Telegram, 1938.
Madison *Enterprise-Recorder*, 1911, 1926.
Madison *New Enterprise*, 1904–1905.
Madison *New Era*, 1884.
Madison Recorder, 1885–1903.
Miami Herald, 1991, 1996.
Miami Metropolis, 1899.
Mobile (Ala.) *Daily Register*, 1873.
Monticello *Advertiser*, 1872.
Newark (N.J.) *Sentinel of Freedom*, 1868, 1873.
New Orleans *Daily Picayune*, 1872.
New York Age, 1888–1889, 1891, 1911–1915.

New York Daily Tribune, 1867–1868.
New York Freeman, 1885–1887.
New York Globe, 1883–1884.
New York Herald, 1867.
New York Times, 1866–1868.
New York Tribune, 1868, 1878, 1880.
Norfolk (Va.) *Journal and Guide*, 1927.
Ocala *East Florida Banner*, 1874–1878.
Ocala *Evening Star*, 1901.
Palatka Daily News, 1883, 1887.
Palatka *Eastern Herald*, 1873, 1875–1881.
Pensacola Advance, 1879.
Pensacola *Advance-Gazette*, 1884.
Pensacola Commercial, 1883–1884.
Pensacola *Daily News*, 1890–1895, 1906.
Pensacola *Echo*, 1878.
Pensacola *Florida Weekly Express*, 1871.
Pensacola Gazette, 1878–1880.
Pensacola Journal, 1905–1912, 1925.
Pensacola Mail, 1872.
Pensacola *Observer*, 1868.
Pensacola Republican, 1874.
Pensacola *Semi-Weekly Commercial*, 1869, 1882.
Pensacola *Tri-Weekly Observer*, 1868–1869.
Pensacola Weekly Commercial, 1882–1883.
Pensacola Weekly Gazette, 1876.
Pensacola *West Florida Commercial*, 1868–1869.
Philadelphia *Christian Recorder*, 1866–1902.
Philadelphia *Journal of United Labor*, 1886–1888.
Philadelphia *Times*, 1883.
Punta Gorda Herald, 1902.
Punta Gorda *Sun-Herald*, 1992.
Quincy Journal, 1875.
Quitman (Ga.) *Reporter*, 1876–1877.
Sanford Herald, 1910.
Savannah *Advertiser-Republican*, 1873–1874.
Savannah Daily Advertiser, 1869, 1873, 1875.
Savannah Daily Herald, 1866.
Savannah *Daily News and Herald*, 1866–1868.
Savannah Daily Republican, 1867, 1870.

Savannah Morning News, 1868–1889.
St. Augustine *Examiner*, 1867.
Tallahassee *Daily True Democrat*, 1919.
Tallahassee *Florida Bureau of Immigration Monthly Bulletin*, 1891.
Tallahassee *Semi-Weekly Floridian*, 1867, 1880.
Tallahassee Sentinel, 1868–1876.
Tallahassee *True Democrat*, 1905.
Tallahassee *Weekly Floridian*, 1867–1893, 1896.
Tallahassee *Weekly True Democrat*, 1911.
Tampa Daily Times, 1927.
Tampa *Florida Peninsular*, 1868–1871.
Tampa *Sunland Tribune*, 1877.
Tampa Tribune, 1912, 1921, 1927, 1994.
Thomasville (Ga.) *Southern Enterprise*, 1876.
Thomasville (Ga.) *Times*, 1876.
Washington (D.C.) *Daily Morning Chronicle*, 1865.
Washington (D.C.) *People's Advocate*, 1879–1880.

SECONDARY SOURCES

Akin, Edward N. "When a Minority Becomes the Majority: Blacks in Jacksonville Politics, 1887–1907." *Florida Historical Quarterly* 53 (October 1974): 123–45.

Anderson, Jervis. *A. Philip Randolph, A Biographical Portrait*. New York: Harcourt Brace Jovanovich, 1972.

Ayers, Edward L. *The Promise of the New South: Life After Reconstruction*. New York: Oxford University Press, 1992.

Beatty, Bess. "John Willis Menard: A Progressive Black in Post–Civil War Florida." *Florida Historical Quarterly* 59 (October 1980): 123–43.

Blakey, Arch Frederic. *Parade of Memories: A History of Clay County, Florida*. Green Cove Springs: Clay County Bicentennial Steering Committee, 1976.

Bond, Gordon C. "The First Negro Politicians of Florida: The Black Delegates to the Constitutional Convention of 1868." *Negro History Bulletin* 38 (1975): 486–89.

Bordelon, Pamela G. "Zora Neale Hurston: Writer on Relief." Ms. in collection of Pamela G. Bordelon, Pensacola.

Boyd, Joseph A., and Randall O. Reder. "A History of the Supreme Court of Florida." *University of Miami Law Review* 35 (September 1981): 1019–66.

Brown, Canter, Jr. "African Americans and the Tampa Bay Area to World War I." In *Things Remembered: An Album of African Americans in Tampa*, by Rowena Ferrell Brady. Tampa: University of Tampa Press, 1997.

———. *African Americans on the Tampa Bay Frontier.* Tampa: Tampa Bay History Center, 1997.

———. "Bishop Payne and Resistance to Jim Crow in Florida During the 1880s." *Northeast Florida History* 2 (1994): 23–40.

———. "Carpetbagger Intrigues, Black Leadership, and a Southern Loyalist Triumph: Florida's Gubernatorial Election of 1872." *Florida Historical Quarterly* 72 (January 1994): 275–301.

———. *Florida's Peace River Frontier.* Orlando: University of Central Florida Press, 1991.

———. *Ossian Bingley Hart, Florida's Loyalist Reconstruction Governor.* Baton Rouge: Louisiana State University Press, 1997.

———. "Prelude to the Poll Tax: Black Republicans and the Knights of Labor in 1880s Florida." In *Florida's Heritage of Diversity: Essays in Honor of Samuel Proctor*, edited by Mark I. Greenberg, William Warren Rogers, and Canter Brown, Jr. Tallahassee: Sentry Press, 1997.

———. " 'Where are now the hopes I cherished?' The Life and Times of Robert Meacham." *Florida Historical Quarterly* 69 (July 1990): 1–36.

Browne, Jefferson B. *Key West, The Old and the New.* St. Augustine: Record Co., 1912. Reprint. Gainesville: University of Florida Press, 1973.

Bruington, Lola Lee Daniell. *St. Michael's Cemetery, Pensacola, Florida, 1807–?* Decorah, Iowa: Anundsen Publishing Co., 1986.

Butler, John Campbell. *Butler's History of Macon and Central Georgia.* Macon: J. W. Burke and Co., 1879. Reprint. Macon: J. W. Burke and Co., 1958.

Caldwell, A. B. *History of the American Negro, South Carolina Edition.* Atlanta: A. B. Caldwell Publishing Co., 1919.

Carson, Ruby Leach. "William Dunnington Bloxham, Florida's Two-Term Governor." Master's thesis, University of Florida, 1945.

Casdorph, Paul D. *Republicans, Negroes, and Progressives in the South, 1912–1916.* Tuscaloosa: University of Alabama Press, 1981.

Clark, James C. "John Wallace and the Writing of Reconstruction History." *Florida Historical Quarterly* 67 (April 1989): 409-27.

Coles, David James. " 'A Terrible and Sad Result': The End of the Civil War in Florida, March–June 1865." In *Proceedings of the 90th Annual Meeting of the Florida Historical Society at St. Augustine May 1992.* Tampa: Florida Historical Society, 1992.

———. " 'They Fought Like Devils': Black Troops in Florida During the Civil War." In *Florida's Heritage of Diversity: Essays in Honor of Samuel Proctor*, edited by Mark I. Greenberg, William Warren Rogers, and Canter Brown, Jr. Tallahassee: Sentry Press, 1997.

Davis, Jess G. *History of Gainesville Florida*. Gainesville: N.p., 1966.

Davis, Thomas Frederick. *History of Jacksonville, Florida, and Vicinity 1513 to 1924*. Jacksonville: Florida Historical Society, 1925. Reprint. Jacksonville: San Marco Bookstore, 1990.

Davis, William Watson. *The Civil War and Reconstruction in Florida*. New York: Columbia University Press, 1913. Reprint. Gainesville: University of Florida Press, 1964.

Dodd, Dorothy. " 'Bishop' Pearce and the Reconstruction of Leon County." *Apalachee* (1946): 5–12.

Drake, J. V. *The Florida Legislature: An Official Directory of State Government*. Jacksonville: Times-Union Book and Job Office, 1883.

Edwards, Lucy Ames. *Grave Markers of Duval County 1808–1916*. Jacksonville: Privately published, 1953.

Elliott, E. J. *Elliott's Florida Encyclopedia or Pocket Directory*. Jacksonville: E. J. Elliott, 1889.

Ellsworth, Lucian, and Linda Ellsworth, eds. *Pensacola: The Deep Water City*. Tulsa: Continental Heritage Press, 1982.

English, Jeanne E. *James D. English, 1816–18–*. Key West: N.p., 1991.

———. *Nelson Francis deSales English, 1848–1914*. Key West: N.p., 1991.

Fahey, David M. *Temperance and Racism: John Bull, Johnny Reb, and the Good Templars*. Lexington: University of Kentucky Press, 1996.

Fenlon, Paul E. "The Notorious Swepson-Littlefield Fraud: Railroad Financing in Florida, 1868–1871." *Florida Historical Quarterly* 32 (April 1954): 231–61.

Fishburne, Charles Carroll, Jr. *The Cedar Keys in the 19th Century*. Quincy, Fla.: Sea Hawk Publications, 1993.

Flynt, Wayne. *Duncan Upshaw Fletcher: Dixie's Reluctant Progressive*. Tallahassee: Florida State University Press, 1971.

Foner, Eric. *Freedom's Lawmakers: A Directory of Black Officeholders During Reconstruction*. New York: Oxford University Press, 1993.

Foster, John T., Jr., and Sarah Whitmer Foster. "Aid Societies Were Not Alike: Northern Teachers in Post–Civil War Florida." *Florida Historical Quarterly* 73 (January 1995): 308–24.

Gibbs, Thomas V. "John Willis Menard: The First Colored Congressman-Elect." *A.M.E. Church Review* 3 (April 1887): 426–32.

Gordon, Julius J. *Afro-Americans of Hillsborough County, Florida, 1870–1890.* Tampa: Privately published, 1993.

Grismer, Karl H. *Tampa: A History of the City of Tampa and the Tampa Bay Region of Florida.* St. Petersburg: St. Petersburg Printing Co., 1950.

Hall, Kermit. *The Magic Mirror: Law in American History.* New York: Oxford University Press, 1989.

Hamilton County Bicentennial Committee. *An Early History of Hamilton County, Florida.* 2d ed. Jasper: Jasper News, 1976.

Hardy, Alonzo. *Brown and Martin Family Reunion History.* Estill, S.C.: N.p., 1994.

Hawes, Leland. "Diary leads to rediscovery: Tampa's first city council had a black member and a Hispanic member." *Tampa Tribune,* May 9, 1993.

———. "One official's untold story." *Tampa Tribune,* February 13, 1994.

History and Souvenir of Bethel Baptist Institutional Church, Jacksonville, Florida. Jacksonville: Bethel Baptist Institutional Church, ca. 1920s.

The History of Local Government in Pensacola and Escambia County. Pensacola: John Appleyard Agency, 1991.

Hoffman, Lynn A. "Westview Cemetery." Typescript, 1985. Palatka Public Library, Palatka, Fla.

Hubener, Hal. "Lakeland Jubilee: The African-American Experience, 1882–1954." Typescript, 1997. Lakeland Public Library, Lakeland, Fla.

Hume, Richard L. "The 'Black and Tan' Constitutional Conventions of 1867–1869 in Ten Former Confederate States: A Study of Their Membership." Ph.D. diss., University of Washington, 1969.

Hunter, Charlene A. *A History of Pensacola's Black Community.* Pensacola: Escarosa Humanities Center, n.d.

Jackson County, Florida, Tombstone Inscriptions, 1777–1960. Sink Creek, Fla.: Genealogy Department, Church of Jesus Christ of Latter Day Saints, Sink Creek Branch, n.d.

Jackson, Jesse Jefferson. "The Negro and the Law in Florida, 1821–1921." Master's thesis, Florida State University, 1960.

Johnson, James Weldon. *Along This Way: The Autobiography of James Weldon Johnson.* New York: Viking Penguin, 1933. Reprint. New York: Penguin Group, 1990.

Jones, Maxine D., and Kevin M. McCarthy. *African Americans in Florida.* Sarasota: Pineapple Press, 1993.

Journal of Proceedings and Year Book of the 47th Annual Session of the South Florida Annual Conference, African Methodist Episcopal Church. Fort Lauderdale: South Florida A.M.E. Church Annual Conference, 1939.

Jupiter, Del E. "Agustina and the Kelkers: A Spanish West Florida Line." *National Genealogical Society Quarterly* 80 (December 1992): 265–79.

Kealing, H. T. *History of African Methodism in Texas*. Waco: C. F. Blanks, 1885.

Kenney, Patricia Drozd. "LaVilla, Florida, 1866–1887: Reconstruction Dreams and the Formation of a Black Community." In *The African American Heritage of Florida*, edited by David R. Colburn and Jane L. Landers. Gainesville: University Press of Florida, 1995.

Kleinberg, Howard. "Discovering black participation in Miami's birth." *Miami Herald*, October 8, 1991.

———. "Miami pioneer Lightburn: Too long forgotten." *Miami Herald*, January 23, 1996.

Klingman, Peter D. *Josiah Walls: Florida's Black Congressman of Reconstruction*. Gainesville: University of Florida Press, 1976.

———. *Neither Dies Nor Surrenders: A History of the Republican Party in Florida, 1867–1970*. Gainesville: University of Florida Press, 1984.

Long, Charles Sumner. *History of the A.M.E. Church in Florida*. Philadelphia: A.M.E. Book Concern, 1939.

McCluskey, Audrey Thomas. "Ringing Up a School: Mary McLeod Bethune's Impact on Daytona." *Florida Historical Quarterly* 73 (October 1994): 200–217.

McDonough, Gary W., ed. *The Florida Negro: A Federal Writers' Project Legacy*. Jackson: University of Mississippi Press, 1993.

McKinney, George Patterson, Sr., and Richard I. McKinney. *History of the Black Baptists of Florida, 1850–1985*. Miami: Florida Memorial College Press, 1987.

McLauren, Melton Alonzo. *The Knights of Labor in the South*. Westport, Conn.: Greenwood Press, 1978.

Maloney, Walter C. *A Sketch of the History of Key West, Florida*. Newark, N.J.: Advertiser Printing House, 1876. Reprint. Gainesville: University of Florida Press, 1968.

Menard, Edith. "John Willis Menard: First Negro Elected to the U.S. Congress; First Negro to Speak in the U.S. Congress." *Negro History Bulletin* 18 (December 1964): 53–54.

Menard, J. Willis. *Lays in Summer Lands*. Washington, D.C.: Enterprise Publishing Co., 1879.

———. "The Negro in Politics." *A.M.E. Church Review* 15 (October 1898): 594–604.

Minutes of the Seventeenth Session of the Florida Annual Conference of the African Methodist Episcopal Church. Marianna: Latimer C. Vaughan, 1882.

Morris, Allen. *The Florida Handbook 1991–1992.* Tallahassee: Peninsular Publishing Co., 1991.

Negro History in Florida. Jacksonville: Works Project Administration, Federal Writers' Project, 1936.

Neyland, Leedell W. *Twelve Black Floridians.* Tallahassee: Florida Agricultural and Mechanical University Foundation, 1970.

Neyland, Leedell W., and John W. Riley. *The History of Florida Agricultural and Mechanical University.* Gainesville: University of Florida Press, 1963.

Osborn, George C., ed. "Letters of a Carpetbagger in Florida, 1866–1869." *Florida Historical Quarterly* 36 (January 1958): 239–85.

Otey, Frank M. *Eatonville, Florida: A Brief History.* Winter Park: Four-G Publishers, 1989.

Payne, Daniel Alexander. *Recollections of Seventy Years.* New York: Arno Press and the *New York Times*, 1969.

Peeples, Vernon. Telephone interview, July 18, 1993. Notes in collection of the author.

Proctor, Samuel. *Napoleon Bonaparte Broward, Florida's Fighting Democrat.* Gainesville: University of Florida Press, 1950. Reprint. Gainesville: University Press of Florida, 1993.

Richardson, Barbara Ann. "A History of Blacks in Jacksonville, Florida, 1860–1895: A Socio-Economic and Political Study." Ph.D. diss., Carnegie-Mellon University, 1975.

Richardson, Clement. *National Cyclopedia of the Colored Race.* Vol. 1. Montgomery, Ala.: National Publishing Co., 1919.

Richardson, Joe M. "Jonathan C. Gibbs: Florida's Only Negro Cabinet Member." *Florida Historical Quarterly* 42 (April 1964): 363–68.

———. *The Negro in the Reconstruction of Florida, 1865–1877.* Tallahassee: Florida State University Press, 1965. Reprint. Tampa: Trend House, 1973.

Rivers, Larry E. "Baptist Minister James Page: Alternatives for African American Leadership in Post–Civil War Florida." In *Florida's Heritage of Diversity: Essays in Honor of Samuel Proctor*, edited by Mark I. Greenberg, William Warren Rogers, and Canter Brown, Jr. Tallahassee: Sentry Press, 1997.

Rivers, Larry E., and Canter Brown, Jr. "African Americans in South Florida: A Home and a Haven for Reconstruction-era Leaders." *Tequesta* 56 (1996): 5–23.

Schafer, Daniel L. "Freedom Was as Close as the River: The Blacks of Northeast Florida and the Civil War." *El Escribano* 23 (1986): 91–116.

Shofner, Jerrell H. "Florida." In *The Black Press in the South, 1865–1979*, edited by Henry Lewis Suggs. Westport, Conn.: Greenwood Press, 1983.

———. *History of Jefferson County.* Tallahassee: Sentry Press, 1976.

———. *Jackson County, Florida—A History.* Marianna: Jackson County Heritage Association, 1985.

———. *Nor Is It Over Yet: Florida in the Era of Reconstruction 1863–1877.* Gainesville: University of Florida Press, 1974.

Shuften, John T. *A Colored Man's Exposition of the Acts and Doings of the Radical Party South, From 1865 to 1876.* Jacksonville: Gibson and Dennis, Steam Book and Job Printers, 1877.

Smith, Charles Spencer. *A History of the African Methodist Episcopal Church.* Philadelphia: Book Concern of the A.M.E. Church, 1922. Reprint. New York: Johnson Reprints, 1968.

Smith, Julia Floyd. *Slavery and Plantation Growth in Antebellum Florida, 1821–1860.* Gainesville: University of Florida Press, 1973.

Speed, Willie. Personal interview, Apalachicola, Florida, February 14, 1995. Notes in collection of the author.

Stanaback, Richard J. *A History of Hernando County 1840–1976.* Brooksville: Action '76 Steering Committee, 1976.

The Struggle for Survival: A Partial History of the Negroes of Marion County 1865 to 1976. Ocala: Black Historical Organization of Marion County, 1977.

Talbert, Horace. *The Sons of Allen, Together with a Sketch of the Rise and Progress of Wilberforce University, Wilberforce, Ohio.* Xenia, Ohio: Aldine Press, 1906.

Tebeau, Charlton W. *A History of Florida.* Coral Gables: University of Miami Press, 1971.

Thomes, Sidney Phoenix, Jr. *Early Vital Records of Pensacola, Florida.* 3 vols. Pensacola, 1988–1989.

Thompson, Camilla, and Reginald Thompson. *Capers Michael Vaught, Sr.: A Shaper of the Early History of Jacksonville.* Jacksonville: Privately published, 1986.

Trefousse, Hans L. *Andrew Johnson, A Biography.* New York: W. W. Norton and Co., 1989.

Varick, Florida Duke, and Phyllis Rose Smith. *Tallahassee and Leon County, Florida, Cemeteries.* Tallahassee: Privately published, 1979.

Wallace, John. *Carpetbag Rule in Florida: The Inside Workings of the Reconstruction of Civil Government in Florida After the Close of the Civil War.* Jacksonville: Da Costa Printing and Publishing House, 1888. Reprint. Kennesaw, Ga.: Continental Book Co., 1959.

Warner, Lee. *Free Men in an Age of Servitude: Three Generations of a Black Family.* Lexington: University of Kentucky Press, 1992.

Wayman, Alexander W. *Cyclopaedia of African Methodism.* Baltimore: Methodist Episcopal Book Depository, 1882.

Webb, Wanton S. *Webb's Jacksonville Directory, 1882.* New York: W. S. Webb and Co., 1882.

Welch, W. Curtis. *Tampa's Elected Officials: A Narrative Chronology of Municipal Elections and Tampa's Elected Officials from 1849 to 1886.* Tampa: City of Tampa Archives, 1997.

Whitfield, J. B. *Florida State Government, An Official Directory of the State Government.* Tallahassee: Florida Steam Book and Job Office, 1885.

Williamson, Edward C. *Florida Politics During the Gilded Age 1877–1893.* Gainesville: University of Florida Press, 1976.

Womack, Miles Kenan, Jr. *Gadsden: A Florida County in Word and Picture.* Quincy, Fla.: N.p., 1976.

Woodward, C. Vann. *The Strange Career of Jim Crow.* 3d ed. New York: Oxford University Press, 1974.

Work, Monroe N. "Some Negro Members of Reconstruction Conventions and Legislatures and of Congress." *Journal of Negro History* 5 (1920): 63–72.

Wright, Richard R. *Centennial Encyclopaedia of the African Methodist Episcopal Church.* Philadelphia: N.p., 1916.

INDEX
to Chapters 1–5

About the Author

Canter Brown, Jr., Historian-in-Residence at the Tampa Bay History Center, has won many awards for his historical writing, including the 1992 Rembert W. Patrick Memorial Book Award of the Florida Historical Society for his *Florida's Peace River Frontier* (1991). He has served in government for more than fifteen years and holds a Doctor of Jurisprudence degree and a Doctor of Philosophy degree from Florida State University. Some of his most recent publications include *Ossian Bingley Hart, Florida's Loyalist Reconstruction Governor* (1997), *Florida's Clerks of the Circuit Court: Their History and Experiences*, cowritten with William Warren Rogers (1996), and *Fort Meade, 1849–1900* (1995).